FIRE OVER ULSTER

FIRE

OVER

ULSTER

BY

PATRICK RIDDELL

HAMISH HAMILTON
LONDON

First published in Great Britain
by Hamish Hamilton Ltd 1970
90 Great Russell Street London W.C.1

SBN 241 01912 5

PRINTED IN GREAT BRITAIN
BY EBENEZER BAYLIS AND SON LIMITED
THE TRINITY PRESS, WORCESTER, AND LONDON

TO

KATHRYN AND JANE

In the hope that when they are older they will read this book and learn from it that in Ireland nothing is ever as simple as it seems

Acknowledgements

I AM in considerable debt to Mr. Harry Calvert, Reader in Law of the Queen's University of Belfast, and to Dr. A. T. Q. Stewart, Lecturer in History of the same University. They were kind enough to read each chapter of the book as it was written and their knowledge and advice were invaluable.

I was also given outstanding help by Mr. James Vitty, Librarian, and Mr. James Gracey, Sub-Librarian, of the Linenhall Library, Belfast, who, as always, were unfailingly patient and efficient in dealing with the many demands I imposed upon them.

Without the constant aid and guidance of these four men, I doubt if the book could have been written and I ask them to accept my sincerest thanks.

I also most gratefully acknowledge the kindness of those who allowed me to include material from books and journals protected by copyright: Mr. Sean O'Faolain, from his biography of Mr. De Valera; Mrs. Brighid O'Hegarty, from *The Victory of Sinn Fein*, by the late P. S. O'Hegarty; Messrs. George Allen and Unwin Ltd., from *Craigavon, Ulsterman*, by Dr. St. John Ervine; The Mercier Press of Cork, from *The Civil War in Ireland*, by Mr. Eoin Neeson; The *Irish Times*; The *Church of Ireland Gazette*; Century Newspapers Ltd. of Belfast; The *Financial Times* of London, and the *Belfast Telegraph*.

Foreword

W HEN the affairs of Ireland explode on the Western World it is proper for the informed Englishman to maintain a repentant silence. He usually does, as he is aware that each explosion— there have been many Irish political explosions—has been triggered off in a continuing chain reaction to the behaviour of Englishmen in Ireland from somewhere around the middle of the fifteenth century to the twenty-second year of the twentieth. But the number of Englishmen who are informed on Ireland and what happened there is small. The uninformed constitute an overbearing majority. How many Englishmen know or care today that Ireland had to be partitioned in 1921 because of the mistaken policies of their forebears, and that the official designation of Britain changed from the United Kingdom of Great Britain and Ireland to the United Kingdom of Great Britain and Northern Ireland? The responses of the present-day English as a whole to events in Ireland declare an ignorance and a superior disapproval which make the well-read Irishman wince.

It is not only the English, of course, who are generally uninformed on Ireland or misinformed or both. The other countries of the Western World are similarly unenlightened and prejudiced. In the United States, for instance, thanks to Irish immigrants and their descendants, with inflexible Republican Irish sympathies, there is a formidably numerous, articulate, untaught, bitter and persistently anti-English and anti-Northern Irish lobby, which will stoop to almost any lie to blacken Britain and Northern Ireland in the eyes of Americans if it will somehow push forward a dissolution of the semi-autonomous Northern Irish state and the unification of the Irish people, north and south, in an all-Ireland Republic. They have formed organizations like the American Congress for Irish Freedom, which has issued propaganda material of such scurrility and untruthfulness that even Members of Parliament in the Northern

Ireland House of Commons who work openly for Irish unification have repudiated it.

The story of Ireland is a sorry one. The English, throughout the centuries of their oppression of Ireland, never really tried to understand the Irish. They showed generosity and foresight in other countries of their empire, but were seriously lacking in vision in their relationship with Ireland. The Irish, in their turn, never tried to understand the English, although the moves in power politics are not difficult to interpret and on several occasions a reasonable accommodation acceptable to both countries could have been reached. The Irish could never see the imperative English need of a reliably secure back door, the English could not grasp the justifiable Irish claim to nationhood or recognize the Irish as heirs to an early learning and cultural achievement considerably ahead of anything of the same period in England. The English have shown themselves in the past to be a great people, but too frequently insensitive in their dealings with other countries. They have characteristically forgotten what the Irish did for them, especially the Northern Irish who gave them important help in the First World War and decisive help in the Second.

It has never been easy to deal with the Irish, of course. The native Irish have ever been a fickle, feuding race, given to political assassination and related murder, lacking the national purpose and tenacity which the inheritance of Norman blood developed in the English. There was no Norman Conquest of Ireland, unfortunately. A number of Norman knights and men-at-arms landed in Ireland in the twelfth century on the invitation of a dispossessed and disgruntled Irish chieftain, but the impact of the Normans on Ireland generally was limited. If they had arrived in prevailing strength and had made as thorough and as disciplining a conquest of the Irish as they had made of the Saxons in England, the subsequent story of Ireland would have been happier. It would have been happier, too, whatever the Republican Irish may say, if the English successors to the Normans had made a thorough and reforming conquest. Any intervention by a resolute and more advanced race that imposed order on the murderous Irish clans and septs and welded them into an enduring national coherence would have been a godsend to the unhappy country.

For a variety of reasons, however, neither Norman nor Englishman prevailed and the story of Ireland from the twelfth century is one of half measures. The Normans and the English did not conquer, the Irish did not win. The English brought flame and sword, but perhaps the principal policy instrument in their effort to subjugate the Irish and build that reliably secure back door they so badly wanted was the implantation of Protestant English and Scottish settlers throughout Ireland, on escheated and confiscated lands which had belonged to the native Roman Catholic Irish. The most concentrated and systematically executed of these many implantations—or Plantations, as they were called—was launched in the year 1610 in the northerly Province of Ulster, later reduced from nine counties to six and known as Northern Ireland. No fewer than four million statute acres of fertile Ulster soil, the best in the Province, were seized from 'the mere Irish' and largely granted to Protestant English and Scottish settlers, mostly Scottish, by the King of England—'a greater extent of land than any prince in Europe has to dispose of'.

The several Plantations all over Ireland—Elizabethan, Jacobean, Caroline, Cromwellian—were a sowing of dragons' teeth, inevitably followed by a springing up of armed rebellious men. Rebellion on rebellion, massacre on massacre, death by musket, pistol, sword and pike, death by hanging, death by famine, diminishing the population of the wretched country from nine million to four million—such was the dreadful pattern until the engineered partition of 1921. Even then the killing, the burning and the hatred did not cease. Anyone who thinks that picture overdrawn has only to read Irish history to see that it is not. A sorry story, indeed, and one the English should call to mind, particularly in the light of recent happenings in Northern Ireland where, mainly as a result of that ruthless Jacobean Plantation of 1610, the population of about one and a half million is divided into two antagonistic communities—one million Protestants, mostly of settler stock, and half a million Roman Catholics with some claim to native Irish descent—each of them, as far as can be seen at present, irreconcilable with the other.

The half million Roman Catholics argue that, through parliamentary and municipal discrimination by the determined and better-off Protestant majority, they are thrust into the position of second-class citizens and kept there. The Protestants argue that the Roman Catholics, who benefit equally from the provisions of the British Welfare State by virtue of the fact that Northern Ireland is a full tax-paying part of the United Kingdom, are not interested in displaying constructive citizenship but are dedicated to bringing about the incorporation of Northern Ireland in an all-Ireland Republic, where there would be a permanent Roman Catholic and inward-looking majority obdurately opposed to political association with Britain. The fear behind this reasoning may not be soundly based, as attitudes in the Irish Republic are thought by some observers to be changing or likely to change. Certainly the Republican leaders insist that Northern Ireland would have nothing to be afraid of, but this is doubtful to say the least and in Ulster the fear persists.

The accusation of discrimination against the Roman Catholic minority in Northern Ireland has substance, but not as much as the world has been persuaded to believe. The minority propagandists have been effective—far more so than the publicists in the money-starved public relations services of the Northern Ireland Government, which for a long time has been parochially unalert in the matter of projection—and the image has been successfully blurred. The discrimination has been exaggerated and distorted, while nothing has been publicized by the minority, of course, concerning their own discrimination and obstinate insistence on segregation. Their grievances were unarguable and serious but many of the minority leaders have raised the stakes and are now playing their traditional Republican game of disruption. This is tactically understandable, as the Irish Nationalist Party in the Northern Ireland House of Commons—there were nine members prior to the last parliamentary election, pledged to further the objective of an all-Ireland Republic, and none of them men of calibre—has never been effectual. In early 1967, therefore, or thereabouts, a Civil Rights Association, led at first by moderates, was formed by mostly Roman Catholic men and women throughout Ulster to demand equality of treatment for the minority and to secure the greatest possible amount of publicity for the demands. The Association staged a big protest demonstration in the ancient

Ulster city of Londonderry on October 5, 1968, which resulted in a violent clash with the Royal Ulster Constabulary. National and international newspaper and television services were represented and the news value was brilliantly exploited by the demonstrators and their astute leaders.

There were other Civil Rights marches afterwards, many of them accompanied by violence or ugliness of some description. There were provocative Protestant back-lash counter-demonstrations, also accompanied by ugliness and riot. Things came to an evil pass. That they did so was due to omission by the early Northern Ireland Cabinets, which could and should have prevented the situation from arising by introducing the necessary reforms many years ago. The Cabinet Ministers were shortsighted, however, and the uncommitted men and women of both sides in Northern Ireland are now paying the price. Yet the Ministers had a case. It was a good case to begin with but declined in credibility as time moved on. I shall do my best to explain it.

Indeed, in this book I shall do my best to explain those political and religious facets of life in Northern Ireland—or Ulster, as I prefer to call it—which outsiders find so puzzling. I shall try to convey the case for the Protestant majority as well as that of the Catholic minority. Ulster has been excessively and unfairly blackened and damaged in the eyes of the world and her splendid story has not been told. I shall try to tell it. I have perhaps some qualifications for making the attempt. I am an Ulsterman, with a deep love of my small and beautiful country and with a knowledge of its past. My Ulster ancestry goes back over many generations but there is Southern Irish blood in me, too, and I shall be fair-minded. I admire the fine qualities of the Ulster stock but I think of myself as an Irishman. I have no liking for extremists on either side of the fence. I am independent, I have no connection with any Irish political party or order. I belong to no Church. I have studied the history and watched the conduct of the Christian Churches in Ireland and have disliked what I have read and seen. I am not a hatchet-man. All I am anxious for is that the Irish people should live together in peace.

I am especially interested in setting out the truth about Ulster and the causes of its troubles, that all who will may learn of aspects they were unaware of, facts they had not heard of. I shall be accused of having written a controversial book, for the Irish in the main are an emotional race, addicted to myth, unloving of disenchantment. Some will swear by the book, many will curse it, but I shall not mind the attacks. Everyone who writes a book on Ireland is attacked. I hope the book succeeds in putting reality in place of the versions preferred by my countrymen and by others equally credulous, but I have no certainty that those who read it will agree that it has done so. Who could write a book about the Irish and be certain of anything? A strange people. They so often behave like the beings in their darker folk-lore that I sometimes wonder if they are real.

PART ONE

Chapter One

The 27th of Foot saved the centre of my line at Waterloo.
Duke of Wellington

I am not an Ulsterman, but yesterday, the 1st July, as I
followed their amazing attack on the Somme, I felt I would
rather be an Ulsterman than anything else in the world.
Sir Wilfrid Spender

One of the finest examples of human courage in the history
of mankind.
Sir Philip Gibbs

At half-past seven in the bright summer morning of July 1,
1916—the signalled opening minute of the Battle of the Somme,
the greatest and most violent direct assault on strongly held
enemy positions ever attempted up to that time—battalion on
battalion of the 36th (Ulster) Division, embarking on their first
attack, their first compelling test in war, emerged from their
heavily shelled assembly points in Thiepval Wood, formed
themselves up in No Man's Land as though on parade and
walked steadily and calmly through artillery and machine-gun
fire of such murderous concentration and intensity that it all but
obliterated platoons and even whole companies in an instant.
The Ulstermen, although wave after wave of them disappeared
in the annihilating fire, kept their formation and disciplined
approach—'no fuss, no shouting, no running, everything
orderly, solid and thorough'—until they came close to the first
German trench. Then, with a wild Ulster yell, they swept into
it and over it and through an even more appalling fire to the
second German position and the third. When the officers fell—
they were conspicuous and few of them lived—the sergeants and
corporals took over. When they fell, too, the men went on
without them. They had been told to take four of the enemy
positions in depth, including the dominating and formidably

3

defended Schwaben Redoubt, and they meant to do so, whatever the cost.

The cost was terrible. Unfortunately for the British Army, and tragically for the Ulstermen, the 32nd and 29th Divisions on the right and left of the Ulster Division were bloodily repulsed. The successful 36th found itself so far forward and so exposed that the Germans were able to bring to bear on it the decimating fire that should have been spread over three divisions. The Ulstermen were mown by frontal fire, by enfilading fire from both flanks and by a particularly maddening fire from pockets of surviving Germans behind them. But nothing could stop the 36th. They swarmed into the third enemy position, killed every German who opposed them, and held it. They rushed the Schwaben Redoubt and captured it. There remained the fourth enemy position, a distance away over open country devoid of cover. The sweating Ulstermen gathered up their grenades and ammunition, eyed the position calculatingly and prepared themselves to take it. Fighting not far from them, but unable to help, were the men of the Royal Inniskilling Fusiliers, one of the finest of the Ulster regiments, formerly known as the 27th Regiment of Foot.

It was the 27th that went into the fight at Waterloo with a combatant strength of 750 Ulstermen and came out of it at the end with no more than 306, the highest casualty rate of any British regiment engaged in that battle. At the most critical moment, when Napoleon was almost through the middle of Wellington's pounded and reeling line, it was the steadiness and superb Ulster fighting quality of the 27th—in 'the post of honour', which meant that they had been placed in the most important and dangerous position, with nothing to shelter them from the French cannon and musketry fire—that saved Wellington and turned the battle in his favour.

But on the dreadful day in 1916, not all the sacrificial bravery and persistence of the Inniskillings, successors to the 27th, in attack after attack on the impregnable German flanking machine-gun strongholds, could save their fellow Ulstermen if they decided to move on their final and distant objective. The Divisional General, realizing that if they did so they would be unsupported on either side and would assuredly be destroyed, tried to call them back. He sent runners, but one after the other

4

they were killed before they could get through. When one did at last get through, it was too late. The assault had been launched, the Ulstermen were on their way. The crossing of one thousand yards of open and death-swept area in daylight was a desperate venture and few returned. Those who did told of the last determined thinned-out dash, the savage hand-to-hand fighting in the trench, the overpowering enemy reserves, the inevitable and stubbornly resistant retirement to lines already captured and the continuing efforts throughout the seemingly lengthened hours of night, without possibility of reinforcement, to beat off German bombing raids.

At seven o'clock in the morning of the 2nd, as the ground mists dispersed, it was seen that the Ulstermen were still holding out in captured German trenches, without food and water, without adequate supplies of bombs and ammunition, at the last stretch of endurance. A collection of 400 men, many of them wounded, was scraped together from shattered regiments of the Division to struggle through the enemy artillery barrage with supplies. A hundred men were lost but the remainder reached the trenches and aided the defence. That night the exhausted Division was relieved. The battered, dirt-grimed remnant of worn-out Ulstermen marched heavily to the rear until they got to the village of Martinsart and flung themselves down to sleep. They did not know then that the Division had won in a single day the astonishing number of four Victoria Crosses. They did not know that if the penetration they had made had been equalled all along the front, the Battle of the Somme would have been the first great British victory of the war. They knew not and cared not. They slept, and for many days after they were very silent. They had cause to be silent. Almost three-quarters of the Division was out of action. No more than 2,500 of the 9,000 Ulstermen who had gone into the attack, which lasted no more than forty hours, answered the roll-call two days later. The Division was never again to be the one the survivors had known, and they themselves, or most of them, were to die in subsequent battles.

At home in Ulster the news of the opening of the battle was received with excitement and pride. It was known in high quarters that the Division was engaged and the word got around. The local newspapers appeared with such headlines as—

Great Anglo-French Offensive, A Brilliant Opening—Battle of the Somme, All Still Going Well—The Great Offensive, Thrilling Stories of the Fighting—Progress of the Great Battle, Advance Beyond Second German Lines. The excitement rose, the pride rose with it. But when the British War Office began to send its harrowing telegrams to the next-of-kin of the killed and missing—many of the missing were later found to be dead—the euphoria vanished. Almost the whole of the little Province, not much bigger than a single major English county, was in mourning. Scarcely a fair-sized family escaped. The Lord Mayor of Belfast, the principal city, about the same in area and population as Bristol, asked the citizens to observe a five-minute silence at noon on July 12, the traditional procession day of the Orangemen, normally a holiday. The procession was cancelled and, as the clocks struck twelve on that day of pouring rain, business was halted, all traffic came to a stand, and the people—hundreds of them weeping—stood still and voiceless in the streets. The young men of Ulster had fallen in thousands and could not be replaced.

How had it happened? There was never any compulsion, conscriptive or otherwise, on the Ulstermen to fight and die for England in the Valley of the Somme or in any theatre of the war. There was no compulsion on the men of Southern Ireland, either, yet thousands of them joined the specially formed 16th (Irish) Division, fought finely in France and died there. They mostly enlisted, when war broke out, on the appeal of John Redmond, leader of the Irish Home Rule Party in the British House of Commons and an Irishman of vision, who urged his Nationalist followers in Ireland to show, by helping England, that they could shake themselves free from obsession and take the larger view. Redmond felt that all Irishmen, whatever their political and religious differences, should come together in the necessary effort to defeat Germany, that this would lead through a shared sacrifice to a better understanding and tolerance among Irishmen everywhere, and result eventually in the Ulster-Irish accepting the unification of Ireland as a self-governing state. Events were to prove him wrong, or seemingly wrong. They were to prove, too, that he was out of touch with and indeed unaware of a rancorous element in Ireland intent on rebellion and blood-letting. The 1916 Easter Rising in Dublin, led by the fanatical idealists Pearse and Connolly—'England's danger is Ireland's opportunity'—dismayed him. Yet the fact remains that the cream of the men of Ireland, north and south, Protestant and Catholic, Nationalist and Loyalist, bore side by side the maiming and killing in Flanders, aided one another when aid was needed—the 16th Division lent officers to the stricken 36th after the fall of so many of the Ulster officers on the Somme—and Irishmen from both Divisions who survived and returned to Ireland, north and south, did so with respect for one another, the respect that is achieved by soldiers the world over who have known the common experience of a terrible ordeal in war. If power of decision had rested with those tired men, if the English could have kept the Irish question out of their party-political struggles and could have learnt to honour their word to the Irish—something for which they cannot be depended on, even today—Redmond might have been proved right and the later savageries in Ireland might have been avoided or at any rate lessened.

But it was the absence of the silenced young men of the Lost Generation that had perhaps a diminishing effect in Ireland as in England. Men of better initial quality, and later of lengthened horizons, than those who stayed at home remained in France for ever. Southern Irishmen like Tom Kettle, Irish Home Rule Member of Parliament at Westminster and a poet with a heart as wide as his thinking, remained there, too. Willie Redmond, brother of John Redmond and a middle-aged man when the war broke out, insisted on joining the 16th Division in the name of the truer manhood of Ireland and was also killed in action. Many of the very best young Ulstermen were stopped by death in battle from bringing their broadened outlook to the service of their troubled Province. The ancient Irish enmities would probably have been little affected—they are so deep-seated and implacable as to make most thoughtful Irishmen despair—but there is no country that is not the lesser for the loss of its men of generous mind. The Ulstermen fought gladly in France to prove to England that their loyalty to her, their determination to continue as part of her, should never be mistaken for a statement of alterable faith; yet the finest of those who fell could have come to see at the last, as in Kettle's lines written shortly

7

before his death from a German bullet, that they fought not 'for king nor flag nor emperor, But for a dream born in a herdsman's shed, And for the secret scripture of the poor.' There is no man who can say what influence those men from Southern and Northern Ireland might have had on their country had they lived. Companionship in war brings trust.

The story of Ireland in every century is marked with saddening imponderables, however, and it is not the intention of this book to elaborate on profitless might-have-beens or to write a history of Ireland as a whole. The intention is to explain the causes and almost insoluble dilemmas of the latest world-publicized troubles in Ulster and to tell the story—characteristically unremembered by the English and unknown to other nationalities—of the splendid overall Ulster achievement from which the world in general and the English in particular have gained so much. That is why the book begins with the slaughter of the Ulstermen at the Somme, for no one who regards that superbly brave attack of more than fifty years ago as irrelevant or is ignorant of the events in Ireland and in London that led to the formation of the Ulster Division at the outbreak of the 1914–18 War will ever understand the intractability of the Ulster-Irish problem. So, then, how did the 36th (Ulster) Division come into existence? And why?

The answer lies in the uneasy and variable English mind, the guilty conscience of the educated radical English in the early years of the twentieth century, who regretted the English treatment of Ireland in the past, misread the depths of the Ulster-Irish contradiction—as the radical English of today are misreading it—and were anxious to make amends by acceding to the clamorous Southern Irish demand for Home Rule. A restricted form of Home Rule had been granted to Ireland by England in the eighteenth century under Henry Grattan, one of the few worthwhile Irish patriot leaders of his day, but the two countries were legislatively united by the Act of Union of 1800, a parliamentary manœuvre made possible by the venality with which the dominant Anglo-Irish landed gentry sold their country's privileges for money or lucrative office or both. The ease with which they were suborned into betraying the independent interests of their country and accepting the extinction of the Parliament of Ireland, although not exceptional in the

8

murky light of eighteenth-century politics, is one of the many repellent episodes in the Irish story. The Roman Catholic majority amongst the people, suffering severe deprivation of political and other rights, were given to believe that the passage of the Union measure would soon be followed by removal of the disabilities. William Pitt, Prime Minister of England, in his efforts to honour the implied undertaking, was frustrated by the obstinacy of King George III who believed that, if he agreed to the proposed emancipation of the Irish Roman Catholics, he would be in breach of his Coronation oath to uphold the Protestant faith. This was not the first or the last undertaking, implied or categoric, made to the Irish and broken by the English.

However, onward to the early years of the twentieth century. The British Prime Minister at the significant time, prior to the 1914–18 War, was Asquith, head of the Liberal Party which had tried more than once under Gladstone to give Ireland self-government but had been foiled by the English Tories and other opposing elements. Asquith was a man of high intellectual and political ability who knew that the deeds of the English in Ireland down through the centuries were of a pattern with the power-political methods then received as normal practice throughout Europe. He knew that, in the eras of enforcement of policies stemming from strategic necessity, from the need to ensure survival, every nation that found itself subject to possible danger had no qualms in using the sword to acquire immunity from invasion by conquering and holding in repression a near-by, small and inadequately defended country that could serve as a springboard for invaders. Ireland was just such a springboard and the attempt to use it as one had been made many times by strong military and naval powers—Spain and France, for example—hostile to England and resolute to defeat and occupy her. England had certainly much to be ashamed of in her handling or mishandling of Ireland but not to such an extent as the Republican Irish maintain. The Irish of this third quarter of the twentieth century who are pursuing their dream of an all-Ireland Republic in isolation from Britain will disagree with that view, of course. They are depressingly untutored in European history, even more depressingly in the history of their own country, and they are generally unable to understand, as an

9

instance, that Soviet Russia has seized Czechoslovakia for precisely the reasons that originally prompted the English to seize Ireland.

Asquith also knew, though, that the Irish claim to self-government had justification. In 1912, he introduced into the Westminster House of Commons a Bill which was to be passed by both Commons and Lords two years later, after a ferociously contested journey, and be known as The Government of Ireland Act. It was a mild little Act, granting Ireland self-government of a limited kind, under the British Crown. It received the Royal Assent on September 18, 1914, but was not to come into effect until after the end of the war, which had begun on August 4 of that year. But for all its mildness, the Protestant Ulstermen fought it with increasing anger from the moment it was first tabled in the House as a Bill. England, they argued bitterly, had put them in Ulster to help her in assuring her own safety, yet now she meant to abandon them to those who hated her and to a powerful and adamantly reactionary Church notorious for intolerance of Protestantism. Their fear of the Roman Catholic Church in Ireland and its politically conditioned priesthood largely recruited from the ill-educated Irish small-farmer class was the most important factor in the Ulster determination to resist Home Rule. It could never be too strongly stressed that the Ulster-Irish question has always been primarily a religious quarrel, especially laden and intense during the critical Parliamentary years leading up to the 1914–18 War. Home Rule meant Rome Rule, said the Ulstermen, although the Irish Roman Catholic Home Rulers and the English radicals denied it.

There was to be irrefutable evidence[1] years later of dictatorial interference in democratic Irish Government statutory matters by the Roman Catholic Hierarchy in Dublin, which substantiated the initial Ulster prophecies and caused the sons of the pre-1914 Ulstermen to shake their heads and say, 'Our fathers told you so!'; but today it looks as if the Cabinet Ministers of the Irish Republic have gathered enough courage to ward off encroachments by their Church in legislative affairs, although their

[1] 1951. The 'Mother and Child' Bill, introduced by Dr Noel Browne, Minister of Health in the Dublin Government. The Catholic Hierarchy intervened behind the scenes to have the Bill altered or withdrawn. Dr Brown resigned from the Cabinet and the matter became public.

steadiness if pressed hard enough is by no means established. The Ministers are almost all of them good Catholics themselves, loyal and dutiful in their faith, and should their Church firmly voice unaltering disapproval of some measure or other, there is not a Protestant Ulsterman who would risk so much as an opinion on the outcome. There is further irony in the reproval of the Ulstermen by radical Englishmen in 1912 for refusing to become a minority in a Roman Catholic-dominated state, in view of the safeguards against Roman Catholicism imposed in England by the English constitution and the conditions concerning English monarchical religious belief and succession. Those safeguards and conditions still obtain in England, the Ulstermen still distrust the Roman Catholic Church in Ireland or anywhere, and the Ulster-Irish question is still essentially a religious one. A long long time must pass before the Protestants of Ulster agree to unite with the Roman Catholics in an all-Ireland Republic, if they ever do. There is no certainty that they will, despite the usually swallowed argument that old hatreds naturally and ultimately die away. In Ireland, only the warm, soft rainfall is predictable—and the continuing toughness of the Ulster-Scottish stock.

If Asquith and those of his committed Liberal Party colleagues who were helping him to force through the Home Rule Bill had remembered that toughness or taken the trouble to inform themselves of it, they would not have made the mistake of thinking that the massively staged Ulster resistance was no more than a manoeuvre in the game of political bluff. Asquith brought all practicable pressure to bear on the Ulstermen to break their nerve but they were accustomed to beleaguerment. They had been a defensive minority for generations, drawing their hardness from their seventeenth-century ancestors who had farmed their granted Ulster acreage with muskets slung from their shoulders or within speedy reach, ready to repel such dispossessed and vengeful native Irish as might swoop on them. Those ancestors had been prepared to fight to the death for their families and their faith—many of them did—and the Ulstermen of 1912 were of the same unweakening determination. They made two decisions of telling importance in modern Irish history. They decided to pledge themselves and they decided to arm themselves. The pledge was couched in language that even those politically opposed to it agreed had quality—it derived its phrasing and style in part from the Scottish Covenant of the seventeenth century, when the English tongue had dignity, the century of the Authorized Version of the Bible—and, in scenes of extraordinary unanimity and gravity, which should have opened the eyes of every Liberal Cabinet Minister in London, it was signed by Protestant Ulstermen all over the Province and in Dublin, London, Edinburgh, Glasgow, Manchester, Liverpool, Bristol and York. The grand total of Ulstermen who signed was 237,368. No fewer than 234,046 Ulster women signed the accompanying Declaration, specially written for them, making an overall total of 471,414, almost half a million men and women of Ulster pioneering stock and fervent adherence. The Covenant they gave their names to informed the mainly amused and under-estimating world that:

Being convinced in our conscience that Home Rule would be disastrous to the material well-being of Ulster as well as the whole of Ireland, subversive of our civil and religious freedom, destructive of our citizenship, and perilous to the unity of the Empire, we, whose names are underwritten, men of Ulster, loyal subjects of His Gracious Majesty King George V, humbly relying on the God whom our fathers in days of stress and trial confidently trusted, do hereby pledge ourselves in solemn Covenant throughout this our time of threatened calamity to stand by one another in defending for ourselves and our children our cherished position of equal citizenship in the United Kingdom, and in using all means which may be found necessary to defeat the present conspiracy to set up a Home Rule Parliament in Ireland. And in the event of such a Parliament being forced upon us we further solemnly and mutually pledge ourselves to refuse to recognize its authority.

Thousands of Ulster people abroad, especially in such countries as Canada—Toronto today is a city with a near-dominant proportion of Ulster men and women in its population—supported the Covenant and Declaration, although unable actually to sign them; but the English, conditioned by their traditions and their respect for legal process, could not believe that Ulster would disobey the lawful ordinance of their democratically elected Parliament at Westminster. They were taken aback when the Ulstermen put into effect the second of their two major decisions by arming themselves in preparation to resist attack by the Crown forces to a degree which would have made them pause and bind their unexpected wounds. Of a surety the Ulstermen would have resisted Home Rule to the death, fighting obstinately in their cities, towns, villages, valleys and mountain areas, however paradoxical it might have seemed that loyalists to the British Crown should have fought the forces of the Crown in order to stay as citizens of that Crown.

The story of Ireland is chaptered in paradox, however, and the Ulstermen knew all about defiance of the British Government. They had formed in the eighteenth century the secret society—betrayed by an Irishman,[1] with typical Irish treachery —known as The United Irishmen, with the object of compelling the English to accede to a liberalizing and friendly nationalism in Ireland. The rebellion of 1798 was inspired by the United Irishmen. It failed, as Irish uprisings before it had failed, through the congenital incapacity of the native Irish to unite, through lack of purposefulness, endurance and organization, through meanness of mind and heart. On several occasions in the Irish past, and most strikingly during the Elizabethan reign, an Irish military leader[2] had the English soldiers with their backs to the sea. One combined attack would have finally freed the country of them, but it was never delivered. The Irish preferred to fight their fellow-countrymen. Leader after leader was betrayed when on the verge of success and the English forces were allowed to recover their strength and the lost ground. Those who regard the native Irish as an inferior race have found much in history to support their argument. However, the rebellion of 1798 was sufficiently dangerous and startling to goad the English into persisting in joining the two countries politically, economically and defensively under the famous Act of Union of 1800—accepted, incidentally, by the Irish people generally to an extent that disturbed the revolutionary element in the nation. The Society of United Irishmen disappeared into history, bequeathing to the Protestant Ulstermen of 1912 its unafraid spirit. There was nothing unprecedented, then, in the decision of the inheritors to turn an obdurate front to the English

[1] Leonard MacNally.
[2] Hugh O'Neill, Earl of Tyrone, was one.

13

and prepare to fight Home Rule. They reached for their weapons—and discovered they had none. This did not dismay them, for they had ideas about that. They formed an Ulster Volunteer Force, which was immediately thronged by thousands of Ulstermen, young and middle-aged. The world smiled as it watched the unpractised battalions, drilling in civilian clothes, belted and bandoliered, with dummy rifles made of wood. Then, suddenly, the smiling faces changed expression. The Ulster Volunteer Force had acquired, as if from nowhere, no fewer than 40,000 rifles, with millions of rounds of ammunition. Where had they come from? Smuggled, of course. But how had they been smuggled into Ulster under the eyes of the British Government and its Royal Navy?

The answer is simple. The Ulstermen were efficient. The contrast between the Ulster gun-running and the later ludicrous gun-running by the Southern Irish Home Rule Volunteers marks the difference between the two peoples. The Southern Irish amateurishly and slowly unloaded, in full daylight, a derisory number of 900 rifles at Howth Harbour near Dublin, marched exultantly and irresponsibly with them along the open road to the city, still in full daylight, and were compelled to open fire on such soldiers and unarmed police as were sent out by the British authorities in Dublin to stop them. The Ulstermen ran their guns into Ulster at night. They did so with speed, daring, steady nerve, brilliantly executed deception measures which successfully misled the British authorities in Belfast, and, above all, characteristic organizing ability. The story is one of the most extraordinary exploits in the book of Irish history. At the centre of it were three resolute men. The first, and the political leader of the Ulster anti-Home Rule movement, was Sir Edward Carson,[1] a Dublin barrister with a seat in the British House of Commons at Westminster, a convinced and formidable protagonist in the Parliamentary battle, a man with a mesmeric personality, an outstanding lawyer and debater, who sacrificed the principal objectives of his career in order to help the Ulster cause. The second, although not in importance, was Major Fred Crawford, ex-Royal Artillery officer, an Ulsterman who counted a day wasted that was not at risk, an adventurer in the class of Buchan's Richard Hannay and probably ahead of him.

[1] Later Baron Carson of Duncairn.

The third was another Ulsterman, James Craig, a former active service captain in the Royal Irish Rifles, who was to become the first Prime Minister of Northern Ireland and be raised in later years to the peerage, as Viscount Craigavon, by the English (they usually admire their successful antagonists), a massively built man who looked as if he had been chiselled from an Ulster mountain, determined and immovable in anything that concerned the interests of the people he knew so well and cared so much for, imperturbable and wise throughout his public career, liked and trusted by all who came to know him, including his Irish Home Rule political opponents—the most remarkable figure in the creation and development of the Northern Ireland State. Carson held the Parliamentary front at Westminster and was worshipped by the Ulster Defence Volunteers, who would have given him their lives. Most of them did. Crawford, the skilful and nerveless cloak-and-dagger man of many aliases, the undercover agent, slipped into European cities to negotiate behind mysterious doors with the arms merchants, found the guns and delivered them to the Ulster coast.[1] Craig, who had shaped the Ulster Volunteer Force on modern army lines—it had an efficient signal battalion, numerous motor-cycle despatch riders and an intelligence section with secret codes and code-breaking experts—was the organizing brain of the whole complex and dangerous gun-running operation. And it was certainly dangerous, very dangerous. Craig and his friends were engaged in a treasonable conspiracy and the military would have every right under British law to fire on them. If they did, many lives would be lost. But the coin had been tossed, the time had arrived.

On the night of Friday, April 24, 1914, the military and civil authorities in Belfast were puzzled and on edge. The Ulster Volunteers were out in force and the city was electric with expectancy. There was nothing exceptional in the appearance of the Volunteers on the streets, of course, it was just another test mobilization—or so the authorities were informed—and the men were as usual unarmed. But why had a thousand of them taken up position around and inside the railway station that served the County Antrim coast? Why was another large

[1] The story is exceptionally well told in A. T. Q. Stewart's admirable book *The Ulster Crisis*.

detachment of disciplined and resolute Volunteers lining one of the best-equipped landing berths in Belfast Harbour? There had been rumours that a ship loaded with illicit arms was due to arrive. Was this the appointed night? Belfast Harbour seemed the obvious place for the unloading of heavy crates of arms as it was well fitted with the essential cranes. Were the Volunteers on the dockside ordered to resist any official approach to the ship until its cargo of guns had been discharged and taken away? If they were approached by troops or police or both and if they did resist, there could be bloodshed and very serious trouble.

The authorities, who suspected much and knew little, were further perturbed when they learned that a darkened ship showing only her navigation lights was cautiously steaming up Belfast Lough in the direction of the Harbour and sending flash-lamp signals to persons on shore. They watched her carefully to see where she would berth and when they saw that she had tied up alongside the very berth the Volunteers had some hours earlier lined in hundreds they decided to send aboard her a senior officer of Customs and Excise, accompanied by some of his juniors. The officer, with his juniors, threaded his way through the capacious horse-drawn carts, coal-lorries, motor lorries which the Volunteers had made a point of bringing with them. The Customs officers were carrying lanterns and formid-able-looking staves and, as they walked up the gangplank, they noticed that the ship was the S.S. *Balmarino*. They demanded to see her papers, but the master had mislaid the keys of the locked cabin-desk in which they were kept. They demanded that the hatches be opened. The master refused on the grounds that he had no instructions in the matter of opening the hatches. The Customs men asked him to tell them the nature of the cargo. The master again declined on the grounds that he had no instructions, but offered to allow them to inspect the cargo when the hatches were removed next day. The unfortunate Customs men applied to the police for help. The police, possibly in secret sympathy with the Volunteers, gravely drew attention to the absence of evidence of any illegality. All they could do was to note the registration numbers of the motor lorries and the names that were painted on the horse-drawn carts. Time wore on. At last, hours later, the Superintendent of Customs was called in and angrily insisted on the hatches being opened.

The ship's second mate obeyed the order but Colonel Couchman, commanding the Volunteers, had them quickly slammed down again. And so it went on, hour after hour, with the Customs authorities convinced that the *Balmarino* contained the rumoured arms consignment, and the police—who were Irish and understood their fellow-countrymen—equally convinced that the *Balmarino* was a blind and that the real gun-running was taking place elsewhere. They were right.

At the little town of Larne and at Larne Harbour, twenty-five miles from Belfast on the County Antrim coast, the well-laid plans of the Volunteers were being put into effect without a hitch. At 8 p.m. exactly, the Volunteers had taken control of the town and harbour. The police believed that it was yet another test mobilization and paid no attention. Volunteers in strength were posted on all the roads leading into Larne and, on the hills above the sea, check-points were set up. At 9 p.m. all telephone communication with Belfast was cut and the railway telegraph put out of action. The Volunteers were in full possession. Everything now depended on the prompt arrival of the S.S. *Mountjoy*, with Crawford and the arms and ammunition. There was suspense as the selected Volunteer commanding officers scanned the sea with binoculars. At last, to their relief, a small ship was sighted. The officers flashed the agreed signal and received the agreed reply. It was the *Mountjoy*. At 10.30 p.m. she crept slowly into the harbour. At 11 p.m. she made fast, the hatches were removed and the work of unloading the rifles and ammunition was begun. Waiting to carry the arms to their hidden destinations were scores of motor cars, their engines throbbing impatiently. As fast as a car was loaded it drove off and its place taken by another. The Volunteers, sweating but exultant, worked like Pharaoh's slaves. The final crate was swung from the *Mountjoy* to the quay, the last car drove off with its load, the *Mountjoy* crept out to sea again and headed for the small dormitory town of Bangor on the County Down coast on the opposite side of Belfast Lough to deliver the Down consignment and, although the plan had run two hours behind schedule, all had gone well. The police had not stirred, the troops had not appeared. In Bangor and in Donaghadee— another little County Down harbour where a consignment was expected—all was in readiness. The arms arrived and were whisked away. When the people of Larne and Bangor and Donaghadee had finished their morning meals and made their way to their daily work there was not so much as a grinning Volunteer in sight, although there had been thousands of them in and around the three little places up to an hour or so before. 40,000 rifles and several million rounds of ammunition had been landed and spirited away as though by the wave of a wand. Telephone and telegraph communication was restored and, in Belfast, Colonel Couchman advised the Customs authorities that they might now open the hatches of the S.S. *Balmarino.* Their report on what they found when they acted on the invitation is not available.

The landing of the guns and ammunition became known, of course—it was impossible to hide the fact of the operation completely from the many experienced English newspaper correspondents who were in Ulster in anticipation of just such an event—and the leading London journals came out with special editions conveying the news. Asquith informed the assembled House of Commons of the 'grave and unprecedented outrage' committed by the Ulstermen and the Government had to be dissuaded from making a series of arrests which would have been fiercely resisted by the now well-armed and defiant Ulster Volunteers. On a strict interpretation of constitutional and common law, the Ulster leaders had been guilty of treason, but Asquith knew very well that they had the sympathy of many of the most prominent and influential men in England together with that of a great proportion of the British electorate. Earlier, before the gun-running had taken place, such men as Lord Milner, the famous 'proconsul of Empire', Walter Long, a distinguished politician, Field-Marshal Lord Roberts, Lord Balfour of Burleigh, the Duke of Portland, Rudyard Kipling (who had written in 1912 a very angry poem in favour of the anti-Home Rulers in Ulster), and Leo Amery had openly encouraged the Ulster standpoint. In March 1914, Milner had issued his British Covenant, to be signed by those who opposed the imposition of Home Rule on an unwilling Ulster:

I . . . of . . . earnestly convinced that the claim of the Government to carry the Home Rule Bill into law without submitting it to the judgment of the Nation is contrary to the spirit of our Constitution, do hereby solemnly declare that if the Bill is passed I shall hold myself justified in taking or supporting any action that may be effective to prevent it being put into operation, and more particularly to prevent the armed forces of the Crown being used to deprive the people of Ulster of their rights as citizens of the United Kingdom.

By the end of July 1914, when the lists had to be closed, Milner had collected no less than two million signatures and could beyond doubt have gathered many many more. The Ulstermen knew of this, naturally, and were strengthened to an even greater extent by the knowledge. The historic year drew on, the Ulstermen steeled themselves to seize the Province and form a Provisional Government[1] which would declare itself as implacably against Home Rule in Ireland as ever before and implacably resolved to fight it, if fight they must. Come what might, they would not give in. As usual, they organized methodically and thoroughly for the inevitable struggle, actually making arrangements for the evacuation of the Ulster women and children to Scotland and—with characteristic Irishness—to England. Then came August 4, 1914, the long-threatened war with Germany—and the fateful alteration in the purpose and service of the Ulster Volunteer Force.

Immediately, James Craig offered the Force to the British War Office for service in the British Army. After some obstinate and unwise opposition from Lord Kitchener, the British Secretary of State for War, the offer was accepted. So, too, was the demand from Craig that the Force should be formed into a cohesive Division and that the word Ulster should be associated with it. Thus did the 36th (Ulster) Division come into existence, go into training and prepare itself to fight in Flanders instead of in Ulster. The Division was indeed cohesive, more so than any other in the Army. Men from the same Belfast district would be in the same battalion, which would consist entirely of them. Battalions would be formed exclusively of men from the same countryside area, companies and platoons of men from the same small town and village. Every man in the Division was surrounded by his friends, men he had known for years, men he understood and relied on, men he had served with in the

[1] See Chapter 17 of *The Ulster Crisis* by A. T. Q. Stewart.

Volunteers. No other Division throughout the whole of the British Army had such a homogeneity, such a close-knit comradeship. They were all of them men of the same religious faith, the same political opinion, the same unarguing loyalty to their Province, the same intensity, the same determination to honour the Ulster name. They went into training in Ulster itself, a training eased by the experience of their earlier discipline and military practice in the Volunteer Force. Kitchener later consented to inspect them and was so impressed that he described the Division as the best he had seen. King George V inspected them and was similarly impressed. They were fit, perhaps the fittest Division of all the Divisions in the armies that Kitchener, who had foreseen a long war, was forming. They trained for a time in their Ulster camps—the men grumbling because they were not in action in France—and then at last they marched through the streets of Belfast, their rifles at the slope, their bearing high, on their last parade before the final training phase in England. As they marched through Belfast, which most of them knew so well, the people of the city and thousands more who had journeyed from the country towns and villages to bid them farewell wrapped them in a great roar of cheering. There was sadness in the cheering, of course, for the wives and fathers and mothers had laden hearts, but there was a near to bursting pride as battalion after battalion marched past and disappeared from sight.

Arrived in France, the Division was soon in the line, seeing some scattered and unimportant action but destined, unknowingly, for the great attack on the Somme which was designed in the main to take the terrible pressure from the French at Verdun and, it was hoped, break through the German lines and carry the fighting to open country. Haig, commanding the British Armies, was assembling Divisions of cavalry to exploit the expected break-through. The Artillery, enriched with more high explosive and mortar shells than they had possessed since the beginning of the war, were certain that the bombardment of the German trenches would be so devastating that few if any enemy infantry could emerge alive, let alone defend their positions effectively. For a week before the troops were to advance, the British heavy guns, row upon row of them for

20

thousands of yards, almost wheel to wheel, blasted the German trenches as they had never been blasted before. The watching assault troops felt that the gunners were right and that nothing could live under such a weight of metal. The din was tremendous, shattering to the ears and nerves, almost unendurable, and the attack divisions longed for it to stop as one after the other they moved up to their assembly points to get ready for the assault.

The central mass of the 36th found themselves in Thiepval Wood and under increasing shellfire from the German artillery. One company was almost blown to pieces. The men, grim-faced and silent, were confident of taking their objectives. They knew their officers and had trust in them and all they asked was a pause in the hellish roar of the gun-fire. The bombardment suddenly ceased and the hours of night that preceded the attack were unexpectedly and blessedly still. The Divisional chaplains moved from company to company and there were heard the age-old words the Ulstermen knew so well—'I will say of the Lord, He is my refuge and my fortress, in Him will I trust'—and then, as dawn drew near, the steadying assurance given out on so many Sundays in the parish churches of the Ulster towns and villages—'Yea, though I walk through the valley of the shadow of death, I will fear no evil, for Thou art with me, Thy rod and Thy staff they comfort me.'

The men, on edge, taut, forced themselves to talk, some of them to joke. Most of them sweated, many of them prayed. Many wondered what their families were doing at that moment, if they knew what was about to happen or if they were asleep. Mostly, though, they longed for the final bombardment from the guns to open and for the attack to begin, whatever it might bring. They had not too long to wait. And the weather favoured them. 'The dawn came with a great beauty,' wrote Philip Gibbs, one of the British war correspondents, 'there was a pale blue sky flecked with white wisps of cloud. But it was cold and over all the fields there was a floating mist which rose from the moist earth and lay heavily on the ridges.' No rain, no mud, good fighting conditions. The time grew close, the Ulstermen braced themselves. Then, with a roaring crash that made them jump, the final bombardment opened and seemed for an hour and a half to rip the very heavens, as man upon man crouched in the

21

assembly-trenches and waited for the command that must shortly come.

It came. The bombardment stopped, the whistles blew, the German machine-gunners hurried from their unsuspected deep-down bunkers to position themselves—and wave upon wave of Ulstermen, their rifles at the slope, their bayonets glistening in the bright new day, their disciplined ranks magnificently in line, went forward to their deaths as brave men should.

Chapter Two

IT is the dream of many far-seeing Irishmen today who love their appealingly beautiful little country, north and south, with all its contradictions and all its faults, that the twenty-six counties of the Irish Republic and the six of the tiny State of Northern Ireland shall join together, that Republican Irishman and Unionist Ulsterman shall unite in a cleansing effort to make of their country as a whole a land in which the economic absurdity of two expensive governments has been removed, a land in which the ancient and horrible hatreds are forgotten, the killings forgiven. To men of other and less emotional nations, men who prefer to solve a problem through the application of reason, it is incomprehensible that in the second half of the twentieth century an un-Christian quarrel between two branches of the Christian Church and a reconcilable political difference should continue to divide a warm-hearted, instinctively generous and kindly people, high on the list of the world's most friendly races. It must be possible, say these men of other nations, for half a dozen intelligent, informed and moderate Irishmen from each side to sit at a table under the chairmanship of an intelligent, informed and impartial statesman from a disinterested European country and settle the matter on a basis that sensible living Irishmen and all Irishmen to come will accept. Surely, they say, the Irish can see what they are doing to themselves? Is common sense to be ignored for ever?

The Southern Irishmen would be more likely to agree to such a conference than the Protestant Ulstermen. The Southern Irish insist that the Ulstermen would have nothing to fear from joining an all-Ireland Republic, that the Protestants already resident as citizens in the Irish Republic have openly declared that they are not discriminated against and have never been discriminated against since the Irish Free State came into existence in 1922, that some of the Republic's Cabinet Ministers are Protestants. They also insist that the moment of realization of an all-Ireland

Republic would be the moment when the centuries-old enmity of the Republican Irish towards the English would cease, when co-operation between the two nations would begin on a foundation of friendship, trust and loyalty. They then produce what they regard as their most telling argument—that the Ulstermen who hold out for retention of Ulster's privileges as a part of the United Kingdom of Great Britain are in a minority where the overall wishes of the Irish people are concerned, as a referendum in Ireland would inevitably result in a vote of some three million in favour of Irish unity and a million in favour of the British connection. From this they maintain that the Irish question could be settled fairly, peaceably and honourably if the Ulstermen would not be so recalcitrant, if they would abandon their stubbornness and show a juster sense of the over-riding well-being of Ireland and the reasonable aspirations of the mass of the Irish people at home and abroad.

This argument has been skilfully and very effectively propagated around the world with the result that most or many of the watching countries are inclined to accept it. The Ulstermen, in their refusal to accept it, are almost isolated. They in their turn argue that their vision of unity with Britain and consequently with the continent of Europe and the world is outward looking and in accord with modern economic developments and international trading trends; that Ireland is so situated geographically that she can never be independent of England either politically, monetarily or militarily—the official army of the Irish Republic is small, ill-equipped, ill-trained and inexperienced in war, while the Irish Navy consists of no more than about three corvettes; that the ambition of many Southern Irishmen to bring into being an isolationist and self-contained all-Ireland Republic is typical Celtic nonsense; that the true background to the much-trumpeted undiscriminatory attitude towards the Protestant citizens of the Irish Republic is to be seen in the fact that they constitute less than five per cent of the Republic's population, a very uninfluential minority.

Will the Irish Roman Catholic Hierarchy and the Irish Republican Government remain undiscriminatory when an all-Ireland Republic, inclusive of the million Ulster Protestants is formed and the Protestant minority rises from five to twenty-five per cent? The Ulstermen doubt it. In the matter of assurances, they point out that their own assurances have been proved to be reliable but that Irish Republican assurances have been proved to be unreliable. They distrust the Republican Irish. The Irish hatred of the English, the Ulstermen argue, has persisted and will stay in the native Irish mind for generations to come. They quote as only one illustration of this hatred the neutrality of the Irish Republic during the war against Nazi Germany, a neutrality that incontrovertibly stemmed from the lasting native Irish enmity towards England, from the native Irish inability or unwillingness to see clearly, think fairly and rise above their inborn pettiness and inadequacy. The Ulstermen gave England all possible help in that war, immense and critically important help, while the Republican Irish stood meanly and sullenly aside, although, if England and her Allies had been beaten, the Nazi troops would have instantly and brutally occupied Ireland to prevent her territory from being used as a springboard by the re-gathered and re-invading Allied armies. The Republicans would not see this at the time, they refuse to see it now. They still justify their neutrality in the shyster lawyer language they used in 1939. Their repeated hand-on-heart assurances, put out before and since the war by their Cabinet Ministers and other leading figures, of friendly and loyal co-operation with England from the moment she engineers for them an all-Ireland Republic are taken by the Ulstermen with a large grain of salt. As for the referendum argument, the Ulstermen cite the known disinclination of the Ulster Roman Catholics to forgo the generous social benefits for which they qualify through living in a part of the British Welfare State. The Catholics, because of their large families, have particular need of State aid and would suffer from the inevitable and serious fall in the definition, scale and value of the benefits should they accede to an all-Irish Republic.

So say the Ulstermen but, in the opinion of those men of other and less conditioned nations who believe that the Irish problem can and should be solved through the application of reason, they are no more infallible than the Republican Irish. Reason could undoubtedly be applied in Ireland with advantage. There are some who try it but they are few and they are not listened to. The standards of education throughout the country are unequal, thinking is generally insular and parochial, men of

25

able and trained mind are reluctant to enter Irish political life, which is why almost all the northern and southern Irish politicians today are of a wearying mediocrity. A very large number of the most highly qualified and valuable Irish university graduates from middle- and upper middle-class families, the families more traditionally inclined towards service of the state, immediately and thankfully quit the country on acquiring their degrees. Ireland is no place for clever young Irish men and women of vision who wish to help in forwarding a national intelligence. They go abroad, they work hard and well, they enrich their adopted countries. This is proclaimed by Irishmen at home as a loss to Ireland. There is a dilemma here, which looks as if it will be insoluble for many years. If the young people stay in Ireland, they are subject to the urgings of ancestral voices and the deadening pressures exerted in every Irish stratum, hindered in the all-important growth within themselves of better values. They are blinkered, hampered in the personal effort to see their native land in proper perspective. If they go overseas, they deprive their own country of a potential it very urgently needs. If they stay at home, they are unlikely to grow taller. There is much in Ireland that is permanently stunted. It is one of the last countries in which, as things are at the moment, reason can profitably be applied in the solving of problems, so the Irish both north and south—those of them, that is, with knowledge and capacity for thought—are in the main unimpressed by suggestions of conferences at tables of whatever size and shape. The Ulstermen, being generally of a more pragmatic mind than the Republican Irish, prefer to look facts in the eye and draw their conclusions from them rather than from emotionalism and wishful-thinking. They know what they want, they know what has happened to them in the past, they are a cautious race, they like to lift the lid of the attractive package and examine the contents closely and for an adequate time before they will buy. They remember what happened when the State of Northern Ireland was born in 1921, they remember the horrible happenings in Ireland as a whole from 1919 to 1923 in particular.

It was in Southern Ireland that the Sinn Fein movement started. The phrase Sinn Fein is Gaelic Irish for Ourselves Alone, and those words, in the Irish–English context and contest, are self-explanatory. The movement was founded to secure the independence of Ireland from England and out of it grew the Irish Republican Army, led by such men as the famous Irish guerilla fighter, Michael Collins, later killed—characteristically—by his own countrymen. The Irish Republican Army, containing in its ranks many splendid and clear-headedly patriotic Irishmen as well as many incapable of seeing further than the range of a rifle, began to fight the 'occupying forces' in or around 1919. The 'occupying forces' were, at first, the Royal Irish Constabulary, just as much native-born Irishmen as the Irish Republican Army men. Later, the 'occupying forces' embraced regiments of the British Army and a scratch force of police auxiliaries, the detested and over-blackened Black and Tans who fought the Irish Republican Army with its own methods of ruthless warfare and have been subsequently described by the Southern Irish propagandists as the most vicious terrorists ever thrown by the English at the Irish throat. There is truth in this, but the propagandists are careful to say nothing of the viciousness with which the Irish fought. The methods of both sides were horrifying. The Irish have never been squeamish in the matter of killing and the Irish Republican Army, for all the sentimental and emotionally admiring ballads sung throughout the country today in praise of its heroic Freedom Fighters, shared the belief of violent revolutionaries the world over that any kind of killing in the name of a national revolutionary cause is sanctified. It declared itself as fighting a war but callously disregarded the agreed conventions of war. Much of its fighting against the English forces and certain Irish social classes in Ireland itself was nothing other than cold and conscienceless murder. Its practice of blowing uninvolved English men, women and children to pieces by planting time-bombs in English city shops and postal pillar-boxes, its 'military executions' without reasonable trial, its 'legitimate ambushes' with the odds overwhelmingly in its favour, its avoidance of fair-matched open warfare, its slaying of unarmed solitary men conveniently labelled as spies, its killings of old men and older women, its pitiless burning of the beautiful and ancient houses of uncommitted long-established Irish families innocent of offence —all in the name of Ireland and contrary to the teachings of the Catholic Church its soldiers so fervently attended and believed in—have been carefully concealed in a cleverly contrived fog. The world has been deceived. The English themselves, with typical forgetfulness, have been persuaded to accept the statement that they should be ashamed of the 'one-sided brutality' with which they fought the chivalrous Irish, whose only crime was to struggle with inadequate arms and equipment for the independence of their country.

It was a dreadful time. It seemed as if the whole of Ireland were aflame. The war-hardened men of the Black and Tans, with their British Army khaki uniforms, their black berets and grim black belts, their rifles forever at the ready, their heavy revolvers in open holsters tied to their thighs to facilitate a quick draw, appeared to be everywhere, tramping the streets, firing discriminatingly or undiscriminatingly at open windows, speeding through the cities, towns and villages and along the countryside roads in armoured cars and wire-netted Crossley tenders, shooting, shooting, shooting. Houses and tenement blocks were raided, suspected Irishmen dragged from them and shot, villages were burned to the ground, most of the city of Cork reduced to acrid rubble. Ireland was a place of curfew and terror, quarter on both sides was unwanted and ungiven, the fight was savage and to the death. It was one of the darkest and most shameful passages in the Irish story. Michael Collins discovered that a number of British Army intelligence officers had arrived secretly in Dublin. He ordered their 'execution' and, in the course of an hour, fourteen of them were hunted down in their hotels and lodgings, caught unarmed and shot dead, one of them in the presence of his young and pregnant wife although he begged his executioners to let her go into another room and close the door before they killed him.[1] The English Government, under the premiership of David Lloyd George, saw that a settlement of some description must be reached. A truce was arranged, the Ulster leaders—James Craig, in particular—and the Irish rebel leaders were summoned to London. Conference after conference broke down and the horrible struggle renewed itself. Then Lloyd George framed a Bill for the Better Government of Ireland, later known as the Government of Ireland Act,

[1] Mentioned in many of the books by Irish authors of the time; also recounted to the author by a Major in the British Intelligence Corps, who escaped the I.R.A. gunmen by diving through a french window and climbing the garden wall.

1920, providing an intended temporary partition of the country between north and south and—it was hoped—an ultimate pacification and unification of both parts under a single government for the whole of Ireland. There were to be, to start with, an Ulster Parliament and a Southern Ireland Parliament, with a linking Council for consultative purposes in matters affecting the interests of each. Provision was made for the establishment of an all-Ireland Parliament, subject to the consent of both Northern and Southern Ireland. This fell through. Later, in 1921, Ulster was given the right to opt out of another proposed all-Ireland government, if she so wished. She did so wish. In view of what she had seen of the Southern Irish bitterness, she exercised the option.

Fighting flamed again in Southern Ireland and it became obvious that the immediate settlement provisions of the 1920 Act and its hopeful longer-term objectives were unacceptable not only to the Ulstermen but to the Southern Irishmen as well. The Ulstermen had never wanted Home Rule in any form but decided in the circumstances to accept it for themselves as being preferable to a government of all Ireland in which they knew for certain they would be out-voted and their political faith frustrated. They knew, through their insight into the thinking of the Southern Irishmen, that they would be forever stripped of the British connection that meant so much to them. They set up their small Parliament and resolutely proceeded to make the best of it, with a warning to all concerned that they would resist any pressure that might be brought on them to abandon it. They give the same warning today and the English would be wise to heed it. The Ulsterman is not of the kind that weakens on a question of principle.

Lloyd George had to try once more to settle with the Southern Irish. After long and hard negotiation, the English Government managed to gain the signed assent of Michael Collins and the other Southern Irish plenipotentiaries to a Treaty drawn up in December 1921. Collins and his colleagues signed reluctantly, as they knew that their consent to partition would be resented and fiercely opposed by many obdurate elements at home in Ireland who would look on the division of the country as a betrayal of Republicanism. However, the Treaty was taken back to Ireland and submitted to the members of the clandestine

Provisional Government of Republican Ireland, set up by the Republicans when they were fighting the English. The President of this Provisional Government, Eamon de Valera—one of the strangest figures in modern Irish history, although not himself an Irishman, and one of the most stubborn and narrow, a man so mistaken in many things that his value to Ireland has been questionable—rejected the Treaty and, with his equally obstinate and visionless followers, prepared to fight in order to stop it being put into effect. Collins and his supporters knew that the Irish Republican Army was in straits and could not possibly continue fighting in the face of the additional military strength Lloyd George had threatened to send against it.[1] Many of the Sinn Fein leaders agreed with him and decided to swallow the Treaty.

Their decision led to the creation in 1922 of the Irish Free State under its Parliament in Dublin, known as the Oireachtas in Dail Eireann. A Boundary Commission confirmed to the Southern Irish Parliament three of the counties in the original area of the Province of Ulster and left to the Ulster Parliament the six counties of Antrim, Armagh, Down, Fermanagh, Londonderry and Tyrone. The Southern Irish, although partition is never a satisfactory way of solving the problem of a country in which political philosophies and allegiances held by its people are opposed, had at last achieved self-government. The Home Rule so long and so honourably sought by John Redmond and the men of his Irish Party in the British House of Commons was to some degree a fact and the Southern Irish could run their limited household as they pleased. Elections were held and Dail Eireann came into open and acknowledged Parliamentary operation. The English gave a sigh of relief. They had finally had enough of the Irish and their country. They looked forward to seeing them establish themselves, they wished them luck in learning the uncomfortable craft of governing their own Irish people. They hoped that the Irish, north and south, would now settle down and live in peace, that there would be a long and healing period of tranquillity, that both sides would come to respect each other as time passed and would eventually merge in friendship and enduring trust under

[1] See *Michael Collins and the Making of a New Ireland* by Piaras Beaslai and *The Victory of Sinn Fein* by P. S. O'Hegarty.

a single Irish Government. They were disappointed. The Southern Irish celebrated their new-found freedom from English control by embarking on a civil war of even greater ferocity than the war they had waged with the English.

The Southern Irish talk little and write less about their civil war. They keep silent about it, in the main, because they have shrewdness enough to sense how gravely it discredits them. They will speak willingly and unendingly of the atrocities committed by the Black and Tans, they are understandingly loth to speak of atrocities committed by Irishman on Irishman lest their words shall be heard and lead to a diminishment of their success in spreading across the world their stories of the savagery of the English in Ireland and the unique bigotry of the Ulstermen. The Southern Irish are surprisingly and formidably expert propagandists but not so expert at looking inside themselves and assessing fully and honestly what they find there. They are intellectually astigmatic, strongly flawed by a capacity for self-deception, unversed in the truth about their country and their race and unwilling to be made aware of it, opting for romanticism, perhaps afraid. They are an odd mixture, with their cloudy thinking, their business ability—there are no sharper traders in Europe—and their head-in-the-sand wishfulness in the world of political realities, their ignorance of what goes on in the corridors where matters of global importance are decided. They are immature.

Some of their wiser men readily admit this, some of their less wise men can be driven to admit it. Most Southern Irishmen, however, when they are brought to the admission of anything that tells against their race, are near unanimous in blaming the defect on England. The English, they argue, applied to the Irish the policy of 'divide and rule' and thus were enabled to maintain their domination in Ireland. It does not seem to occur to the Irish that the ease with which they were divided is a reflection on them, on their national character. The Swiss and the Finns were not easily divided, or the Dutch and other small races that set out to gain independence. Each population, when engaged in its struggle, stood firm in racial unity. Serious betrayals of the national cause by fellow-countrymen were few, if any. In Ireland they were numerous. But, where Ireland is concerned, all, all, is the fault of the English. Again and again supposedly educated Irishmen are heard to complain that their country suffered '800 years of oppression by the British Empire', despite the fact that 800 years ago there was no such thing as a British Empire. How could the Irish mature, they ask, when the boot of the British Empire was on their neck for 800 years? It is this sort of thing that makes intelligent and well-informed Irishmen, who think deeply and with clarity on the present and future problems of their country, come very close to giving up. They are confronted in Ireland at so many turns by the Irish insistence on clinging to the myths absorbed in boyhood from myth-ridden parents and school teachers. They are confronted, too, by the primitiveness that keeps rising to the surface of the Irish, despite their devotion to their Church. Southern Ireland strikes many visitors as being a strongly religious country, touchingly dedicated to the older Christian faith—and, in certain ways, it is—yet it can truly be said of a saddeningly large proportion of Southern Irishmen that they are of the kind that holds human life to be cheap.

When, during the 1914–18 War, there was a rumour in Dublin that the hard-pressed British were about to apply conscription to Ireland—James Craig had asked for it to be applied to Ulster and the Ulstermen would have welcomed it—an article appeared in *Ant Oglach*, the secretly printed journal of the Irish National Volunteers, and said this:

A conscription campaign would be an unprovoked onslaught by an army upon a civilian population, which would thus be given no choice between murder on the spot and massacre after an interval. If England decides on this atrocity, then we on our part must decide that in our resistance we shall acknowledge no limit and no scruple. We must recognize that anyone, civilian or soldier, who assists directly or by connivance in this crime against us merits no more consideration than a wild beast and should be killed without mercy or hesitation, as opportunity offers. Any man who knowingly or willingly does anything to facilitate the working of conscription must be dealt with exactly as if he were an enemy soldier. The man who serves an exemption tribunal, the doctor who treats soldiers or examines conscripts, the man who voluntarily surrenders to conscription when called upon to do so by the authorities, the man who in any shape or form applies for exemption, the man who drives a police car or assists in the transport of British Army supplies, all these, having assisted the enemy, must be shot or otherwise destroyed with the least possible delay.

The article was specially printed separately and circulated[1] to all Volunteer detachments on the instruction of Michael Collins. Conscription was not applied to Ireland, of course, but, if it had been, the article—accepted as an order by the Volunteers—would have resulted in the imperilment of the large number of Protestant Unionists throughout Ireland who would have freely wished to obey the conscription command. Many thousands of Catholic Irishmen, in sympathy and agreement with the Allied effort to defeat Germany, would have been similarly imperilled. There is no lack of evidence that human life was indeed held cheaply in Southern Ireland. P. S. O'Hegarty, in his book *The Victory of Sinn Fein*, has this to say:

> As the shooting evolved until it became a guerilla war, the public conscience grew to accept it as the natural order of things . . . the national Press sat on the fence and such Churchmen as condemned the shootings mixed their ethics with politics and made the case worse. The eventual result of that was a complete moral collapse. When it was open to any Volunteer Commandant to order the shooting of any civilian and to cover himself with the laconic legend 'Spy' on the dead man's breast, personal security vanished and no man's life was safe. With the vanishing of reason and principle and morality we became a mob . . . and for a mob there is only one law—gun law.

O'Hegarty was an active member of the illegal and secret Irish Republican Brotherhood before the 1914–18 War and later a member of Sinn Fein, so it is easy to see where his sympathies lay. His description of the gun-law acquiescence by the Southern Irish people is soundly based and may be accepted, as those who lived in Ireland at the time—and they include the

---

[1] The article was written by Ernest Blythe; see *Michael Collins and the Making of a New Ireland* by Piaras Beaslai.

author of this book—are only too sadly aware. They look back on that murderous period with a shudder. There were Ulstermen, too, of course, who thought nothing of allowing the gun to have the first and final word. Ulster also has its unhappy share of violent men but they were then and still are proportionately very much fewer than those of Southern Ireland. The behaviour of the Ulstermen since the foundation of the Northern Ireland State in 1921 has proved this. They have not launched a single attack across the border between Ulster and the Irish Republic,[1] although they have had to endure many armed and vicious cross-border attacks by the men of the South. They had much to endure in particular when the Southern Irish were engaged in their civil war, indeed they had to fight for their very existence as a separate State. The Irish Republican Army—mostly the anti-Treaty elements of it, those who were opposed to the Irish Free State forces supporting the Treaty—made a determined and deadly attempt to bring it down and the consequent death-roll in Ulster was heavy. The Ulstermen defended their State fiercely but they have never, in something like 200 years, perhaps not since the seventeenth century, shown such ferocity as the Southern Irish displayed when they fought their appalling civil war. Ulstermen will strike back but they are rarely cruel and they have to be very seriously provoked before they will strike back at all.

When the civil war broke out, almost the whole of Southern Ireland was again aflame. Men like De Valera, Rory O'Connor, Oscar Traynor, Liam Lynch and Erskine Childers—an Englishman and author of that famous book *The Riddle of the Sands*—led the Irregulars, as the dissident Irish Republican Army faction were known. Sean Lemass, Prime Minister of the Irish Republic from 1959 until succeeded by Jack Lynch, was another Irregular leader. W. T. Cosgrave, first Prime Minister of the Irish Free State, and Michael Collins were the political and military leaders of the pro-Treaty Government party. The Irregulars seized the Four Courts in Dublin, a beautiful eighteenth-century building containing the Public Record Office and the irreplaceable

[1] This is still true, although ultra-extreme Ulster Protestants have attempted (1969) to blow up certain buildings and installations in the Irish Republic; they did not make an armed attack on fellow-Irishmen, although nothing excuses their would-be terrorism.

historical documents of Ireland. It was shelled by Government troops and the Irregulars blew it up before they evacuated it. The documents were lost in the flames. Father fought against son, brother against brother. Towns were set ablaze, villages burnt down, personal animosities led to personal murders. Fathers and uncles of leaders, elderly relatives who were not in any way involved, were murdered merely because they happened to be related. Reprisal followed reprisal. Brigadier Sean Hales of the Government forces was assassinated by the Irregulars. At dawn next morning, Rory O'Connor and three of his fellow Irregulars, who had earlier been captured, were taken from their cells on Government orders and shot without trial—'as a reprisal for the assassination of Brigadier Sean Hales and as a solemn warning to those . . . who are engaged in a conspiracy of assassination against the representatives of the Irish people'. All over the country Irishman murdered Irishman in the name of Ireland.

When the Irish Rebellion of 1916 in Dublin was suppressed by the British troops, fourteen of the Irish rebel leaders were captured, tried by courts martial and executed by firing squad, on the grounds that they had been proved guilty of high treason in time of war. None of them denied his active participation in the rebellion, there was no injustice, the courts martial were legal and were fairly conducted. The executions angered the Southern Irish people, at first strongly and angrily opposed to the Rebellion, and much has since been made of the shootings by way of propaganda. Here again the English have been cleverly put in the wrong, yet they did no more and probably less than other countries engaged in a life-and-death war with a powerful enemy would have done. No country, fighting for its life, likes being attacked in the back, and Germany would not have hesitated to take much severer action against any rebels.

But the protesting Irish still complain to the world about the 1916 executions, yet say very little about the executions carried out by both sides in their civil war. They totalled considerably more than fourteen and the legal process under which they took place was more often non-existent and, at the best, very questionable indeed. According to a book by Eoin Neeson, published in 1966,[1] something like eighty executions took place, not to

[1] *The Civil War in Ireland*, published in Cork.

mention an unascertainable number of even more unpleasant killings of prisoners. No one knows or ever will know how many men were shot in the course of the struggle. Thousands of Irishmen were killed by the guns of their fellow Irish. The hatred and the savagery were intense. The Catholic Church was horrified and referred in a joint pastoral letter to 'unauthorized murders', a very Irish phrase to use. Diarmuid O'Hegarty, Military Governor of Mountjoy Gaol in Dublin, a Government pro-Treaty officer, warned Irregular soldiers imprisoned there that 'any resistance to guards . . . revolt, mutiny, conspiracy, insubordination, attempt to escape or cell wrecking' would render them 'liable to be shot down'. In what civilized country, the Ulstermen asked, is a captured soldier 'liable to be shot down' for insubordination or cell wrecking, apart from trying to escape, which, provided a parole has not been given, is legitimate under the recognized articles of war? The fact is that the civil war was a disgrace to the Southern Irish name and they are wise to keep as quiet as possible about it. The Government side were faced with an appalling situation, admittedly, and had to take the draconian action of setting up Military Courts and outlawing all Irishmen in arms against the State. This gave some legal standing but it was a merciless and bloody fight, watched grimly by the unsurprised Ulstermen in the north. Torture was commonplace. Neeson describes the killings of some captured Irregulars:

In March 1923, nine Irregulars, one of them with a broken arm, another with a broken wrist and one unable to walk from spinal injuries, were taken by lorry to Ballyseedy Cross near Tralee. The hands of each prisoner were tied behind him, each was tied by the arms and legs to the man beside him and a rope was passed completely round them so that they stood in a ring facing outwards. In the centre of the ring was a landmine. The Government soldiers who had tied the prisoners took cover and the mine was exploded. The remnants of the prisoners were flung far and wide, bits of bodies hung from the trees in the wood that bordered the roadside. By some explosive freak, one man, instead of being blown to pieces, was blown into a ditch and escaped. Several of the prisoners had been interrogated that day in Tralee

Barracks by officers armed with hammers, hence the broken limbs.

Breaking the limbs of prisoners to coax them into revealing what military information they may possess is not in accord with the accepted usages of war, nor is it accepted that they shall be disposed of in such a manner as to decorate the surrounding trees with torsoes. A few days after, five other Irregulars, captured nearby, were interrogated in the same way and killed in the same way. To ensure that none of them should have the misfortune to be blown into a ditch and compelled to run for his life, each prisoner was thoughtfully shot in the legs before the landmine was exploded. The various families concerned were doubtless gratified to learn later that the bits and pieces had been respectably coffined. Indeed the matter of burial was usually attended to. There was a Government order—'Prisoners in military custody in the Kerry Command shall be interred by the troops of the area in which the death has occurred'. What could be more explicit? Furthermore, Government officers in charge of Irregulars detained in crowded prisons where insubordination and cell wrecking were disapproved of showed particular understanding. The next-of-kin were invariably ignorant of the whereabouts of their combatant menfolk, although aware, of course, that they were fighting on the side of the Irregulars. The Prison Officers sent telegrams, which read: 'Remains of . . . have been coffined and buried in consecrated ground.' The considerate sending of such information relieved the next-of-kin of distress and reassured them on an important aspect.

It is not to be thought, of course, that the barbarous killings were confined to the Government side, although Neeson suggests that they were. He implies that the Irregulars fought with the nobility of Arthurian knights. The fact is that there was nothing to choose between the two sides. The Irregulars, with even less ability than the Government troops to house and guard their prisoners, resorted to murder as freely as their opponents. They, too, were Irish Republican Army men and it was men of that army who had two years earlier thrown two captured Black and Tans, unwounded and alive, into the blazing furnace of an Irish gas-works.[1] Why should they shrink from

[1] See *Protest in Arms* by Edgar Holt, p. 226.

killing now? Both sides revealed in full the ugliest facets of the Southern Irish mind and instinct, both brought shame to their country. When it came to a killing regarded as a military or political necessity, the law of the land was ignored. Erskine Childers, captured by Government troops and discovered in possession of a small pearl-handled revolver given him originally by Michael Collins as a personal gift before the civil war began, was tried in Dublin, found guilty of being in arms against the State and executed by firing squad despite the fact that the defence was in the process of trying to secure a writ of habeas corpus and the execution should have been stayed until the application for the writ had been decided.

The severity shown by the Government party was essential, however. They saw that the country must be brought back to normality, that the Southern Irish people had endured too many years of warfare, that those who fought the State were injuring the people and defying their will. The people longed for peace and the Government men were determined to secure it for them. They thought more clearly than the Irregulars, who left their thinking in political matters to De Valera, a man of pedantry and persistent unrealism, while they did the fighting. De Valera really believed that an Irish Republic wholly independent of England could be formed and that Ulster could and should be forced to join it whatever the cost in still more fighting, still more killing. The Government party knew that this was an obsession, wrongly informed, unrealizable, though they had some sympathy with it where Ulster was concerned. They argued that the Treaty had conceded three-quarters of what the Irish Home Rulers had struggled for, that the unity of all Ireland necessarily lay in the future and could only be achieved by convincing the Ulstermen of good intention and proved good practice on the part of the South. They had a better appreciation of the attitude of the Ulstermen than De Valera had—he was never able to understand it—although they erred at first in failing to curb the elements of the Irish Republican Army engaged in attacking Ulster and trying to smash it. However, W. T. Cosgrave, political head of the Irish Free State, eventually recognized that the attack was a mistake. He was a quiet-spoken and seemingly diffident man, deceptively so, a man of vision and firmness, capable of taking difficult and stern decisions and enforcing them as the hour and the crisis demanded. He and James Craig, the monolithic and reticent Ulsterman, learnt to respect each other and to work sensibly behind the scenes in matters of common Irish interest, with no sacrifice of opposing ideals and objectives. Had the Cosgrave policy of common-sense dealing with Ulster been consistently followed by his successors, the situation between the north and south of Ireland might have been different today. Indeed, it would almost certainly have been different and better. The successors were lesser men, however, who too often lacked tact and patience, talked too much and talked foolishly. Cosgrave, although frequently compelled to talk down to the level of his political supporters throughout Southern Ireland, usually knew—in regard to Ulster—when to speak and when to keep silence. He was a good Irishman, strong and fair.

He certainly had need of his strength as the civil war went on. Michael Collins, on an inspection tour of the Government troops in his native county of Cork, was ambushed by the Irregulars and shot dead. Cosgrave had to see the war through more or less on his own from the political aspect. It was a daunting task. The fighting had put much of Dublin in ruins, many country towns and villages were in like plight—a few of them escaped damage—and, as the war continued, the new-born State fell more and more into chaos. Steadily, however, the Government troops succeeded in capturing and holding the principal ports, which enabled them to keep renewing their munitions of war, the vital quantities of rifles and ammunition, guns, shells and bombs, which—the story of Ireland is ever ironic—they were as glad to receive from the English as their former enemies were to ship them. The Irregulars, deprived of the ports and the all-important major towns in which they found both food and defensive shelter, were driven to reverting to the hit-and-run tactics of flying-column warfare, inevitably ineffective against the always increasing numbers of better armed Government troops, and at last surrendered. The civil war was over.

The victory had been dearly bought. Many thousands of Irishmen lay in known and unknown graves, thousands more were maimed.[1] The war had cost the Irish Free State no less a

[1] See Eoin Neeson for casualties.

sum than £17,000,000 and an army of 60,000 men had been enrolled to defeat the Irregulars, a very large and expensive army for so small and so poor a country to maintain in the field.[1] However, in the spring months of the year 1923, the Government was at last in sole control of its twenty-six counties. The long and dreadful time which had begun in the morning of Easter Monday 1916, when Pearse and Connolly and their men had seized the General Post Office in Dublin as their rebellion headquarters, had ended. The bitterness of it all, especially the bitterness born of the viciously waged civil war, is felt to this day in Southern Ireland by those who are old enough to recall the era and lucky enough to have survived it. Many elder Southern Irishmen who took part in the fighting of that terrible period and emerged unscathed by bomb or bullet or deliberate maiming are particularly embittered. The two principal political parties in the Dublin Parliament are known as Fianna Fail and Fine Gael. The first was founded by De Valera and his fellow Republicans who argued and fought on the side of the Irregulars, the second arose in the interests of Cosgrave and his fellow supporters of the Treaty and the Irish Free State. There is still a flow of recrimination between them on the floor of Parliament and even outside Parliament, what the Irish call 'up-casting', each accusing the other of responsibility for launching the civil war and for sins of commission in the course of it. Truly is it said that the Irish have long memories.

The Protestant Ulstermen have long memories, too. They remember the flame and the smoke they could see from the north as they shaded their eyes and stared across the border towards the south, they remember the civil war gunfire, the pitiless bloodletting which for all their faults at the time they had not been guilty of and have not been guilty of since. Then, when trouble broke out in Ulster in 1968 through the activities of the Civil Rights Association and continued to disturb the life of the Province, they, too, felt bitterness as they read in the newspapers of the world the one-sided attacks on them, the feature articles blaming them exclusively for what had gone wrong, the English and American editorials that patronized them and insulted them and ignored their achievements and put

[1] See *Protest in Arms* (Holt), p. 307.

forward solutions in accord with the wishes of the men of the Irish Republic, in forgetfulness of what Southern Irishmen had done in the past and might very well do in the future. They resented the slanted television pictures of Ulster rioting, introduced by uninformed men devoid of understanding of what had led to the rioting, they resented the superficiality, the biased assumptions, the susceptibility to Irish Republican propaganda and they particularly resented the holier-than-thou attitude of the political leaders of the Irish Republic in their appeals to the United Nations to despatch a peace-keeping force to Ulster with a view to ending the 'horror' there. The Protestant Ulstermen had not descended to such depths of behaviour, such extremes of savagery, as to blow their opponents to pieces with landmines or throw them alive into furnaces.

The troubles that broke out in Ulster in 1968 were bad and the Protestant Ulstermen had brought them on themselves through their own short-sightedness and prejudiced folly, but to compare them with the true horror of the Southern Irish fighting against the English and the atrocities of the civil war would be absurd. The Ulstermen are parochially minded in the main, over-absorbed in their provincial problems, unsophisticated and off-guard in the dangerous world of propaganda, unpractised in the skills of publicity. They have long been unaware of the importance of image-making and of constant maintenance of the image. Money spent on it, in their view, would have been money wasted. They have awakened at last to their mistake but still have pinchbeck ideas on how to set about repairing the damage they have caused the Province through neglect, are still unwilling to vote in their Parliament a sufficiency of money to cover the heavy and ever-increasing cost of modern publicity campaigns as planned and pursued by experienced and influential public relations consultancies today.

The Government of the Irish Republic has made no such mistake. It has shown an intelligent, consistent and calculating appreciation of the value of a good publicity service and lobbying machine in England and in all the principal Western countries, especially the United States of America where the Republican Irish element is so politically significant, and never hesitates to ensure that money is plentifully available for it. In the summer of 1969, when the Ulster troubles were growing and the eyes of

41

the world were turned on the Province, the Dublin Government astutely reinforced its overseas embassies with something like twenty trained publicists to assist the experts already in post, with the result that the Republican interpretation of the rioting in Londonderry and Belfast and elsewhere in Ulster is widely known and the Ulster version is not. The additional publicists sent abroad from Dublin have been very effective and the opportunities of the Dublin Government illustrates how far ahead it is of the Ulster Government in the art of making and enhancing an image. It is possible, of course, that the Ulster Government may come to realize fully the danger it has brought upon itself and its people through its foolishly skimping attitude—the outlook of a village ironmonger weighing a bag of nails—and will somehow, despite its lack of direct representation abroad in the way of embassies, bestir itself to tell the Ulster story. It had better do so, if it prefers to survive, for many English Members of Parliament at Westminster have been displaying the all too familiar English ignorance of the realities of the situation since the Ulster troubles broke out and have been throwing petrol on the fire.

But the fire in Ulster today is small, however, compared with the one the Ulstermen had to face and subdue when their Government was founded in 1921—and for a near desperate year or so afterwards—as the men of the Irish Republican Army flung themselves on the infant State and strove to kill it. The flames that had lighted Dublin and other Southern Irish cities and towns were seen then in Belfast, the same language of machine-gun, rifle and grenade was heard in its streets and from its rooftops, there was the same ruthless and cowardly and horrible killing. The Ulstermen had been in no way provocative, they had not attacked their fellow Irishmen of the south, they had merely asked to be let alone, to be allowed to run their minute corner of Ireland in peace and to the best of their ability. They had a Governmental apparatus to set up, a Civil Service to create. They had a Parliament House to design and build, an electoral system to bring into being, a police force to reorganize and re-name, a code of law to frame and institute, a Law Courts to erect for the housing of the judges and the legal administration. They had no experience in such fields, they had to learn. They were walking slowly, tentatively, sometimes mistakenly, but always determinedly. They were busy with their own affairs, very busy indeed, they had neither the time nor the wish to interfere with others. Others, however, had both the time and the wish to interfere with them. Thousands of well-armed Irish Republican Army men infiltrated secretly into Ulster, coalesced with those already there, found concealment with resident sympathizers and prepared to strike.

Chapter Three

BELFAST, the capital of Ulster and a city that has had more disapproving fingers pointed at it of late than perhaps any other in Europe, is claimed by its citizens, with all the confidence that marks the uninhibited and untravelled Ulstermen, to be the equal of any in the world and probably superior. The claim is unjustified. It is an unlovely city, of mushroom growth, dully painted—the Belfast people, or most of them or too many of them, have a deeply embedded Presbyterian predilection for the respectability of front-door brown—and it is architecturally unattractive. It lacks the superb and internationally famous Georgian terraces and squares of Dublin, built in the eighteenth century by the unthanked English. The Belfast atmosphere is commercial and over-burdened with industrial smoke, its civic planning is unimaginative and incompetent, but it has charming suburbs and is rewardingly situated on the beautiful Belfast Lough with the splendid headlands on one side and gently wooded hills on the other. It has admirable schools, maintaining sensibly moderate fees and syllabuses that result in the pupils being more advanced in progress than those of equivalent age in a lot of the top-ranking schools in England and the United States. It has a good university, prudently and generously helped by grants from the Ulster Government, possessed of outstanding faculties of medicine, science and law, numerously and happily attended by many coloured students from many overseas countries. Such discrimination as Belfast may be guilty of is rarely conditioned by colour prejudice. The race antipathy that has faulted England and will almost certainly fault her even more in the future is unknown in Belfast or anywhere in Ulster. Also, however questionable Belfast may be in certain aspects, it has a considerable advantage over other and more polished cities. You can get out of it with gratifying speed and ease. Provided you have a car, and almost everyone has a car nowadays, you can find yourself teeing up a golf ball on a first-

44

class course or setting a spinnaker on the Lough within thirty minutes of leaving the office. Even without a car, you can get clear of the city in a surprisingly short time.

It is a hard-working city, yet for all its indigenous preoccupation with the pursuit of money and its determination to acquire as much of it as possible as quickly as possible, the tempo of life is sensibly slower than in most leading contemporary cities. The people, too, are remarkable in their kindliness and unaltering instinct for hospitality, despite the inclination of a segment of them to crack the skulls of fellow citizens in Christian disapprobation of errant doctrine. It is a small segment, disproportionate to the main mass of the Belfast and Ulster population and the cause of a damaging reproach which the Province overall has not deserved. Men and women from other countries who stay in Belfast for even a short while are struck by the fact—and it is fact—that nowhere do they encounter any prejudice in their relationships with such Ulster people and Belfast people as they meet. They are struck, too, by the fact that family doors are instantly open to them. There are countries, and possibly England is one of them, where you have to be known for years before you are invited into a household for a cup of morning coffee. Not so in Belfast or anywhere in Ulster, but there you will be given tea not coffee as a rule. The Ulster people are prodigious tea drinkers and their hospitality is immediate and warm-hearted. Whatever the family you may meet, whether well-off or harassed by unemployment and the hardships that go with it (all too rife in Belfast), you will hear the women of it saying with quiet command as you prepare to go—'Now, now, you'll not be leaving this house till you've had a cup of tea'—and if you refuse, you will hurt them.

Belfast households are never closed to those who come in friendship. There is the cup of tea for them in the little front parlour or there are chairs for them at the family lunch or dinner table, there is an observed tradition of pot-luck invitations and evening laughter with fine Ulster whiskey and good conversation. The people have both humour and wit, whichever social class they come from. This is especially true of the working-class men, although they have suffered dreadfully from the endemic under-employment that has for so long afflicted the Province generally and Belfast in particular. Their womenfolk are hard-pressed but they have pride. The working-class wives and mothers have faced their difficulties and continue to face them with character, dignity and unselfishness, ensuring that whoever in the family may be in want it will not be the children. This can be said, of course, of all decent women throughout the world, but it is extensively true of the women who live in the speckless little parlour houses of the back streets of Belfast. A cheerful, courageous, blunt-tongued race, admired and liked by all who come to know them.

No city in Ireland has grown so swiftly as Belfast. In 1769, its population totalled a mere 11,000, in 1869 there were 173,000 and in 1969 the population had reached a figure of around 400,000. It owed this unusually rapid increase to the rise of several major industries. For generations, Belfast housed the world's leading and most skilful manufacturers of fine linens. Ulster linen had a quality that was unbeatable. In the eighteenth century there was founded in Belfast a small wooden-ship construction concern which developed into the world's largest single shipbuilding yard, Harland and Wolff. Later, there was founded the Belfast Ropework Company, which supplied the British Navy and innumerable other navies with countless miles of the best and most reliable rope; and then came the famous firm of Davidson and Company—The Sirocco Works—for long the world's greatest manufacturers of tea machinery, sufficient to produce three hundred million pounds weight of tea leaf every year. In 1857, a young man called Thomas Gallaher set up in business in the tiny front room of a tiny house, making twist tobacco himself on a hand-operated tobacco spinning machine, acting as his own traveller and delivering the orders personally. When he started, he had to put down £3 for the goodwill of the business he was buying and, having only six shillings to his name in ready cash, he was compelled to borrow the balance. Today, Gallaher Limited is one of the world's giants in tobacco and cigarette making, with an annual sales intake of approximately £450,000,000. These are some of the industries built up in Belfast, in ever-growing need of workpeople. The workers came into existence—presumably in the normal way—and the population climbed.

When the 1914–18 War came at last to an end, the Belfast people were tired. For four and a half years they had been working extremely hard, helping England on aspects that were vital to her. The Harland and Wolff yard had provided the British Navy with more than half a million tons in the way of critically needed warships—heavy cruisers, light cruisers, armed merchant cruisers, destroyers, heavy monitors, light monitors, oil carriers, fast patrol boats—and another huge tonnage in merchant ships to replace the losses from U-Boat sinkings, together with troopships, hospital ships and other big ships for varied use. The din of the riveters and of crashing hammers in the yard had never ceased as the Harland and Wolff men not only built ships but repaired many of those that had been heavily damaged in action, built and fitted ships' engines and installed special deck armaments. It had been seven days and seven nights a week non-stop and a construction speed never before achieved in the realm of shipbuilding and shipwork generally. The other but much smaller Belfast shipyard, Workman and Clark, had worked equally hard and well and had turned out a further much-needed tonnage of ships. The English were under a deep debt of gratitude to both yards or should have been. They had been magnificent.

But the yards had not been the only contributors to the war effort. Every one of the hundreds of Royal Air Force fighters and bombers of the time had linen stretched on its wings and fuselage and the Belfast mills had woven every foot of that linen and indeed almost all the linen used by the British during the war, an astronomical quantity. Gallahers and Murrays—Murrays were another long-established Belfast firm, dating from the early nineteenth century—had produced hundreds of tons of tobacco and cigarettes for the armies in France, the big engineering concerns had helped in the making of munitions, the clothing firms with the making of uniforms, the whole of the significant industry of Belfast had been adjusted to war output. As the sirens sounded for the Armistice of November 1918, the Belfast people gave as great a sigh of relief and thankfulness as any heard from the British all over the rest of the United Kingdom. They had given of their best blood and best endeavour and they were tired. They were soon to be angry. Thanks to the Irish Republican Army, no fewer than 232 men, women and children were to be shot dead in a single year in Ulster, mostly in Belfast, a thousand were to suffer wounds, and property worth £3,000,000 was to be destroyed by bomb and flame. The appeal of King George V, as he formally opened the Ulster Parliament in June 1921, to all Irishmen 'to pause, to stretch out the hand of forbearance and conciliation, to forgive and forget, and to join in making for the land which they love a new era of peace, contentment and goodwill', was to fall on ears deaf to all but the sound of gunfire.

The period of the main Irish Republican Army attack on Ulster, unprovoked, unjustified and murderous, which the English of today do not trouble to recall and which the present Government of the Irish Republic takes very good care to keep quiet about, covered roughly the years 1921, 1922 and 1923. They were years of horror, a time of martial law, when soldiers of the British Army and the men of the Royal Ulster Constabulary and Special Constabulary fought and died in the struggle to save the Province from being ruined by men ruthlessly resolved to wreck it, however much misery they might bring to their fellow-Irish in doing so. There were between eight and nine thousand Irish Republican Army men in Ulster, armed with revolvers, rifles and grenades and possessed of supplies of materials for incendiarism, hidden in the cellars and buried in the backyards of the houses of local Nationalist sympathizers. Eight to nine thousand armed men are almost the equivalent of a regular army Division, which usually totals about ten thousand.[1] There the comparison ends, however, for the Irish Republican Army men operated in civilian clothes, as they had done against the British forces in Dublin and elsewhere in Southern Ireland. This made them inconspicuous and thus able to stroll up behind an unsuspecting and unarmed man in a central and busy city street—more often a man of some civic prominence, marked down for killing on the grounds that his death would be 'salutary'—pull revolvers from their pockets, shoot him in the back and escape in the immediately gathering crowds. The methods of the Irish Republican Army were despicable—let there be no mistake about that and no sentimentality—and they remain despicable to this day. When it launched its bitter assault on Ulster in the 1920s, men who had fought bravely and openly in the war against Germany despised it as a faction of fanatical assassins, devoid of claim to the

[1] See *Protest in Arms* (Holt), p. 291; also Eoin Neeson's *Civil War in Ireland*.

honourable status of soldiers, devoid of claim to membership of a legitimate military organization.

The men of the Irish Republican Army argued that they were outnumbered and that, as they lacked and had always lacked the equipment and armaments that could be employed against them —armoured cars, wire-netted fast motor tenders, light artillery and mortars—they could not possibly wage open warfare with an equal chance of winning and were consequently compelled to adopt guerilla tactics. This was true enough and in the fight against the English forces in Southern Ireland and against the Ulstermen of the Ulster countryside the argument had a reasonable and acceptable basis. Guerilla fighting has been used by many elements in many struggles and, provided it is conducted with observance of recognized rule, there is no substantial objection to it. Deliberate terrorism against innocent civilians in the public thoroughfares of a city, however, and indiscriminate firing into thickly peopled shopping and housing areas with no concern for whomsoever might be killed or wounded—the very crime for which the Black and Tans had been blamed by the outraged Irish—cannot possibly be justified in the name of patriotism or in the name of anything, if those who would justify it especially claim to be faithful to a Christian Church. The tenet that the end justifies the means has brought evil upon evil to humankind. It is a doctrine that has been repeatedly quoted by the Irish Republican Army and it is the doctrine it followed in Belfast during the years of savage violence its men inflicted on the Ulster people.

It was a ghastly violence, laden with hate, peculiarly and mercilessly horrible. The Belfast air was electric with tension, so thick it could almost be leaned on. The people became grimly angry. By day, there was lethal Republican sniping from cleverly concealed places on the rooftops. Many an elderly man and elderly woman, engaged in nothing more antagonistic than buying the weekly groceries of a household, would be shot dead on emerging from the shops. The Republicans were highly skilled in sniping, an art they had learnt and practised in Dublin and other Irish cities. They brought unexpected death to many in Belfast. There were shocking murders of shipyard men returning from work and reading their evening newspapers in the packed trams, equally cowardly murders of policemen on traffic

49

duty or going home to their families or on the steps of their churches as they were entering them. No one could guess when the shooting would break out or where. Shoppers in the city centres or in any of the various shopping streets would have to throw themselves flat to escape a burst of bullets that would suddenly and terrifyingly sweep the thronged pavements as a group of Republican gunmen would round a corner, aim and fire their revolvers and disappear as swiftly as they had appeared. At night there was curfew and the roar and crackle of burning houses and factories, the tramping footfalls of patrolling British soldiers and Ulster policemen wearing steel helmets, the screaming brakes of Crossley tenders pulling up quickly, the shouted challenges, the sound of rifle shots and running feet and more rifle shots and the moans of dying men. People were dragged from their beds by Republicans and shot dead on their own front doorsteps, attempt after attempt was made to assassinate James Craig and his Cabinet Ministers, women were killed in their homes by shots deliberately fired at them, gatherings of children were fired on, grenades were thrown into streets where children were playing and many of them were killed, wounded and maimed. The figures of 232 people killed and 1,000 wounded have been given by the Headquarters Archivists of the Royal Ulster Constabulary. It is possible that they are an under-estimate. They refer to one year only—1922—but St. John Ervine, in his biography of James Craig,[1] states that in the year 1921 the number of killed was 109 and in 1922, or by 1922, it had reached the figure of 294. Whatever the exact toll may be, it is known that many many Ulster people died.

The Protestant mobs in certain notoriously backward districts, provoked to fury, behaved dreadfully, attacking and killing innocent Roman Catholics. The reprisals by the Roman Catholic mobs, from their backward districts, were similarly dreadful. Every city has its guttersnipes and none will claim to be free of them. Belfast should not be singled out as being exceptional. The inhabitants of any English, Welsh or Scottish city would be unlikely to respond differently if they were subjected to such a terrible and undeserved attack as the Irish

[1] St. John Ervine's biography of Craig, *Craigavon, Ulsterman*—see bibliography at end of this book—gives a harrowing picture of the I.R.A. attack on Belfast and the dreadful scenes it led to.

Republican Army brought to bear in Belfast. It is an historical fact that the Protestant Ulstermen did not want the violence in Belfast and did not start it. They reacted to it shamefully in many instances but it was begun and carried on by the Irish Republican Army and its sympathizers, without scruple for human life, without conscience. The men and women who live in the Irish Republic today, if they know of the terrible things that were done in Belfast and Ulster generally in the name of the Republic of Ireland, prefer to forget them. The Ulster people— not unnaturally—remember. A very long time indeed will have to pass before they can forget what happened. Such things do not fade easily from a corporate memory.

A good many years ago the Government of the Irish Republic proscribed the Irish Republican Army and declared it to be an illegal organization. It did so because there was an official army in the service of the State and no government can or should tolerate the existence of an unofficial army dedicated to un-official and improper purposes. Yet the Irish Republican Army still exists and is still determined to operate against Ulster in whatever way it can. It infiltrates and influences any movement capable of embarrassing the Ulster Government and the Ulster people. It has done this despite the proscription of it by the Government of the Irish Republic. This proscription brings a cynical smile to the lips of Ulstermen, as the Irish Republican Army, under the cloak of the Sinn Fein movement, which is also still in existence and is not proscribed, runs an office openly in Dublin—in Gardiner Place—and publishes a kind of newspaper entitled *The United Irishman*. The Government of the Irish Republic turns a very blind eye in the direction of Gardiner Place. It maintains that, if it were to round up all leading Irish Republican Army men, the remainder would go underground and create a great deal more trouble than they are causing at the moment. There is probably something in this argument. The Dublin Government maintains, too, that it could easily counter any harmful action the Irish Republican Army might take. There could be an element of truth in that argument, also. But, if there is, the Ulstermen say, why did not the Dublin Govern-ment put a stop to the armed attacks the Irish Republican Army made against Ulster in the 1930s?

It was the men of the Irish Republican Army, in civilian

clothes as usual, who started the bad rioting that took place in Belfast in 1935 by shooting at an Orange procession as it marched through a section of the city. Twelve people were killed in the rioting and ninety-eight injured. Again the Belfast people became angry, again they reacted in some instances shamefully, again it must be emphasized that they were provoked. Earlier, in 1933, the Irish Republican Army men murdered two policemen of the Royal Ulster Constabulary. In the troubles of the 1920s they had killed thirty-five regular policemen and thirty-eight of the Special Constabulary, which makes seventy-five in all. In 1939, the Irish Republican Army launched its campaign of terror in England, by placing time-bombs in shops and postal pillar-boxes. The Coventry explosion, which killed five English people, including a child, and injured others, was engineered by the Republican Army. Two of their men were caught, tried and hanged. In 1969, their bodies were disinterred and sent back to Ireland for re-burial. They were honoured by thousands of men and women of the Republic and the proscribed Irish Republican Army fired three volleys in the air as the coffins were lowered into Irish soil. In the 1939 episodes this same Army murdered four policemen of the Royal Ulster Constabulary and wounded twenty, killed two members of the Ulster Special Constabulary and wounded two. In 1948, the Army carried out a series of raids against military installations in Ulster with a view to stealing arms and ammunition. In November 1955, it attacked a police station in County Fermanagh with bombs and machine-guns and, from 1956 to 1962, in a series of raids from the Republican side of the border, it killed six Royal Ulster Constabulary men, wounded twenty-one. It also wounded eleven men of the Special Constabulary.

Two of their murders at that time were particularly repellent. These were the killings of Constable Anderson and Sergeant Ovens, both of the Royal Ulster Constabulary. Constable Anderson, a young man of only twenty-six years of age, had strolled across the border into the Republic to see a girl he was fond of. He was wearing a macintosh over his uniform and had left his car on the Ulster side of the border. On his return, he found himself unable to start the car. This was not surprising, as the Irish Republican Army men who were waiting for him behind a hedge had immobilized it. They were armed with revolvers and a sub-machine gun. Constable Anderson was unarmed. The Republicans dragged him up a narrow and little-used lane, forced him to lie down with his face to the ground, emptied a magazine of machine-gun bullets into him, pinned to his riddled back a piece of paper on which was written 'Spy, executed by the Irish Republican Army' or some such words, and departed.

Constable Anderson was not a spy. He was simply a young man who had met and taken a liking to a girl, as young men will, and had gone across the border into the Republic—quite legitimately—to meet her. She lived in the Republic. But even if he had been a spy, the death inflicted on him was both shameful and illegal. Spies are as much entitled to a fair and properly conducted trial as anyone else. This is an aspect the Republican Irish mind usually and indeed almost always fails to see. Recently the author of this book was discussing the Anderson case with an Irishman of Irish Republican Army sympathies. It was hotly maintained by the sympathizer that Anderson was indeed a spy and deserved to be killed. Not for an instant did it even occur to this Republican that there should have been a fair and legally processed trial or that the Irish Republican Army, as a proscribed body, a body declared illegal by the Government of a democratically elected and constituted State, had not the slightest right to execute anyone, still less a citizen of a different State. It had not the right to institute a trial, so Constable Anderson was murdered, coldly and viciously, and no argument to the contrary can be produced.

Then there was the case of Sergeant Ovens, also of the Royal Ulster Constabulary. At 11 p.m. on August 17, 1957, an anonymous telephone message was received at a countryside station of the Constabulary to the effect that a man had been seen acting suspiciously at an unoccupied house not far away. A party of police, led by Sergeant Ovens, went to investigate. A light was burning inside the house but the windows had been painted to prevent anyone seeing into the rooms. Sergeant Ovens, revolver in hand, found that the front door was unlatched, stepped cautiously across the threshold and was blown to pieces by a booby-trap placed there for that purpose. It could not be proved that it had been placed in position by the Irish

Republican Army but the trap had been so efficiently wired that the police had no doubt that it was the work of experts. There were plenty of explosive experts in the Irish Republican Army. This case was also mentioned to the Irish Republican Army sympathizer already mentioned. He merely shrugged his shoulders. His inability to see anything seriously wrong with the elimination of a fellow human being in such a dreadful and cowardly way is characteristic of far too many Republican Irishmen and their supporters inside and outside Ulster, far too many who have failed to think and failed to learn. Very possibly a number of them has managed to do both, but the number does not appear to have grown sufficiently to reassure the Ulster people.

The Government of the Irish Republic showed a marked inactivity when the men of the proscribed Irish Republican Army were slipping across the border on raids into Ulster. It should have moved its regular Army soldiers to positions where they could guard the Republic's side of the border and prevent the raids. This is what every friendly Government would have done at once in such circumstances, but the Irish Republic held back from doing so for a long time. It did not make a move until many murders had been committed, yet, when the 1969 rioting began in Ulster, it ostentatiously rushed its soldiers to various places on the Ulster border and proclaimed to the world that they had been sent there to give all possible help to the mal-treated Ulster Roman Catholics. This, the Ulstermen argued, was palpable dishonesty. The Ulster Roman Catholics certainly had much to fear and complain of in 1969 but so had the Ulster Protestants. It must be stressed once more—it could not be stressed too often, if fairness is to be maintained—that the Protestant people in Ulster since 1921 have been more sinned against than sinning. Throughout the years from 1956 to 1962, when the Irish Republican Army was raiding from across the border, those same Protestant Ulster people were guiltless of reprisal. If they had carried out reprisals it would at least have been understandable, human nature being what it is, but they heeded the appeal of their Prime Minister at the time, Viscount Brookeborough, to keep cool and to refrain from acts of revenge. There was not a single reprisal, although the people were con-siderably and most justifiably angered. No party of armed

Ulstermen slipped across the border to assail the Republicans in a retaliatory raid—every foray was made from the opposite direction by Republicans; no member of the police force of the Irish Republic was attacked, no police or military barracks in the Irish Republic was bombed and machine-gunned. It is a revealing measure of the skill with which the political leaders of the Irish Republic have succeeded in befogging the over-credulous that men and women in interested countries are unaware that not a man of the Garda Siochana, as the police force of the Irish Republic is called, and not a single soldier in the official regular Army of the Irish Republic has ever been fired on by Ulstermen, let alone killed or wounded. From 1921, the attacks have been exclusively suffered by British soldiers in Ulster and by the police in Ulster. The police alone have had almost a hundred killed by gunfire and somewhere around 200 wounded, to which must be added more than 800 injured in the rioting that blazed up in Ulster from October 1968 to August 1969. The total strength of the Royal Ulster Constabulary was then about 3,200,[1] so the 800 constituted a quarter of the force. That all this is unrealized in England and abroad is an illustration of the ineptitude of the Ulster Government. It could and should have brought this out through every available publicity medium. It could and should have brought out, too, the details of the earlier attacks, so that the world would be less condemnatory, but it let its case go by default. If the faces of the present-day Ulster Cabinet Ministers are red, they have no one to blame but themselves.

The Ulster people, as they look back across the years to 1921, 1922 and 1923 and think on all the things that happened in their Province, should be forgiven if they are inclined towards obstinacy in their attitude to the Irish Republic. Those who are old enough can still see the flames, hear once more the shots and the crash of explosions, the screams of women and children, see yet again the bullet-riddled bodies in the streets and alleyways. They have not forgotten and they have told these things to those who are younger. The memory persists. In the summer of 1922, the author of this book was seventeen. One afternoon he was standing in Donegall Place, the very centre of the city of

[1] This figure of 3,200, the author has since been advised, includes policewomen; it is more accurate to give the male strength as 3,000.

55

Belfast, awaiting a friend. He was wearing a trench coat, rather shabby—the popular wear with a lot of the worldly-wise and fashionable young Belfast gentlemen of the period—and not only was the collar of it turned up, gangster style, but the youngster had his hands in the pockets of it. Suddenly, a tall policeman on the same pavement ten or twelve yards away spotted him, whipped out his heavy black service revolver, pointed it at the boy and shouted. Instantly, two other policemen who had been standing inconspicuously and watchfully in the entrance to a nearby department store sprang upon the boy and held his arms. He was searched quickly and efficiently. The first policeman, still pointing his revolver steadily and with meaningful intent, his forefinger almost tightening on the trigger, walked swiftly up and looked inquiringly at his colleagues. They shook their heads. No gun, they told him. Nothing. No weapon of any description in the trench coat pockets or any pocket, but they still held the boy tightly. The first policeman lowered the muzzle of his revolver and demanded that the boy state his name and address. They were stated. The address indicated a 'non-combatant' area. The tall policeman studied the boy carefully, decided that he was not a gunman and unlikely to be connected with gunmen, that he was obviously speaking the truth. 'Go home, son,' he commanded, but in a much more kindly voice, 'go home, now, and stay home like a good lad. If you have to come into town, don't be wearing a coat like that and don't be having your hands in your pockets when you're anywhere near a policeman. If you do, you're liable to be mistaken for an I.R.A. man and be shot on sight. The men who shoot first in this town are the men who live.' The command was obeyed. The boy jumped on a tram that had just pulled up at an appropriate stop, a tram he knew would take him not far from the house he lived in with his parents. As he hurried on board, shots rang out some forty yards away and he saw the three policemen, all of them with their guns in their hands now, leaping for cover. They were joined by other policemen and there was heavy firing. The passengers in the tram crouched down, the driver accelerated. The boy was not sorry to reach his home. When he next put on the trench coat he found he had grown out of it.

That same year of 1922 a most extraordinary noise could be

heard in night-time Belfast. It came from the Catholic working-class district—the Falls Road area, now familiar to so many abroad who have read the newspaper reports of the 1969 rioting in the city, the area of the biggest barricades—and it sounded like nothing so much as the weeping of many women. The weeping was accompanied by what seemed to those who listened to be a strangely rhythmic drumming. Drumming, drumming, drumming. On and on and on. Not every night, but often, as soon as darkness fell on the wretched city, the haunting sound would begin, rising and falling like the wailing of an Irish banshee prophesying death. How the sound was produced the author of this book has never been sure, but he heard it and it made him shiver. Years afterwards he was told that the people of the area had produced the sound by using whistles in an unusual way and by banging in a peculiar musical pattern on dustbin lids. They had done this, it was said, to threaten the peace of all within hearing who were of differing political and religious faith and they had done so on the orders of the men of the Irish Republican Army. How much or how little truth there was in this explanation the author could not say—in Ireland, explanations are customarily coloured by the partiality of the explainer—but after nearly half a century he can still hear the sound when he cares to remember it and, however it may have been produced and for what particular reason, it still makes him shiver. It was a horrible sound. But Belfast was then a horrible and saddening city.

It was a city goaded to fury, a city driven by ruthless attack to a blood-lust madness, a city fighting for survival. Leading Southern Irish Republicans had publicly declared their intention to smash the Ulster Parliament, smash the capital city of Ulster, smash Ulster and the Ulster people.[1] The Protestants of Belfast turned on their attackers and met violence with violence, murder with murder, although they committed far fewer murders than the number committed by the Republicans. James Craig, always a leader of vision, did everything he could to calm his people throughout the city and the Province and had considerable success. But man is a fighting animal and

[1] One of them was Eoin O'Duffy, a notorious gunman; on September 4, 1921, at a meeting attended by Michael Collins, he said of Ulster: 'We will tighten the screw—if necessary, we will use the lead against them.'

lowergrade man especially so. In the poorer districts of Belfast, mob-mentality prevailed. The Protestant Ulstermen were faced with a savage enemy, however, for the Republican Irish had sunk very low indeed. P. S. O'Hegarty, himself a convinced Republican, wrote in *The Victory of Sinn Fein*:

> We adopted political assassination as a principle, we devised the ambush, we encouraged women to forget their sex and play at gunmen, we turned the whole thoughts and passions of a generation upon blood and revenge and death. We placed gunmen, mostly half-educated and totally inexperienced, as dictators with powers of life and death over large areas. We derided the Moral Law and said there was no law but the law of force. And the Moral Law answered us. The cumulative effect was a general cynicism and disbelief in either virtue or decency, in goodness or uprightness or honesty.
>
> We degenerated morally and spiritually.

In Belfast, page after page of the calendar was stained with blood. Armed and masked men burst at night into the home of a Catholic family called McMahon and shot dead five of its menfolk, chasing them from room to room and at last from corner to corner until there was no escape except in death. One member of the family survived, a boy of about five or six years of age, who crawled under a table and lay there in terror, unnoticed, as the murderers, pressed for time in case the next-door people should awake and arouse the neighbourhood to gather round the house in force, fired their final shots and slipped away in the darkness. The floors and walls of the little terrace house were splashed with blood, the bodies lay some on their face and some on their back and beneath the living-room table a child lay sobbing. The McMahons, as far as was known, were in no way tied in with politics, there seemed to be no accounting for the murders, no one has ever stated the names or calling or politics or religion of the killers. The Catholic newspapers, both north and south, blamed the murders on Protestants but there has never been an iota of proof. It may have been a politically or religiously motivated killing or it may have stemmed from personal vendetta. If Protestants were involved in it, the Protestant community of the time should have been more than shocked—as it was—it should have been ashamed.

Some eight days later, a bomb was flung by Republicans into the kitchen of a Belfast Protestant family called Donnelly, terribly wounding Francis Donnelly, the head of the family, mortally wounding two of his sons, aged twelve years and three years, and badly wounding his two young daughters. Again the walls and floor of a peaceful and innocent house were splashed with blood, again the attackers were not caught, but this time the motive was clear. It was political. Francis Donnelly was a member of the Orange Order. The fact that he was a man of moderation in outlook, who had never harmed a fellow human-being and never would have done, was immaterial. He was an Orangeman and the attackers had no mercy on Orangemen or on those who were connected with them. Before running from the scene and mingling skilfully with the crowd attracted by the explosion and the shots, they deliberately fired their revolvers at Donnelly's wife, who was holding an infant in her frightened arms. Some accounts declared that the bullets missed them both, some declared that the infant was maimed by one of them.

O'Hegarty, in his book, wrote soundly. The Republican Irish had indeed degenerated morally and spiritually. In Southern Ireland they murdered an elderly man called Patrick Cosgrave for no other reason than the fact of his family relationship with W. T. Cosgrave, political head of the Irish Free State Government.[1] He was shot dead by men of the Irregulars, opposed to the Government Party. A similar fate befell the father of Kevin O'Higgins, one of the ablest and bravest of the Irish Free State Government Ministers. Not only did the Irregulars assassinate the father, they later assassinated the son in the streets of Dublin as he was on his way to Mass. Age and uninvolvement was no protection. Several towns and villages in Ulster were raided by the Irish Republican Army men, who kidnapped a number of prominent Ulstermen of varying ages, most of them elderly. One of them was Anketell Moutray,[2] a man of over eighty years of age and a Deputy Lieutenant for his county. There is always comedy in Ireland, even in its most dreadful times, and Moutray provided some of it. He was unafraid of his heavily armed captors and troubled them by singing 'God Save

[1] See St. John Ervine's *Craigavon*, p. 378.
[2] See St. John Ervine's *Craigavon*, p. 472.

the King' at the top of his aged and unlovely voice. When he had finished singing the national anthem of England—anathema to an Irish Republican ear—he proceeded to sing innumerable penitential psalms and continued to do so despite all orders to desist. The captors roared at him to desist, they threatened to shoot him if he did not desist, they waved their revolvers beneath his nose, but still he did not desist, still he sang. Eventually, being unable to silence him and unable to bear with any more of the defiant singing, the Republicans released him. He returned to his home, uninjured and triumphant, and is stated to have advised James Craig that the best way to defeat the Irish Republican Army men was to sing an Anglo-Saxon anthem in their ears, together with an adequate number of the Psalms of David, and keep on doing so.

But comedy in Ireland throughout the dreadful times was very occasional. Blood was up and heads were down. The ancient enmity between men of opposing faiths rose in a flame that seemed to be for ever beyond control. Even men with better and kinder and far-seeing minds felt stirring within them the age-old antagonism, the resentment, the unreasoning anger, the unbalanced reaction. Such Protestant Churches as appealed for peace and strove for it went unheeded. They were few, however. All the Protestant Churches were crowded on Sundays but in the main the Protestant people were not firmly given the Christian message. The Catholic Churches were crowded, too, but the Catholics likewise were not given leadership, were not given the message in its fullness and relevance. The Churches, in their approaches to the warring factions, did not determinedly, commandingly and effectively convey the spirit and vision of the Man in whose name they were founded. Never an easy task, of course. Human nature is recalcitrant as a whole. Nevertheless, institutional Christianity in Ireland, in relation to the definitions of Christian understanding and loving practice, has for centuries been one of the more serious misfortunes suffered by the country. That statement, in the view of many devout Irish men and women, will have on it the sign of the generalization which can be shown to be unsound, but those with knowledge will see on it the clearer mark of a generalization which the history of the Christian Churches in Ireland is more likely to sustain. There are splendid and truly Christian priests of the Catholic Church in Ireland and there are equally splendid parsons and ministers of the Protestant Churches in Ireland, but too many priests, parsons and ministers have been religiously and politically conditioned in boyhood, too many have been recruited from the less educated and less intelligent sections of the people, too many have been small of thought and in generosity. On average, the Irish Catholic priest is brought up in doctrinal arrogance and in the mist-ridden world of Irish ignorance and dislike of England, whereas the Protestant pastor is guided to a conviction that the future of Ireland can only be happily discovered in full, unaltering and all-admiring alliance with England. He has been taught, too, that the doctrines and dogmas of the Catholic Church are unarguably in error. Great harm has been done in Ireland to churches and churchmen by churches and churchmen. The eighteenth-century treatment of Catholics in Ireland by the established Protestant Church of Ireland was shocking, the treatment of Catholics in England by the Protestant Church of England in the reign of Elizabeth was appalling, the treatment of Protestants in every European and Latin American country where the Catholic Church gained dominance and power was no whit better. Generally speaking, it can be stated that the Christian Churches have bestowed on humankind a greater degree of hurt than help, and, where Ireland is concerned, it can be firmly stated that, over the worst of the years the country has had to endure since the Dublin Rebellion of 1916, the Christian Churches have failed their faith and failed the country.

They especially failed in Ulster during the time of the Irish Republican Army attack and the disgraceful behaviour of the Catholic and Protestant mobs in Belfast and elsewhere. It was not the Churches that succeeded in diminishing the violence of the Irish Republican Army men, almost all of them Catholics. It was not the Churches that calmed the people and led them to a realization of the horrors they had been responsible for. The violence died away because the British soldiers and the men of the Royal Ulster Constabulary and the Ulster Special Constabulary defeated the Irish Republican Army, whose men were shot in scores, caught in hundreds and interned in hundreds. It is known, too, that James Craig and Cosgrave worked together

61

in secret to bring peace to Ulster.[1] Peace did come to ti at last, for a time at least, but there were to be more shooting, more attacks by the Irish Republican Army, more trials for the people of Ulster and Belfast. They had been a tired people when the 1914–18 War had ended, they were even more tired in 1923, the year in which the Irish Republican Army fell away in retreat. They looked around their battered little six-county State, no more than two years old, they looked around their unlovely and now unlovelier capital city, they counted up the cost. It was heavy. In many homes, stricken by sudden and undeserved death, life could never be the same again. There were widows, there were fatherless children. If the widows were young enough, they would have to support themselves and their families by working, providing they could get work, which was more than difficult. If they were old, they would have to look to their relatives for support. Others, who had been crippled by gunshot and could no longer work, must live as best they could. Many were bitter beyond all chance of change. Business offices, warehouses, factories, churches, and many other buildings were burnt to ground level. In the countryside, beautiful old houses, rich in history, lived in and loved by the famous old families who owned them, had been reduced to rubble by Republican fire-bombs.[2] Over numerous little terrace streets in the poorer Belfast districts which had borne the worst of the mob fighting, there hung a persisting pall of fear and anger, there was a hardening, a setting of the metal in the mould, a withdrawing from the normal kindness and hospitality, there was a Protestant rage against the Irish Republican Army and the Irish Free State and everything it stood for, a Catholic rage against the Protestant State of Ulster and all that it meant. Years would have to pass before there would be a lightening, a lessening of mistrust and fear, and when the friendlier feelings of the Protestants did begin to stir they were to be swept away into rage again through the renewal of armed attacks by the inveterate men of the Republican South, who could not sense

[1] Craig and Cosgrave respected and liked each other; see Ervine's *Craigavon*, p. 480.
[2] Shane's Castle, seat of the O'Neills, was destroyed by the I.R.A. Lord O'Neill, an old man and an invalid, was carried downstairs in a chair with I.R.A. men pointing guns at his head; the Castle was then razed.

and are unable to sense today the iron in the Protestant Ulster character.

The Protestant Ulster men and women were dreadfully tried, unendurably tried. Their control gave way and horrible things were done by them or by a segment of them, the worst segment of them, not the majority, the decent Ulster people all over the Province, who hated the whole loathsome business, obeyed the civil power, stayed in their houses, kept off the streets and away from trouble. But they, too, as they watched and listened, were angered by what they saw and heard of the violence the men from the South and their helpers in the North were inflicting on Ulster. The Ulster people should not be unfairly blamed for their anger and the violent response of a small number of them. The things the Republicans did to them were infinitely worse than the things that were done to the Republicans and to many innocent Catholics. Ulster is not the only country where the people have been enraged by unprovoked and unjustified attack and have jumped to their feet to strike back at the attackers. Were the Ulstermen, successful when beleaguered in the past, to give in tamely to another beleaguerment? Would the English have given in to it? Through a thousand years the English have repelled their enemies and have rightly prided themselves on doing so. They, too, have been guilty of mob violence, mob cruelty. But they forget these things. They are known forgetters of their misdeeds, known forgetters of their friends, known forgivers of their enemies. Today they disapprove of the French, who were their allies and their friends in two terrible wars against Germany, they applaud the Germans or at any rate forgive them, appease the Republican Irish who are most certainly not their friends, and castigate the Ulstermen who have been very good friends to them indeed and ask only that they be allowed to remain so.

Assuredly, it is a contrary and puzzling world.

Chapter Four

IN the morning of an October day in 1935, the body of Edward Henry Carson, known by the style and title of Baron Carson of Duncairn in the County of Antrim, sometime leader of the Ulster Unionist people in their struggle against Home Rule, was borne through the streets of Belfast in a flag-draped coffin on a gun-carriage drawn by blue-jacketed ratings of the Royal Navy. It was watched on its way by thousands of silent and sorrowing men and women, many of whom wept as they heard the muffled drums and the harrowing rise and fall of the funeral march and gave their thoughts to the anxious days of the past, when the old dead man about to be buried in Ulster soil had been younger and had led them so strongly and so well. The gun-carriage eased to a halt with timed precision at the steps of the Cathedral of St. Anne, the coffin was shouldered by eight sergeants of the Royal Ulster Constabulary and carried up the steps and through the big West Doorway into the midst of the huge congregation. Slowly, slowly, the sergeants carried it, preceded by the surpliced clergy, down the centre aisle to the waiting catafalque in front of the High Altar, the beautiful words of the Church of Ireland Burial Service sounding in their ears—'I am the resurrection and the life, saith the Lord: he that believeth in me, though he were dead, yet shall he live: and whosoever liveth and believeth in Me shall never die.'

In the standing congregation, his head bowed, as was every head, could be seen James Craig, Prime Minister of Ulster, the man to whom Carson had handed the leadership some fourteen years before, the man who, in vision and tolerance, had shown himself to be worthy of succession. None can say what he was thinking, as he stood with the others of that saddened assembly. He was ever an uncommunicative man, disinclined to reveal his mind, and he himself is gone these many years so none can ask him. He may have heard again the voice of his dead chief as he addressed the Ulster Unionist Council for the last time and gave

to its members the advice they would have done well to follow—
'From the outset, now that you have your own Parliament in
Ulster, see to it that your Catholic minority have nothing to
fear from you. See to it that you take care to win the trust of all
that are best among those who have been opposed to you in the
past. Maintain your religion, but be sure, be very sure, you
give the same rights to the religion of your neighbours.'

He may have heard again his own voice as he made his first
speech in the Ulster Parliament—'Our duty and our privilege
are from now onwards to have our Parliament well established,
to look to the people as a whole, to set ourselves to probe to the
bottom those problems that have retarded progress in the past,
to do anything that lies in our power to help forward developments in the town and country, so that the Parliament . . . may
at all events be one which has set out upon its task, fully
realizing the responsibility that rests upon it and fully determined to maintain the highest traditions of any Parliament in
the British Empire. Over and above that . . . every person inside
our particular boundary may rest assured that there will be
nothing meted out but the strictest justice. None need be afraid,
the laws must be obeyed. We will be cautious in our legislation.
We will be absolutely honest and fair in administering the law.'
Nothing to regret in that, he may have thought as the service
drew on and the humbling phrases rolled through the largeness
of the unfinished cathedral to where he was standing—'we
brought nothing into this world and it is certain we can carry
nothing out . . . the Lord gave and the Lord hath taken
away . . .'.

Again, perhaps, the voice of the dead man, with its strong
brogue which he had kept to the end of his days, speaking
savagely and sadly in 1921 in the Palace of Westminster, came
back to Craig and fetched from him an unnoticed nod of agreement—'Loyalty is a strange thing. It is something you cannot
get by sitting round a table to find a formula for an Oath of
Allegiance. It is something that is born and bred in you. I often,
when we were threatened because we were loyal in Ulster in
times past, threatened day after day and night after night, for no
crime except that we were loyal, said to myself that I should
give it up. I never did give it up, because loyalty is something
that is inherited. But do not try us too high. Recognize that we

tried to help you . . . and do not, when we want to stay with you, put us out.'

What a hold this Carson, now about to be lowered into his grave, had gained over the independent and defiant Ulster Scots! How had he done it, how had he controlled such men? How had he disciplined the obdurate stock that had again and again opposed the English strength and intention, that had produced the toughest, most effective and tenacious troops to fight on the side of Washington in the American War of Independence? 'If defeated everywhere,' Washington had said, 'I will make my last stand for liberty among the Scotch–Irish of my native Virginia.'[1]

The Scotch–Irish, who gave such all-important help to the struggling Washington, were the sons of eighteenth-century Protestant Ulster emigrants who had quitted Ulster to escape from English pressures. The American Declaration of Independence was written by an Ulsterman in his own hand, it was first printed by an Ulsterman, first read in public by an Ulsterman.[2] In the American Civil War of the 1860s, almost all the leading generals on either side were Ulstermen. Ulysses Grant, 'Stonewall' Jackson, Leonidas Polk, J. E. B. Stuart, George B. McClellan—all of Ulster stock—were only some of them. The fiercest fighting soldiers in that war were the Ulster Scots. General Robert E. Lee, the Confederate commander, one of the greatest military commanders in history, when asked what race in his opinion had made the best Civil War soldiers, replied: 'The Scots who came to this country by way of Ulster. They had all the dash of the Irish in taking a position and all the stubbornness of the Scots in holding it.'[3] The Ulster stock, on either the paternal or the maternal side, has produced many of the Presidents of the United States. Andrew Jackson, James Knox Polk, James Buchanan, Andrew Johnson, Ulysses S. Grant, Chester Arthur, Grover Cleveland, Benjamin Harrison, William McKinley and Woodrow Wilson were all of them men of Ulster descent. And there were other Presidents who shared that blood. It was the Ulster stock, too, that has given at least nine Field-Marshals and more than a hundred generals to the

[1] See *The Scotch–Irish and Ulster* (Eric Montgomery), p. 6.
[2] See *Ulster Sails West*, p. 47 (Marshall).
[3] *The Scotch–Irish and Ulster*, p. 27.

British Army alone. It was an Ulsterman, General Guy Carleton, who had been Wolfe's right-hand man in the campaign that ended in the Battle of the Plains of Abraham, who captured Quebec from the French after Wolfe was killed in the battle and became the first British Governor-General of Canada. Carleton served two terms as Governor-General and it was his wisdom and moderate policy that won over the defeated French Canadians and kept Canada for the British Crown. Another Ulsterman who served Canada for more than one term as Governor-General, an extension seldom awarded, was Field-Marshal Viscount Alexander of Tunis, a member of an old Ulster Plantation family, that had settled in the early seventeenth century on lands granted to it in County Tyrone—the much-loved 'Alex', one of the most brilliant commanders of the Allied Armies in the war against Nazi Germany.

Craig, if his thoughts wandered in St. Anne's Cathedral on that October day of 1935, could not have known this about Alexander, of course, or that five years later the British Expeditionary Force on its desperate march to Dunkirk was to be commanded and saved by yet another brilliant Ulster soldier, General Sir Alan Brooke, afterwards a Field-Marshal, Chief of the Imperial General Staff and the outstanding military strategist of the war.[1] Brooke was a member of the Ulster Plantation family known as The Fighting Brookes of County Fermanagh, a family that has produced many fine soldiers. It was Alan Brooke who appointed Montgomery to lead the Eighth Army that defeated Rommel at El Alamein—Bernard Law Montgomery, also of an Ulster Plantation family, who became Field-Marshal Viscount Montgomery of Alamein, over-all commander of the Allied Armies that landed in Normandy on D–Day in 1944, the third of the trio of great Ulster soldiers who led the British Divisions through the darkness of Hitler's victorious days and directed the British Armies that overthrew him in the Western Desert, in Italy and in Northern Germany. But though these world-famous Ulstermen, to whom England owes such a debt, were of the future, and Craig, as the lovely phrases washed round him in the Cathedral—'Man that is born of woman hath but a short time to live . . . he fleeth as it were a shadow'—could not have allowed his thoughts to play upon

[1] *Turn of the Tide* (Bryant).

them, he assuredly would have foreseen that the Ulster stock would again give of its best in effort and in men on the side of Britain in the war which many now feared was inevitable, and that both would be unappreciated and forgotten as the 1914–1918 effort had been forgotten. It was a stock he knew as few men knew it—a stock, he may have thought with some bitterness, that had given much and had customarily received more blows than thanks. The man, whose coffined body was now being lowered into the grave that Ulster spades had made for it not far from the altar, was not an Ulsterman—he had been born a Southern Irishman—but he had been abused beyond the bounds of fair political controversy, although the time was certainly coming when those who had abused him so cruelly would admit or could be forced to admit that, in his unveering guidance of Ulster and in his warnings to the English, he was right. Craig watched soil from each of the six counties of Ulster being scattered on the coffin as it rested on the bottom of the grave. Then the buglers sounded the *Last Post* and the *Reveille*, the congregation moved through the opened doorways and made its way down the steps to the crowded and respectful street.

Craig, as he was driven from the Cathedral to his home, will certainly have carried in his mind the significant words of the eulogy spoken on the dead Carson by Archbishop D'Arcy, Protestant Primate of Ireland—'It was not for Ulster alone that he fought but for the great world-wide British community, to which he gave all he had.' The idea of such a community is now derided. The British Empire is condemned by many Englishmen as a thing of wickedness, an evil and repressive power, something to be ashamed of. That it was one of the least repressive empires in history and was never at any time a thousandth part as repressive as the Soviet Empire of today, that it brought much of lasting good to many millions of human beings, are facts the Left Wing English and the Southern Irish who sneer at it so strongly prefer to ignore, if they are even aware of them, which is unlikely. Carson and Craig were convinced that the world-wide British community was something that all far-seeing men should wish to prolong until change could be safely made. They were not old-fashioned and immovable imperialists, there was no jingoism in them, but they would have agreed with A. P. Herbert's undertaking in his policy address of 1935 to the Oxford University electors that, if returned to Parliament, he would 'examine with some suspicion any proposals that might be made for the distribution of the British Empire among foreign countries, whatever their birth-rate, insolence and inefficiency'.

The Empire owed much to the ability Carson had shown in the high offices of state he had held in England during the 1914–1918 War. In the war against Nazi Germany it was to owe even more to Craig and the Ulstermen, who played so important a part in it. But before this test was to reach Craig, he was to be personally tested in the affairs of Ulster itself. The years since the Ulster Government was formed in 1921, with their seemingly unending outbreaks of shooting and killing all over Ulster, had been severely difficult for the Province. Craig had not only the Irish Republican Army to contend with, however. An aftermath of the 1914–18 War was an unparalleled and disastrous slump in the major industries of linen and ship-building on which Ulster depended almost entirely for her living and the employment of her work-people. The Ulstermen were new to the craft of government and to the economic problems that beset every administration, they had much to learn and—like other Western countries—they were dangerously slow to learn. They were especially slow to learn the ancient lesson that it is never wise to have all your eggs in one basket or in two; that, if anything goes wrong with the basket-weave, the eggs may fall through the bottom and get broken. Economically, the 1920s were a very bad decade for Ulster. Many of the biggest linen mills went bankrupt and out of business in depressing numbers; the Harland and Wolff shipbuilding yard paid off its men in thousands, those very men who had built so many ships for England throughout the war. Unemployment was distressing and grew ever more so. In the very month that saw the assembling of Ulster's first Parliament—June 1921—the percentage of unemployed in Ulster was 25·40 against 17·81 in the rest of the United Kingdom. Throughout the twenties it remained the highest in the United Kingdom and it is still the highest. In those days, the unemployed were not given the generous State relief that is common now and the workers, skilled and unskilled, suffered cruelly. It was not until after the finish of the Second World War, in 1945, that the Ulster Government grasped the lesson of the basket-weave and embarked on a campaign to bring heavy and light industries into the Province through inducing overseas industrialists, by means of attractive financial grants and various other rewarding concessions, to set up factories in it and thus give badly-needed employment.

That it took the Ulster Government so long to learn the lesson is due to the fact that one of the worst defects of the Ulstermen—and they have many—is a provincial conviction that they have nothing to learn from anyone. They can be men of remarkable vision. They can also be men—and too often are—of remarkable and maddening conceit and blindness. Their reaction to an imaginative idea, one which would give a badly needed lift to the Province, is such that they will laugh with a peculiarly patronizing impertinence at the fellow-Ulsterman who has put the idea before them. That they frequently adopt the idea years later, when it is more costly to develop, assuming credit for it and acting on it incompetently and inadequately, is regarded as sufficient atonement for anything in the nature of initial short-sightedness and rudeness. Many a valuable young Ulsterman, who could have advanced the Province if he had not been discouraged from doing so, has quitted it and given his needed help to some other country. There has been a damaging brain-drain.

Craig had something of this blindness. He was conservative in his thinking on industry, believing that the staple industries of the United Kingdom would swiftly revive in the world's markets and absorb the bulk of the unemployed. He did not see that times were changed and that, in the matter of linens, tastes had changed, that the industry must shed its bourbonism, that the Ulster shipbuilding yards should be rationalized and modernized, that profitable orders had to be sought in the face of formidable competition. This attitude, of course, was common to most leading British politicians and economists of the day. The great Ulster linen industry did not recover its one-time importance and employment significance. The Ulster shipyards stayed far below capacity for many years, right into the 1930s. Old shipyard men argue angrily that grass was growing on many of the slipways. The third vital Ulster industry, agriculture, was struggling. In the 1920s, no one knew how to help agriculture. No one knew, either, how to help industry and when. Maynard Keynes, the best of the British economists, was not yet influential.

Craig was a compassionate man—he knew the Ulster working men, respected them, liked them, talked with them frequently—and the unemployment problem was ever in his mind. He did what he could, subject to his limitations and those of his advisers. The story put out today by uninformed and unpleasant firebrands of the extreme left like Bernadette Devlin—who 'has had the good or ill fortune to find herself present at most of the events in which violence occurred'[1] in Ulster during the years 1968 and 1969—that all Ulster Governments have deliberately held back from solving the unemployment problem in order to ensure a constant and plentiful supply of cheap labour,[2] is untrue of those Governments and especially untrue of Craig and his administration. There is still serious unemployment in Ulster and there is room for vision on the part of the Ulster Government in dealing with it, but the statements and activities of Bernadette Devlin and those who share her shallow thinking will not help to bring a solution nearer. All they do is to make the situation worse by frightening off industrialists who had intended to set up employment-giving factories in the Province. If Craig could have achieved full employment he would have done it gladly. Ramsay MacDonald and Baldwin would have done it gladly, too. They were equally unable to do so and no one, not even the harebrained Bernadette Devlin, has ever suggested that they wished to ensure a constant and plentiful supply of cheap labour.

Craig, as the first Prime Minister of the Ulster State, has also been blamed for setting the pattern of anti-Catholic discrimination. Again, this is untrue. He detested intolerance and did all he could to follow the advice of Carson and see that the Catholic minority in Ulster was given friendly and understanding treatment. When the Royal Ulster Constabulary was formed in the earlier months of his Ulster Government, he reserved one-third of the places in it for Catholic Ulstermen and urged them

[1] See the report of the Cameron Commission, paragraph 202.
[2] She made this statement publicly in 1969; it was reported in Ulster newspapers and she will not deny it.

to join it, so that the force should be fairly balanced. This allocation of places was in accord with the Catholic proportion in the total population of the Province. It was not Craig's fault that a much smaller percentage of the Catholics enlisted in it. He appointed a very distinguished Ulster Catholic lawyer, Denis Henry, as the first Ulster Lord Chief Justice, he encouraged Catholics to join the newly-created Ulster Civil Service and assured them they would be welcome in it, he urged them to accept the reality of the existence of the Ulster State and to help him in making it work for the betterment and happiness of all its citizens regardless of creed. He was firm with rioters, whichever side of the religious and political fences they might be on. Many a Protestant Unionist disturber of the civil peace in the bad times—the times of the 'crossness' as the Irish were characteristically wont to call them—was taken aback to find that his 'affiliations' had failed to save him from prison. Craig, for all his shortcomings, was not a man to follow the long-recognized Irish tradition that a blind eye is ever turned towards the misdeeds of political supporters. There was one condition he firmly insisted on, however, as he strove to establish the little State on a basis that would be sound and enduring. He insisted that those who sought employment in the service of the State should be loyal to the State, that there should be no reservations. This was in no way unreasonable. Why should the State pay a salary to a man intent on destroying it? Would the English have insisted on less? Do they insist on less today? All men and women seeking to enter Crown employment in the United Kingdom, anywhere in the United Kingdom, are required to take an Oath of Allegiance to the reigning monarch, as well as the customary oath under the Official Secrets Act. In Ulster, many Catholics found this to be insuperable and were debarred accordingly. They wished to draw the benefits of State protection and State employment while remaining free of obligation. A great many of them feel the same way today. One of the persisting difficulties in Ulster is to persuade the Ulster Catholics to think clearly and fairly.[1]

[1] Catholic Nationalist Members of Parliament in the Ulster House of Commons —Austin Currie and John Hume—complained on television in November 1969 that it was unfair to Ulster Catholics to expect them to take the Oath of Allegiance required of all men wishing to join the Ulster Defence Regiment which is to replace the Ulster Special Constabulary.

Craig had little if any rancour in him. 'We in Ulster,' he said in an early speech, 'are prepared to work in friendly rivalry with our fellow-countrymen of Southern Ireland, to vie with them in good government of our respective areas, to vie with them in the great trade markets of the world. We are prepared to work with them for the bettering of the people of Ireland, all of the people of Ireland. It is not our wish to quarrel, it is not our wish to continue in political strife.' He made this speech as the Irish Republican Army was at the height of its attack on Ulster. He could look wisely and far ahead, he could look closely, too. He looked at the Ulster educational system, knowing that it was in the schools where the Ulster and Southern Irish curse of intolerance could first and most hopefully be dealt with. In the debate in the Ulster House of Commons he said: 'I cannot help thinking . . . that our educational system in Ulster is not one that can even be amended, but one that requires to be rooted out of the soil so that we may plant a better growth in its place.' That was not the remark of a man with a narrow outlook, the remark of a bigoted Protestant Ulsterman who believed that only in the Ulster Catholic schools would religious bias be found. He would have liked to bring about an integrated schools system in Ulster, under which Protestant and Catholic Ulster children would have attended the same schools from the age of five and would have learnt naturally, as children do, to be friendly and remain friendly. In this he was frustrated by the obstinate and arrogant determination of the Irish Roman Catholic Hierarchy to maintain its educational segregation. That segregation has been kept in being ever since and the Ulster Prime Minister of today is equally frustrated by it.

Craig was truly tolerant, a man of considerable good-nature who liked and got on well with a very large number of his fellow-men. He could not keep his eye and his admonishing finger on everything as the Ulster State was being built, however, and there was much patronage and jobbery on the part of the lesser Ulsterman below him, there was much discrimination. If the Catholics had played a sensible part, though, as Craig asked them to do, if they had not persisted in standing aside, the discrimination would necessarily have been less. Craig did his best. Many of the Southern Irish have written and spoken of him as a small-minded Ulster Protestant doctrinaire, perpetually bellowing from platform after platform the Orange slogans of 'No Surrender' and 'Not an Inch', so popular with Ulster Protestant extremists then and now. He used those slogans, of course, on many occasions. He was a politician, a man engaged in the political game, and such men have to temporize, have often to give their audiences what they want to hear. But Craig was very far from being a man of doctrinaire mind. He was not just an Ulsterman, he was an Irishman and always thought of himself as an Irishman. He loved Ireland and wanted few things so much as for the Irish people to be at peace and working together to ensure that they would remain at peace.

He was not adamantly opposed to Ulster becoming part of an all-Ireland self-governing entity, provided there were a firm, unchanging and mutually advantageous alliance with England, which could not be abrogated at whim. In his view, there could be no safety or economic hope for Ireland in any other arrangement. He had no use for sentimentality, no use for Celtic dreaming, he could see no derogation of Irish aspirations and self-respect in a close association with England, he was a realist who ever kept in mind the lines of latitude and longitude which inexorably decide that Britain is the all-essential market for the Southern Irish exports and the supporting basis of the Southern Irish currency. Ulster in his day had already developed many rewarding export markets overseas for her manufactured goods. Southern Ireland was far behind Ulster in this aspect of trading, however, and is still behind her. It was peace, though, that Craig most set his heart on, a lasting peace for Ireland. He knew that the ultimate re-unification of Ireland was inevitable, that unification could only take the shape he envisaged—association with Britain; and he confided this conviction to his friends.[1] Unification, he felt, was a long long time away in the future. In the meantime, let there be peace, let the soil recover and mature, let the tree grow—and, above all, let the Ulster Roman Catholics shelve their political aims, drop their hostility and co-operate in making a worthwhile place of what, after all, was their homeland: Ulster. If there were anything he could person-

[1] Including the late J. W. Good, a famous Irish journalist and a fine Irishman of moderate Irish Nationalist sympathies, who was a close confidant of the author's father.

ally do to forward peace in Ireland, he would do it, whatever the political or physical danger to himself.

Craig cared nothing for danger. When an Ulster Member of Parliament called Twaddell was shot dead by Irish Republican Army gunmen in a Belfast street in daylight for no reason other than terrorism, Craig attended the funeral, walking openly behind the hearse, although he knew from the Special Branch of the police that his name was at the top of the murder list. In 1921, shortly before the first election for the Ulster Parliament, he was secretly invited to Dublin for a talk with De Valera, who was then involved with the Irish Republican Army in the fight against the English forces and was a much hunted man.[1] The invitation was conveyed to Craig by Alfred Cope, an English Assistant Under Secretary posted to Dublin by Lloyd George with instructions to do everything possible to bring the opposing northern and southern leaders together in the hope of finding a formula on which peace negotiations could be opened between the three contending sides. Craig at once accepted the invitation and journeyed to Dublin for the talk, although that city was an extremely dangerous place for an Ulster leader to visit and he could easily be shot by some trigger-conscious and insubordinate Southern Irish fanatic. After one or two mysteriously delivered directions were received at the Viceregal Lodge in Dublin, where Craig had arranged to stay, he was taken on a cloak-and-dagger car drive over a deliberately circuitous and confusing route, during which the elderly and placid Ulsterman, armed with nothing more than his briar pipe, was squeezed on to the back seat between two bulgingly revolvered Irish Republican Army escorts, until he was brought face to face with the elusive De Valera in a house which Craig understandably imagined to be about thirty miles away in the Wicklow Mountains but was in fact no more than five miles from the centre of Dublin.

The two leaders settled down for what Craig hoped would be a useful exchange of views resulting in a clarification at least and perhaps in something of immediate and permanent value to the wearied Irish people, but he discovered that De Valera preferred monologue to discussion, provided the monlogue were delivered by himself. 'De Valera began to talk,' said Craig years

[1] See p. 404 and subsequent pages of Ervine's *Craigavon*; Ervine gives a full and accurate account of the famous meeting.

later, describing the encounter, 'and after half an hour he had reached the eleventh century and the era of Brian Boru who beat the Danes at the Battle of Clontarf. After another half hour he had advanced to the period of some Irish king or other a century or so further. By this time I was getting a little tired, for De Valera hadn't got himself within six hundred years of the points at issue. Luckily, however, a fine Kerry Blue suddenly trotted into the room. This gave me a chance to interrupt the lecture and put forward a few points of my own.' Nothing of worth came of the meeting. It was rare for anything positive and profitable to come of any meeting with De Valera, ever a humourless, obsessive and wearyingly discursive pedant. A communiqué signed by both men was issued to the newspapers, saying simply: 'Sir James Craig and Eamonn de Valera have held an informal conference at which their respective points of view were interchanged and the future of Ireland discussed.' Craig was driven back to the centre of Dublin by the same cautious and tiring route to his anxiously awaiting friends.

When he returned to Belfast he was reproached by several of his most prominent and reactionary Ulster Unionist supporters for having consented to speak to De Valera, whom they detested and distrusted. 'Speak to him?' cried Craig. 'I was with the fellow for an hour and a half and could hardly open my mouth.' Craig had not only taken a serious physical risk in going to Dublin, he had taken a considerable political risk as well, for the Protestant Ulstermen were quick to cry treason if an Ulster leader stooped to a meeting with a man associated with what they referred to as 'The Murder Gang'. But this mattered not a whit to Craig. He was an unshiftable man who always did what he thought was right in the overall interests of Ireland, however much disagreement with his actions there might be. In his opinion, it was manifestly right that he should have consented to see De Valera in the hope that something of good to Ireland, however minute, would come of the meeting. De Valera, although in arms against the civil power and liable to execution if caught, was the chosen leader of the Irish Republicans and, when a settlement of the Irish question was achieved, would be elected President of the new Southern Irish State. Craig knew that a settlement was bound to be reached—although he could not have foreseen that the Southern Irish civil war would upset so many calculations—and that he would then have to deal with De Valera anyway, in some manner or another. So why not see him? It might—just might—have helped. Alfred Cope, for one, had been not unhopeful that the meeting would be productive:

Whether the meeting was a wasted effort or not is a matter of opinion. Personally, I think it was not. It might have opened the door for further consultation if the [Catholic] minority leaders in Ulster had taken the long view and applauded the meeting, but they failed to do so. Things might have been different if the Roman Catholic Bishop of Down and Connor, Dr. MacRory, had made himself more approachable, could have been more tolerant and on speaking terms with the Unionist side. He seems to have a deep-seated hatred of England, which has always saddened me in view of his high position in the Church of the Prince of Peace.[1]

The Bishopric of Down and Connor was and still is the most important Roman Catholic See in Ulster. Dr. MacRory, who later became a Cardinal and the Roman Catholic Primate of All Ireland, died a good many years ago. He could have done much to help in reconciling the Ulster Catholics with the Ulster Protestants but made no effort to do so. He was a small man, of narrow and bitter political motivation.[2]

Craig shrugged off the petty-minded Unionist criticism of his meeting with De Valera. He had an election to run and he meant to win it. He did win it. For the first time in Britain the voting system used was that of Proportional Representation and the Unionist Party, of which he was the leader, achieved a considerable victory, winning forty-one of the fifty-two seats which constituted the Ulster House of Commons. The men of the Opposition or of what should have been the Opposition—the remaining eleven constituencies returned eleven Irish Nationalists—refused to take their seats, preferring, as a matter of policy, to remain outside the Ulster House of Commons and thus show that, in their disapproving view, it did not exist. No

[1] See p. 413 of Ervine's *Craigavon*; the extract is from a letter Cope sent to St. John Ervine.
[2] See Chapter Five for MacRory's attitude towards the arrival in 1942 in Ulster of the United States Army troops.

Unionist or other obstacle of any kind was put in the way of their taking seats they had won, but—sullenly and mistakenly—they declined to do so. The Unionists—triumphantly and equally mistakenly—rejoiced in the size of their majority. They rejoiced because they were too inexperienced and too short-sighted to realize that such a majority is unhealthy. The mass of the Unionist Party were unimpressed by the argument that a credible Parliamentary Opposition, capable of forming a responsible alternative administration and of governing the country in the expressed interest of the main body of its citizens, is essential to every viable democratic system. They would have been in no way disturbed if all the fifty-two seats in the Ulster House of Commons had been won by Unionists. They pointed out that the voting strengths in the Province generally reflected its division into two-thirds Protestant Unionist, one-third Catholic Nationalist; and that this made it a normal certainty that the only near-substantial opposing group in the House would be constituted by the Irish Nationalists, who could never be regarded as a credible Parliamentary Opposition capable of governing the country in the expressed interest of the main body of its citizens, as they were implacably committed to the minority wish that the Ulster State should be absorbed in an all-Ireland Republic. The argument was well based and is still valid, for the Irish Nationalist Party members in the Ulster House of Commons today are as deeply pledged to an all-Ireland Republic as ever they were.

This is the major dilemma of the Ulster Parliamentary situation and Ulstermen are irritated by the failure of nearly all the English politicians at Westminster to understand it. Where the Unionist Ulstermen of Craig's long political reign were mistaken, however, was in their inability to see that an Opposition Party could and should have been built up throughout the country by Ulster men and women who agreed unalterably with the need to preserve the British connection and Ulster's place within the United Kingdom but did not agree that only one party had the necessary vision and administrative skill. There should have been an effective Labour Party, perhaps—although the existent small and not very effective Ulster Labour Party damaged its prospects by being indeterminate in the matter of the British connection—or a Liberal Party or a Progressive

Party. There was no unclimbable barrier against the formation of a credible Opposition—there was the deplorable and injuring lack of able Ulster men and women prepared to enter public life, of course, but this could have been remedied. The constant hammering from the Unionist Party propaganda and the influence of its constituency associations, however, ensured that the Protestant electorate was led to believe in the main that only the Unionist Party could be trusted to keep Ulster as a part of the United Kingdom. Any other political party, the Unionist Party men insinuated and shouted, would be unreliable and could be tempted into apostasy.

So the Unionists of 1921 gave praise to Heaven for their heavy victory at the polls, the Irish Nationalists remained intractable in the matter of taking their seats and for the first four years of its existence the Ulster House of Commons consisted entirely of Unionist members, a very unhealthy situation indeed. Craig was aware of the undesirability of this lop-sided representation, however, and did all he could behind the scenes to persuade the Nationalists to attend the House. He was unsuccessful. The times were against him. The Province was under attack from the Irish Republican Army, the Protestants were angry and more inclined to throw the Nationalists into the Irish Sea than to waste time on coaxing them to do their duty by their constituents, the Nationalists were hopeful that the State would disintegrate and convinced that attendance at the Ulster House of Commons would weaken their cause by implying recognition of the very State they wished to see destroyed.

It was not until after the second election, in 1925, that the Nationalists consented to take their seats and their share in the proceedings of the House. When they did so it was found that they had no suggestions to make in the way of economic policy for the struggling Province—their election speeches and pamphlets had been noticeable for a content more emotional than helpful; and they had little to contribute to the larger debates beyond the accustomed assertion that the fortunes of Ulster would take an immediate turn for the better if she would agree to inclusion in an all-Ireland Republic.[1] When asked politely to

[1] Not so long ago, an Irish Nationalist member of the Ulster Senate—Dr. Patrick McGill—gave this very answer to the author in the course of a television debate.

elaborate, they impolitely refused. The men of the Unionist front and back benches were not remarkable, either, apart from Craig. All but a very few of them were above their ceiling and would have been more appropriately seated in the chamber of a Rural District Council. But the Nationalists were a particularly unimpressive lot, regimented, frightened of getting out of Party line, plodding and suspicious, none of them of Cabinet calibre. With one exception, the sand has covered their names. The exception was Joseph Devlin, known to everyone as Wee Joe, who had been a member of the old Irish Party in the Westminster Parliament.

Joe believed strongly in the Nationalist cause—it could be said in a way that he believed in it picturesquely—but he was a moderate, sensible, experienced man, a first-rate Parliamentarian who brought needed wit, intelligence and fun to the House. He was greatly liked by James Craig. The two men would discharge the most lethal broadsides at each other when in action on the floor of the House and be found an hour later in the Members' Bar sitting together at a table, glasses of good Ulster whiskey in their hands, laughing at some story one or other of them had just heard. James Craig and Joe Devlin could have settled the Irish question in a morning, if they had been allowed to. Unfortunately for Ireland, they were not allowed. At every election until Joe passed beyond the point of being vexed by the contrarinesses of Irish politics, he was given by rote the First Preference votes of all the faithful Nationalists in his constituency, which meant that he was automatically certain of election as the Nationalists outnumbered the Unionists of the constituency, who equally automatically gave their First Preference votes to the Unionist candidate opposing Joe. But the Unionists of the constituency liked Joe so much and knew so well that he was a better man and better whiskey drinker than their own aspirant that they gave him their Second Preference votes, with the result that at election after election Joe was returned with majorities so enormous as to be almost historic in British political life. Proportional Representation is no longer the voting system used in Ulster, which has gone over to the straight vote method. This should make matters easier for the professional pollsters, but not even the top-flight pollsters of today—and they have tried—can correctly forecast or analyse or even begin to understand the voting in an Ulster election.[1] We Ulstermen have our own way of doing things. Joe Devlin, however, in the 1920s, was the only pebble on the Nationalist beach. His colleagues were grains of sand. The Nationalist members of the Ulster House of Commons today are as unimpressive as their forebears, probably more so. They still have nothing to suggest of economic benefit to the Province, they still maintain that all will magically improve when Ulster thankfully enfolds herself in the welcoming arms of an all-Ireland Republic—and again not one of them is of Cabinet calibre.

It was in those faraway and troubled days of the 1920s, then, that the Ulster Unionist Party became possessed of the conviction that the aim in every election should be to secure the largest possible Unionist membership of the Ulster House of Commons and the smallest and least effective Opposition. Craig knew better, but each subsequent Prime Minister of Ulster, until Terence O'Neill became Premier in 1963 and annoyed the Unionist Party by trying to make it think, felt that the Party was right in this and failed to grasp that successive steam-rollering majorities were bringing the Party a complacency and an ill-health that would inevitably result in decline.

James Craig was Prime Minister of the tiny Ulster State from 1921 until his sudden death in 1940 at the age of sixty-nine. He led the individualistic and often headstrong Ulstermen for nineteen years against the nine or ten of Carson's leadership. He made mistakes in many matters, minor and major. On the critical issues, however, the issues that most concerned his fellow-Ulstermen and especially the issue of their survival as citizens of Great Britain, he made no mistakes, showing at all times in Irish matters a level-headedness and a foresight which British Cabinet Ministers at Westminster in the later 1930s could well have done with. As Ulster struggled in her early days to learn the job of government, Craig set her on a decided course and kept her on it. His judgment was undisturbed by provocation—and he possibly had to deal with greater internal provocation than any British Minister of the past hundred years —he was under continuous strain yet never lost his steady understanding or his resolution to take what he considered was

[1] The British pollsters were badly wrong in forecasting the result of the election called by Terence O'Neill, then Ulster Prime Minister, in early 1969.

the best and most honourable action in the interests of the Ulster people, regardless of personal popularity or quick political profit. He did not build or seek to build the authoritarian and bigoted state his enemies accused him of building. Such authoritarianism as Ulster has been guilty of (and she has indeed been guilty of authoritarianism) is attributable to Prime Ministers who followed him in office but not in wisdom and who allowed the metal to harden in the mould when the need for metal had disappeared. The Ulster that Craig strove to found would not have blundered into the follies that brought it to the point of shipwreck through the Civil Rights agitations of 1968 and 1969. He cannot be blamed for the blindness of some who sat in his vacated chair. He had stature, others who came after him had not. And in the last two years of the 1930s—the last two years of his life, within a few months or so—he was to show that stature even more clearly than before.

Chapter Five

ENGLAND, in the year 1938, under the political direction of her inexperienced but confident Prime Minister, Neville Chamberlain, seemed no longer possessed of the intelligent diplomacy and the united will and purpose that had once made her formidable. Her Army and Air Force had been allowed by successive and similarly miscalculating Labour and Conservative Governments to fall into dangerous weakness. Even her Navy, for centuries vital to her safety, was seriously below its essential strength. Many, looking thoughtfully and expertly at her from abroad, felt that she was unlikely to survive the coming war with Nazi Germany. It was the year of the Munich Agreement, when—with France, also weakly armed, also unready—she perforce surrendered Czechoslovakia to Hitler, the year when the appeasement policy of Chamberlain reached its heights of concession and the year when a growing number of leading Englishmen, led by Churchill, strove their hardest to wake and warn the British people. It was also the year in which Chamberlain demonstrated, as other Englishmen had demonstrated before him, the persisting inability of the English race to understand the Southern Irish, by seeking, against the advice of those who knew the Irish better than he did, to win from them a friendship they were not prepared to give and to place on them a reliance their record did not justify.

If England were to go to war with Nazi Germany, Ireland, because of her geographical position on the fringe of Europe, was of considerable strategic importance. The main Southern Irish ports and harbourages would be of near-decisive value in the struggle to prevent the German submarine packs from starving England of food and much-needed war supplies. These ports and harbourages were Cobh, formerly known as Queenstown, the port of the city of Cork, on the south coast of Ireland and relevant to the Bay of Biscay; Berehaven, not far from Cork and also on the southern coast; Waterford, again on the southern coast; Kingstown, restored to its original name of Dun Laoghaire by the Irish, a port near Dublin, on the eastern Irish coastline; Galway Bay and Blacksod Bay, two large natural harbourages on the western Irish coast, looking out on to the Atlantic Ocean towards America; and Lough Swilly, another big natural harbourage, on the northerly coast and also looking out on to the Atlantic. In the 1914–18 War against Imperial Germany, these ports and harbourages had been of critical importance in fighting the German U-Boat submarines. Queenstown and Berehaven were the most significant strategically and it was at Queenstown, in 1915, that the Headquarter Base for all the British Navy's Western Patrol Areas had been established. In the negotiations and in the legislation which confirmed the formation of the Irish Free State in 1922, it was laid down by the British and agreed by the Southern Irish that these Irish ports and harbourages should remain under the control and at the service of the British, who reserved and in fact exercised—in the case of the main ports—the rights to continue in naval use and occupation of them. They were of particular importance because they enabled the submarine-killer craft of the British Navy to get nearer the U-Boats lying in wait for incoming and outgoing convoys rounding the southerly tip of Ireland. They helped the British to extend the patrolling zones to such a distance from the United Kingdom's life-line port facilities in the Bristol Channel, Merseyside and the Scottish Firth of Clyde as to give greater protection to the supply-carrying ships that must daily and nightly use them.

A policy of appeasement is not necessarily mistaken. Chamberlain was to an extent naïve but his belief that the defeated Germany of the 1914–18 War was dealt with unfairly in the Treaty of Versailles had justification, although Hitler's account of the wrongs committed by it against Germany were magnified. Chamberlain felt that, if the wrongs were rectified, the Germans would show themselves to be reasonable and friendly and war could be averted. This might have happened if he had been dealing with a reasonable man, but Hitler was not a reasonable man, he was implacable. The moment a concession was made to him by England, he demanded another and then another, or he broke a promise, explicit or implicit, which Chamberlain, as a man of honour, had naturally expected him to keep. Whatever the errors of Chamberlain's appeasement policy, however, it led to England entering on the 1939–45 War with clean hands. She had gone to the furthest and most dangerous brink in her effort to save the peoples of Europe— and they included the people of Ireland—from the deaths, the terrible destruction and the wretchedness a second world war, waged with even more powerful weapons and explosives than those that had been used in the 1914–18 War, would inflict on them. She had done her best and had nothing to be ashamed of.

The remark of many of the Southern Irish in 1939 that her struggle against the Nazis was 'just another of England's wars' could only have been made by men with minds as unreasonable as that of Hitler. It was all the more irresponsible and ungenerous in view of the fact that, during the 1930s, England had gone to considerable lengths to atone for wrongs committed by her in the past against the Southern Irish. Those wrongs had been enlarged by the implacable Irish, as the Allied wrongs against Germany after the 1914–18 War had been enlarged, but England had unquestionably much to blame herself for in her relationship with Southern Ireland and she knew it. So, throughout the decade, she made accommodation after accommodation in favour of the Southern Irish.

In 1937, the ever-hostile De Valera, head of the Irish Free State Government, arbitrarily drew up and put into effect a new Constitution for Southern Ireland that abrogated several important existing legislative arrangements with England. Under this Constitution, the Irish Free State became known as Eire and, in all but name, shed its status as a British Dominion, describing itself as a sovereign, independent, democratic state, with a national territory consisting of the 'whole island of Ireland, its islands and the territorial seas'. This last claim, asserting that Ulster was a part of Eire, angered the Ulstermen, of course, but they ignored the claim and continued on their way. The English also ignored the claim to Ulster but generally and without recrimination acquiesced in the principal terms of the new Constitution and made the necessary arrangements in the Westminster House of Commons to adjust the relationship between Britain and Eire in accord with the Irish wish. They allowed Eire to retain the special privileges extended to member-countries of the British Commonwealth—a matter of economic importance to the Irish—and they decided to settle a dispute over Land Annuities, which had been dragging on for some time. They also decided that they were prepared to discuss with the Irish the question of British retention of the strategically placed ports and harbourages. In the spring of 1938 the two sides met in London to discuss and settle outstanding differences. Chamberlain—urged by Malcolm MacDonald, his Secretary of State for the Dominions, son of Ramsay MacDonald, the first British Labour Prime Minister, and one of the most convinced supporters of the policy of appeasement—agreed to withdraw all British naval personnel from the occupied ports and to hand them over to Eire, free of any condition whatever, in the hope, as he announced from Downing Street, that Southern Ireland would now be friendly; that her territory would not be used as a base by any foreign power for an attack on England; that the concessions would lead to 'an ending of a long quarrel, the beginning of better relations between Northern and Southern Ireland, and the co-operation of Southern Ireland with England in trade and defence'.[1] It was a generous gesture that could and should have been given a generous response.

Voices were heard in protest against the return of the ports so unconditionally. Chief among them was that of Winston Churchill, then out of office, regarded by head-in-the-sand Conservative politicians as an alarmist and generally unheeded. 'You are casting away real and important means of security and survival, for vain shadows . . . these ports are the sentinal towers of the western approaches by which the people of this island so enormously depend on foreign food for their daily bread . . . the first step an enemy might take would be to offer complete immunity to Southern Ireland if she would remain neutral . . . the De Valera Government may, at some supreme moment of emergency, demand the surrender of Ulster as an alternative to its neutrality . . . De Valera may not be able to hold in check the dark forces of the Irish Republican Army, a whole organization of secret men bound together.'[2]

Another voice was that of James Craig, who was aware from

[1] See Keith Feiling's *Life of Neville Chamberlain*, p. 310.
[2] Westminster House of Commons Reports, columns 1105, etc., May 5, 1938.

many years of experience that no gesture from England would mollify the Southern Irish or budge them in their attitude towards her, that they were ungenerous of heart and scant in foresight, that when the time came they would have no hesitation in endangering her. 'I gave the most solemn warnings to British Ministers,' he said later, 'on the dangers of such an unnecessary action as surrendering these valuable bases for British use as protection not only for Great Britain and Ulster, but for Southern Ireland also.'[1] Chamberlain and MacDonald were unmoved. They knew better than Churchill and, in particular, they knew better than Craig, who was naturally sceptical because, they thought, of his unreasoning and characteristic Ulster prejudice against the Southern Irish. They might be prepared to admit that there could be an element of risk in the ports concession but they were satisfied, on the whole, that their decision was right in principle and would bear fruit. If war with Germany were to come, Southern Ireland would be the more likely to co-operate with England in defence.

War with Germany did come and Southern Ireland did not co-operate with England in defence. She immediately declared herself neutral and, from the start of the war to the end of it, denied to England and her allies the use of the Irish ports, so vitally needed in the critical Battle of the Atlantic.

Chamberlain died, a disappointed and indeed heartbroken man, not long after Churchill became Prime Minister in May 1940. His main mistake had been the trust he placed in others, but that is ever a good fault. He had tried—again and again— and had failed. He was not a good listener. He is to be honoured, though, and it should be remembered that, as Churchill said of him in the Westminster House of Commons after his death, 'The only guide to a man is his conscience, the only shield to his memory is the rectitude and sincerity of his actions'.[2] De Valera and his Southern Irish, when they have looked back on to their neutrality in the war against Hitler's Germany which would have given them such short shrift if it had won, might have done well to ponder that. If the corporate conscience of the Southern Irish is clear, if they feel they could maintain that there was

[1] Interview published in a Belfast newspaper, the *Northern Whig*, November 8, 1940.

[2] Westminster House of Commons Reports, November 1940.

rectitude in their neutrality, then they are indeed a peculiar people.

Let not too fine a point be put upon it. The neutrality of Southern Ireland in the 1939–45 War was a disgrace to the Irish name, a sheltering behind the backs of better and braver men. Some thousands of young Southern Irishmen, shocked by the neutrality and determined to do what they could to redeem the reputation of their race, slipped across the border into Ulster, joined the British forces and fought finely and well against the Nazis. Many of them were killed. They recovered for their country some of the honour it had lost. But, while innumerable English, Welsh, Scots, Ulster–Scots, Australians, Canadians, New Zealanders, French, Americans, Poles, Danes, Dutch, Belgians, Norwegians and others were giving their lives in the effort to defeat one of the strongest forces for evil that had yet confronted humankind, the Southern Irish in their lighted cities, towns and villages were mostly indifferent. 'This war,' said De Valera, splitting hairs and evading the real issue, as usual, 'was not of our making.'[1] It was not of England's making, either, yet the Southern Irish continued, in their peasant-like obsession, to think of England as their principal danger, the main oppressor. It could be said of them that they had neither eyes to see, minds to think, nor hearts to feel. They knew, as other countries knew, of the many promises Germany under Hitler had given and broken, they knew of the barbarities of the Nazi Brownshirts in hunting down and disposing of all who opposed them, of the burning of the books and the crushing of cultivated liberal opinion, of the flight from Germany of such decent men and women as could get away. They knew what was happening to the Jews in Germany and in every other land where the Nazis had gained control, they knew as well as everyone else of the seizure of small countries like Austria and Czechoslovakia and of the Nazi cruelties there. They were aware, as all the world was aware, of the terrible blitzkrieg on Amsterdam and Rotterdam, of the longer and even more terrible blitzkrieg on the guiltless people of Poland, a people as devoutly Catholic as the Southern Irish themselves and for that reason, if for no other, especially deserving of Southern Irish pity and help.

[1] This statement was made more than once when he was addressing the Dublin Parliament in 1939 and 1940.

Nothing of all this stirred the main mass of the Southern Irish. They hated England and the war was not of their making. They called it The Emergency and many of the younger men of Southern Ireland responded to the call by joining the Eire Army and standing guard at a few places on the Irish coastline with British rifles on their shoulders and British ammunition in their pouches. When The Emergency had been overcome, De Valera gave them a campaign medal.

It was repeatedly said by De Valera in the past and has been said by him and by other Southern Irishmen that, if the injustice of the partition of Ireland were removed, the relationship between the Irish and the English would be transmuted into one of friendship and trust. This was the most prominent of the many excuses put forward in justification of the Irish neutrality. How could England claim to be fighting for the rights and freedom of nations, it was argued by the Southern Irish, when she was ignoring the rights and freedom of a nation in her own garden by allowing the partition of Ireland to continue, a partition she had herself engineered? It was implied again and again that, were England to insist on Ulster abandoning her separate status and joining in a united Ireland, all would be well and a satisfied Irish people would be firmly on the side of the angels.

The English and Ulster Governments had taken this with a very large grain of salt. They were wise to do so, as De Valera had been intent for years on a policy of neutrality in the event of England becoming involved in a war. On February 16, 1939, in a debate on the question of the defence of Southern Ireland generally and on the 1938 Agreement under which Chamberlain and MacDonald had ceded the Irish ports, he said this in the Dublin Parliament:

I am asked about neutrality and the people who talk to us about neutrality are those who know that, before the Agreement was made last year, neutrality was impossible. By the terms of the Articles of the Treaty which we got cancelled, Britain was entitled to claim in time of war or strained relations with any foreign power any facilities that she might require, whether they were for air purposes or on land or sea for the coastal defence of this country and Great Britain. I pointed out here on many occasions that we thus could not be regarded and would not be regarded as neutral. The Irish Government would either have to refuse to accept that claim, refuse to give the facilities and be involved in a conflict with Britain, or it would have to give those facilities and be open to attack from elsewhere. If we were to go out of office tomorrow and another Government were to come in here, that Irish Government would find itself uncommitted by any agreements with Britain in regard to defence, perfectly free to take any policy that would seem good to them in the national interest. That is the position we have been trying to get for this country . . .

As long as Ireland is divided there will be those who will hate Britain's interference here and many of them will be wishing Britain's downfall, even though there might be a risk for themselves in Britain's downfall, because, by her downfall, the forced separation of this country might be put right. This had been our argument all the time—the argument that has been expressed in public and in private with regard to the relations between Ireland and Great Britain—and there has been no change as far as our attitude in that regard is concerned. I believe that, no matter how we may differ as to the immediate means towards that final end, until it is secured, whether it be secured in this Assembly or in any other Assembly or by any group of Irishmen throughout this country who may come together, there will be a large section of them that will not be reconciled to Britain and who will wish, as it was wished in the past, for Britain's destruction if that destruction were the only means of getting the country united and securing the independence which our people are entitled to expect.

The English of today, still wishful in their thinking on Irish matters, still ostrich-like, should study that speech in full. In the thirty odd years since it was delivered by De Valera in Dail Eireann, the attitude of the mass of the Southern Irish towards England has changed little, if at all. The Ulstermen will say that it is as bitter as ever it was. They do not like saying so, do not want to say so, they wish they were wrong. They are realists, however, and have good sight and hearing. They are in the best position to judge, for they are the closest neighbours of the Southern Irish and are in constant touch with them. They know that for the Southern Irish it is still the case that England's danger is Ireland's opportunity and that, should England find herself in any way again in peril, the Irish would strive to gain advantage. An Ulsterman who was very well aware of this—James Craig—said in 1940:

> However deeply the attitude of the Southern Irish Government may be deplored, no one who has studied closely each successive stage in the policy of Southern Ireland can be in the least surprised. It has been evident all along that she has been accepting concession after concession from Britain with the intention of giving nothing in return. In the midst of a war in which Britain is fighting for her existence, Southern Ireland clings to her neutrality. De Valera's announcement that he would not allow Britain the use of the Irish ports marks the culminating point in the process which we in Ulster have foreseen for the past forty years.[1]

Craig was willing to work with De Valera, though, in the matter of the defence of Ireland, subject to certain conditions. In another speech he made in June of the same year, he said:

> The supreme consideration for all of us is the safety of the whole United Kingdom. In the Dublin Parliament, Mr. Sean T. O'Kelly, Vice Premier of Eire, referred to partition in a way which clearly indicates that Mr. De Valera is once again blackmailing the British Government to end it, at the very moment when the enemy is at our gates. It is evidence that something serious is afoot. I wish, therefore, to declare that I will be no party, directly or indirectly, to any change in the constitution conferred upon Ulster. Nevertheless, in the interests of North and South Ireland, I am prepared to enter into the closest co-operation with Mr. De Valera on matters of defence, provided he takes his stand, as we are doing, on the side of Britain and the Empire, clears out the German and Italian representatives from Eire, and undertakes not to raise any issue of a constitutional character. I have never been a stumbling block, but I will never put my hand to any plan that will imperil the United Kingdom and the Empire.

[1] *Daily Express*, London, November 15, 1940.

If an all-Ireland Parliament had been in existence at the outbreak of hostilities, I am persuaded that Great Britain would have been faced with an all-Ireland neutrality today and British troops would have been unable to land on Irish soil except by force.

The offer to co-operate in the defence of Ireland was rejected by De Valera, of course, and Craig's suspicion was confirmed when De Valera later made nonsense of the original argument that Southern Ireland's neutrality necessarily resulted from the unjust partition of the country by admitting that even if partition were ended a united Ireland would still be neutral.[1] He had already implied this in his speeches on neutrality, delivered to the Dublin Parliament in 1939. Those speeches reveal to a depressing degree the jesuitry of Southern Irish thinking on the relationship with England. The people of the Irish Republic, for all their famous charm, are ungracious. They are insistent on rights, uninterested in obligations. That lesson, learnt by so many who have dealings with the Southern Irish, was eventually absorbed by Malcolm MacDonald, whose idealistic gesture over the Irish ports had failed in its object. Speaking in Canada during the war, he remarked: 'Southern Ireland's neutrality has exposed Britain to great dangers. It has increased the possibilities of enemy espionage by our shores, aggravated the danger of U-Boat attacks against our Atlantic convoys, and left open a flank in our defences against invasion.'

Yet MacDonald and Chamberlain, misguided and perilous though the gesture turned out to be, were not altogether wrong to have made it, to have hoped it could lead to a healing 'of a long quarrel' and to a friendly Irish response, a mature and reconciled reaction. The world would be intolerable if everyone were to distrust everyone else, if there were to be nothing in the way of open-handedness, no generosity in feeling and in approach. In the case of the Irish ports, the approach was bound to fail because it was made to a man of mistaken and unalterable mind. 'If only De Valera would come out of the clouds,' said President Roosevelt, 'we would have a higher regard for him.'[2]

[1] Clearly spelt out in an interview given by De Valera to Harold Denny of the *New York Times* and published by that newspaper on July 5, 1940.
[2] Memoirs of Cordell Hull, U.S. Secretary of State, vol 2, p. 1355.

Wherever a man may live in Ireland, be he a Protestant Unionist or a Catholic Nationalist, he is an Irishman and instinctively feels himself to be an Irishman. He loves his country, all of it, however it may infuriate him, however great the follies it may commit. He can forgive it much. The Ulstermen find it hard to forgive the 1939–45 neutrality, though. They look on it as a betrayal of the entire Irish race, a shaming failure in moral and physical courage. Staring back across the years at De Valera's withdrawal of Southern Ireland from the fight waged by the free and resolute Western countries against Nazi Germany, they see much that makes them angry. They know that the Eire people generally were in favour of neutrality through their age-old enmity towards England, that De Valera knew this, was reinforced by it and saw to it that they got their wish. But this is an excuse the Ulstermen will not accept. De Valera should have known better, they argue, he should have opened the eyes of the people and shown them the better way, he should have led them as Churchill had led the British. Churchill pointed out to the British the road they should take and they took it. He roused them, inspired them, brought out their greatness by speaking to them in words of such quality as none in England had heard since Elizabeth spoke to their forebears on the eve of the Armada; he led them from seeming defeat to one of the most decisive victories in history, while the scowling Irish turned their backs on the battlefield and tended their gardens. James Craig, although not a man of Churchill's greatness, had seen to it that room was made for Ulster on the road the British were taking and that the Ulster people should walk it side by side with them, however long or ultimately disastrous the road might be. 'We will be with you,' said Craig, in an address broadcast to the English early in the war, 'we will be with you to the end.' There was no wavering in Ulster. If there had been, Craig would have dealt with it as Churchill dealt with the defeatism a few of the English showed in the aftermath of Dunkirk. Each man was a leader. De Valera was not.

The Ulstermen, like the rest of the British, were incensed by many aspects of the Southern Irish neutrality that were clearly prejudicial to the Allied cause. They were angered by the fact that the German, Italian and Japanese Legations remained in operation in Dublin throughout the war and in constant communication with their Governments. How much information on Allied convoys, and military and naval dispositions was being conveyed to the enemy through those Legations? Why did De Valera so obstinately refuse all requests to close them down? The Ulstermen could understand his refusal of all British requests to have the enemy diplomats sent home—they did not need to be told of De Valera's dislike of England—but why did he refuse the urgently phrased request from the United States of America, the very country that had shown such outstanding and consistent friendliness towards Southern Ireland's aspirations for Irish unity and had tried more than any other community of people to help achieve that aim? The United States addressed a formal diplomatic Note to De Valera and had it delivered to him in person, asking him to take the appropriate steps for the recall of the enemy representatives in Ireland and bluntly asserting that the Government of Eire, despite its assurance of friendly neutrality, had 'in fact operated in favour of the Axis'.[1] This was awkward for De Valera. He reverted once more to his well-practised ability in double-think. He appealed to leading countries of that British Empire he so detested— Canada and Australia—to persuade the United States to withdraw its Note and thus save him from the embarrassment of answering it. Canada and Australia, however, retorted briefly and almost brusquely that they were 'in accord with the American request'. Both countries felt little but contempt for Eire. De Valera could not wriggle out of replying to the American Note. He delayed as long as he dared, then answered at last in a Note maintaining that 'the removal of the representatives of a foreign state on the demand of the Government to which they are accredited is universally recognized as the first step towards war'. Nothing could make the man think clearly.

There were so many events arising out of De Valera's neutrality and earlier 'separateness' that enraged the British and the Ulstermen. Just as war was about to break out, the ever-feckless and reckless, proscribed Irish Republican Army issued an ultimatum to Lord Halifax, Britain's Foreign Secretary. It was signed by Sean Russell, one of the bitterest and most

[1] See Mary C. Bromage's *Churchill and Ireland*, pp. 168–70.

dangerous of the Irish Republican Army leaders, who was to die later aboard a German submarine while returning from a secret wartime visit to the German Intelligence Service in Berlin.[1] Russell, with another Irish Republican Army gunman, called McGarrity, had been earlier arrested in Detroit, just across the river from Windsor, Ontario, which was being visited at the time by King George VI and Queen Elizabeth.[2] Russell and McGarrity denied an intention to assassinate them. They were not believed and were immediately deported, stating as they left that England was the real enemy not only of the Irish Republican Army but of Ireland. Shortly after Halifax had received the ultimatum from Russell, there was a series of time-bomb explosions in various English hotels, cathedrals, market-places, shops and such railway terminals as Euston, all of them the work of the Irish Republican Army men serving under Russell. Many innocent Englishmen, women and children were killed. An Ulster passenger steamer sank after a heavy explosion on board as she was coming into her arrival berth at Liverpool from Belfast and again many innocent people were killed. This infuriated the Ulstermen. It also, to be fair, infuriated De Valera, who seized as many of the Irish Republican Army men as he could catch and put them in prison or in internment camps he caused to be built for the purpose. One of the men he caught was the Irish Republican Army's adjutant-general, Sean McCaughey, who was discovered to have notes in his possession detailing interviews he had conducted with a German Secret Service agent who had parachuted into Southern Ireland, together with maps showing the dispositions of British army units in Ulster.[3] But De Valera could not catch and imprison all the Irish Republican Army men. Sufficient numbers of them escaped his net to take part in attacks on military installations in Ulster and to machine-gun their own Dublin postmen delivering mail to Sir John Maffey, Britain's diplomatic representative in Eire.[4]

The wartime attitudes of some leading Southern Irishmen and other sympathizers with Irish Nationalist ambitions who

[1] See Mary C. Bromage's *De Valera and the March of a Nation*, p. 276.
[2] *De Valera and the March of a Nation* (Bromage), p. 271.
[3] *De Valera and the March of a Nation* (Bromage), p. 276.
[4] *De Valera and the March of a Nation* (Bromage).

should have known better and, by virtue of their particular calling and position, should more properly have stayed silent, were extraordinary. In 1942, divisions of the United States Army arrived in Ulster to train and, while getting themselves combat-fit for war against the hardened German infantry, to provide an adequate force to handle any possible Nazi invasion of Ireland, whether north or south. An invasion could have come from Nazi parachutists aiming at disrupting various important airfields and military services in Ulster, or there could have been an invasion of Southern Ireland, which the Eire Army would have been too minute and too ill-equipped and untrained to deal with. If there had been an actual invasion of Southern Ireland by the Germans—and it was contemplated[1]—the United States troops would have swiftly crossed the border to engage the Nazis, whatever De Valera might have said or done. He had announced that his Army would fight any invader of Southern Ireland, whoever that invader should prove to be, but if a German invasion had indeed taken place and he had found himself compelled to order his Army to fight two different and opposing forces simultaneously, he and his soldiers would have been in an impossible situation. They would have been overwhelmed. Neither Britain—whose troops in Ulster were set free for other theatres of war by the arrival of the Americans—nor the United States could or would have tolerated a German invasion and occupation of any part of Ireland. De Valera, in his pronouncement, was threatening the storm with a teaspoon. In regard to the landing of American troops in Ulster, he ran true to form. He made a diplomatic protest on the grounds that he had not been consulted and that the Americans were 'infringing the sovereignty of Ireland'.[2] This was to be expected, of course. But the intensely anti-British and pro-Irish Nationalist Cardinal MacRory, Roman Catholic Primate of All Ireland, whose Archiepiscopal Palace was situated in Ulster, also insisted on protesting against the American presence, and on the same grounds. At a religious dedication assembly in County Cavan he referred to United States troops in Ulster as 'overrunning the country against the will of the nation'. It is difficult to see how the matter concerned a Christian priest, however eminent,

[1] J. W. Blake's *Northern Ireland in the Second World War*, pp. 154–6.
[2] Reported in the *New York Times* of January 28, 1942.

but the fact remains. Cardinal MacRory made a strong protest and was probably taken aback to receive a polite but stinging letter from David Gray, the United States Envoy in Eire. The letter is a long one and has had to be edited, but its most telling points are given:

Coming from you, who, as Cardinal Primate of All Ireland, speak with a unique authority, I fear this utterance may have done grave harm to the traditional friendship between our two peoples. News of the attitude of the Eire Government towards the landing of American troops in Ulster came to the American people with a shocked and pained surprise and now your statement that you regard us as invaders will intensify the unhappy impression made by Mr. De Valera's protest. We have asked nothing of Ireland in the past. We have always given, but we have always believed that we could rely on Irish friendship and that in our hour of need we should have Irish help. Now, in our hour of life and death struggle, you warn us off the strategic position so necessary to us and our Allies. Although American citizens are severely rationed in petrol, the American Government is still permitting petroleum products originating in America to go to Eire in sufficient quantities to operate its bus services, to gather harvests, to carry hundreds of thousands of tons of turf to Dublin, to supply transportation for clergy and doctors and to give the poor their scanty ration of paraffin. Without petrol, the Eire Army would be without transport and Eire aeroplanes could not fly. We have witnessed recently the ironic spectacle of Eire Army cars using American petrol, supplied by Britain, to hunt down Allied airmen escaped from Irish internment for having landed on Eire soil, while protecting the ships which brought the petrol from America. We can daily see the most ironic sight of Axis representatives engaged in conspiracy against us happily touring the Irish countryside in cars driven by American petrol, which British sailors have risked their lives to bring to Britain. It is a simple fact that everything imported into Eire, which is everything the Irish people use, except what the soil produces, comes from America or her allies, except what is imported from Spain and Portugal. But even these imports

97

are brought by the coal which we or our allies supply. Not only all this, but, although the Eire Government from the beginning of hostilities had forbidden the sending of Irish funds to the United States, no order has been issued by the American Government preventing the free sending of American funds to Ireland. Americans understand that, in protesting against the arrival of American troops, Mr. De Valera wished to emphasize his claim to Ulster, but they ask why he protested against the arrival of American troops coming as friends for the protection of Ireland and did not protest against German bombers coming to bomb Belfast and kill Irish people. They feel that his attitude has been more friendly to the Germans from whom he obtains nothing but bombs, than to the Americans and their friends from whom he receives what is needed to maintain the Irish economy.

It is not known whether His Eminence replied to that letter.'[1]

The 'Axis representatives engaged in conspiracy' were a serious and ever-present anxiety to the British and Americans. No one can estimate how many Allied lives and valuable cargoes were lost at sea through the constant flow of reports to enemy Intelligence from the Axis Legations in Dublin. When Churchill was proposing to cross the Atlantic by sea to confer with Roosevelt in 1943, the British Chief of the Imperial General Staff, General Sir Alan Brooke, advised against it. The main security risk, he said, would come from the German Legation in Dublin. 'They would soon,' said Brooke, 'be aware of the journey.' Churchill went by air.[2] When all security precautions had to be heightened prior to the Normandy invasion landings in 1944, Churchill became extremely anxious. 'If the German and Japanese Ministers remain at their posts in Dublin,' he minuted, 'it may be necessary on military grounds to sever all contacts between Ireland and the Continent.'[3] Dublin was perilously close to London. Transport and other means of communication were in existence between London and Dublin, also from Dublin to the principal espionage centres in neutral Spain

[1] Gray's letter, dated October 7, 1942, was published by an Ulster newspaper—the *Impartial Reporter*, of Enniskillen, on October 4, 1945, the moment war censorship ended.
[2] *Churchill in Ireland* (Bromage), p. 167.
[3] *Churchill in Ireland* (Bromage), p. 167.

and Portugal. There was an air service between London and Dublin and passenger and cargo ships were still moving in and out of Eire ports. The risk of leakage of Normandy invasion secrets was immense, even more so in Churchill's view than from 'the information betrayed about the movements of Anglo-American troop convoys'.[1] Another source of information to the enemy lay in the fact that the Irish Republican Army was in regular radio communication with the Abwehr and other departments of the German Intelligence Service in Berlin (where Sean Russell, the Irish Republican Army's Chief of Staff, had spent some months receiving instruction in the latest explosives and techniques of sabotage) and was also in contact with Nazi agents who had parachuted into Eire or had managed to enter it some other way, never a matter of difficulty during the war years, especially when there were so many Southern Irish sympathizers willing to aid them.[2] The precise amount of helpful information transmitted to Germany by the Irish Republican Army and the various German agents is unknown, but information was unquestionably sent. There was nothing, as the Ulstermen knew to their cost, that the Irish Republican Army would recoil from if it would injure the Ulster and English peoples. Churchill was also well aware of its malignancy. Throughout the war he was haunted by the possibility, indeed the likelihood, that German U-Boats were being refuelled and generally aided by Irish Republican men in some of the many bays, coves and inlets on the West Irish coastline. If a U-Boat could have slipped into an Irish bay to land Sean Russell, as one of them had actually intended to do, it could have slipped into it to replenish. 'There seems to be a good deal of evidence,' Churchill minuted to the First Sea Lord, 'or at any rate suspicion, that U-Boats are being succoured from Western Ireland—not by the Irish Government but by the men of the Irish Republican Army. If they plant bombs in London, why should they not supply fuel to U-Boats?'[3] To what extent this may have happened is unknown, but there would have been no barrier against its being done. It was always possible, just as it was always possible for U-Boats lying off the Irish coast at night to receive signals and other messages.

[1] *The Second World War* (Churchill), vol. 5, p. 693.
[2] Bromage.
[3] *The Second World War* (Churchill), vol. 1, p. 722.

The neutrality of Southern Ireland was assuredly a deadly danger to the Allies, for all the hand-on-heart reassurances by the Irish that it was benevolent towards them. That is fact. The German Minister to Eire was in frequent touch with Ribbentrop, the German Foreign Minister, conveying De Valera's reaction to varying German overtures and offers of armed help;[1] the Legation was for a while in direct and illegal radio touch with Berlin; there were arrangements with Legation Attachés by which agents in Eire and Irish Republican Army men could have instructions conveyed to them through special flower placings on the Legation window-sills.[2] De Valera took certain steps to temper his neutrality in some slight favour of the Allies, but there is evidence from his career, his speeches over many years and his conversations with friends that he felt the Germans, if victorious, would give Ireland its cherished unity by agreeing to the end of partition and that he would not have been sorry if Germany had won. There was little room in his heart, if any, for friendly sentiment towards England. He had fought her throughout his adult life, he had been one of the most resolute Commandants of the Irish units that had taken part in the Easter Rising of 1916, he had devoted all his political skill to withdrawing Ireland from the Empire and Commonwealth, he had the rigid mind of the fanatic. What else could be expected of him, then, but neutrality when England was fighting for her life? He was not a man who could forget the past, a man who could rise above it and urge his equally hostile people to rise above it, persuade them to join the march of free nations against a tyranny and trust to the future for settlement of the partition of Ireland.

In 1939, De Valera and the Southern Irish had a deciding moment of test. If he and they had possessed quality, if their eyes were clear, if they had judgment, if they had heart and courage, they would have turned to the Ulstermen and said to them: 'The cause in this war is bigger than the cause of either of us. It is being fought to save the things that count most to humankind, that will always be vital to humankind if it is to survive and learn, it is a greater matter than our quarrel with you and yours with us. We will join with you and we will all

[1] Bromage.
[2] See *Spies in Ireland* by Enno Stephan.

fight side by side as Irishmen, until Nazi Germany and its evil is defeated. Then, with better knowledge and appreciation of each other, we shall be able to sit down together as friends and see if our ancient and dividing differences can be settled with honour and closer understanding in the interests of the country which both of us care so much for.' That is what they should have said and the Western World listened carefully to hear if they would say it. They did not say it. In the moment of test they failed. They were given a second test, a second opportunity. In 1941, the United States was attacked at Pearl Harbor by the Japanese and immediately entered the war. The population of the United States included some ten million Irish, who went to arms like the rest of their able-bodied fellow-Americans, and it was then that Churchill sent his historic telegram to De Valera: 'Now is your chance. Now or never. A nation once again. I will meet you wherever you wish.'[1] De Valera did not even answer.

During the latter phase of the 1939–45 War, when the author of this book was serving in the Mediterranean with the Corps of Royal Marines, he found himself on shore leave in Naples and in conversation with a group of Allied sailors and soldiers—Americans, Free French, New Zealanders, Poles and others, some of them wounded. He was asked if he were English and replied that he came from Ireland. At once the group froze. 'What,' asked an American sailor icily, 'what is the matter with you goddam Irish? Are you yellow?' Contemptuous hands brushed aside the author's attempted explanation of the different identity and outlook of Ulster. To the men around him, Ireland was Ireland and Ireland was neutral and that was that. 'Don't you Irish know,' said a young Polish infantryman, whose left hand had been shot away at Cassino, 'that there is a war on? Why aren't you in it?' Again the author tried to explain. It was useless. Many more reproachful questions were flung at him and he still hears the voices of those men as they derided his race for cowardice. He wished bitterly at the time that De Valera could have been present in that Neapolitan bar in August 1944 to hear what that angry group thought of the Irish neutrality. They might have made him think, they might have possibly shamed him into a part realization of what he had done to the great reputation the fighting soldiers of Southern Ireland had

[1] *The Second World War* (Churchill), vol. 3, p. 606.

earned for their country in many a hard-fought war in many a century. But could they have shamed him? The author thinks not. De Valera would still have put Churchill's telegram in a drawer and left it there. He and his Southern Irish of 1939 to 1945 were small.

The Ulstermen were not small. James Craig, ailing and growing old though he was, led them instantly into the war at Britain's side and, in accordance with his broadcast promise to the United Kingdom, they stayed there to the end. Despite all that Germany could do to damage Ulster in attempts to bring her down—and the Nazi Air Force struck hard at her, very hard—she did not draw back by as much as a step. Again she gave of her best in men and endeavour, again her effort—exactly as with the effort she had made in 1914–18—was to be unremembered by the English people who gained so much from it.

Chapter Six

Here, by the grace of God, Ulster stood a
faithful sentinel.

Churchill

From Ulster started the long hard road to
Allied victory.

Eisenhower

THE Province of Ulster, less than a coin in size when looked
at on the map of the globe, has a surprising amount of space
in it.[1] There has been little urbanization, for which the more
truly forward-looking Ulster people are thankful; there is not
too much of what is known today as development. There is
room for a contented man to walk for miles through beautiful
and solitary countryside, from the superb downsweep of the
Mountains of Mourne in the south-east corner, along one of the
finest coast-roads in Europe and past the hushed and lovely
Antrim Glens to the magnificent northerly cliffs at the Giant's
Causeway—one of the Seven Wonders of the World—still
angering, with their age-long indifference, the great Atlantic
rollers. And, if he picks his way, he will encounter on most of it
no more than scattered villages. It is changing now, of course,
but the increasing industrialization is not being allowed to
spread so destroyingly as in over-crowded England. The area of
Ulster is still mainly pastoral and, during the war against
Germany from 1939 to 1945, it was even more so. There was
space for an entire Army Corps to train in and manœuvre; there
was space for erection of the special barracks and hutments
needed for the hundreds of thousands of infantrymen, space in
which to provide cover for the guns, tanks, armoured cars and
military vehicles of every kind; there was space for the making

[1] Roughly 3,500,000 acres, against the approximate 3,800,000 acres of the
County of Yorkshire in England.

of as many additional airfields as the growing struggle demanded
—they could be constructed almost wherever they would be
most strategically and tactically effective; there were large and
easily protected Loughs for submarine-hunting flying-boats to
take off from and return to—and there was an Ulster Government and Ulster Civil Service, immediately reachable, determined that there should be no red tape obstructionism or delay
of any avoidable sort that would result in the withholding of as
much as an acre if it were essential to the winning of the war.
The Ulster people were more than willing to have their
ploughshares beaten into swords.

But it was the Ulster ports that were their most crucial
contribution to the war effort of the Allies. Churchill is on
record in his *The Second World War* as saying that the only
really grave anxiety that beset him in the course of the war, or
perhaps the most serious of his many anxieties, was the Battle
of the Atlantic. If the German U-Boats had won that battle—
and they came frighteningly close to winning it—the war would
have turned against the Allies, probably beyond hope of
recovery. The United Kingdom would have had to surrender.
The British Navy would have escaped to Canada or the United
States. England, Wales, Scotland and the whole of Ireland
would have been occupied by German armies, fortified, and
denuded of all men between the ages of seventeen and forty-five
as laid down in the order signed by the German Field-Marshal,
Wilhelm Keitel, and discovered among the Nazi war papers
when the Reich had collapsed. The Atlantic would have been
formidably policed by an ever-increasing number of German
submarines against the expected convoys of American and
Canadian troops heading for the European fringe in order to
expel the Nazi forces from what had been the British homeland,
then to land in France and conquer there as well. Could this
have happened? Or, with Britain fallen and with Germany, Japan
and Italy in consequent greater strength, could the United
States have survived, as the only power struggling alone in a
war on several fronts and several oceans? No one can say. There
are so many imponderables, including the Russian imponderable,
but no one can deny that the loss of the Battle of the Atlantic
would have been calamitous to the Allies. It was saved for them
by the Ulster people and the Ulster ports. Churchill has said so

and when a man of his genius and experience in war makes such a statement it can surely be taken as conclusive.[1] The vital value of the Ulster ports has been stressed before in this book. No amount of stressing is too much.

The ports were Belfast, with its additional fine natural anchorage of Belfast Lough, its knowledgeable Harbour Commissioners, its numerous and roomy berths, invaluable to the British Admiralty, its great Harland and Wolff shipyard of many slipways, graving docks, engine shops, repair shops and resourceful skills inherited from generations of practised ship-building and engine-building craftsmen; Larne, on Larne Lough, another natural anchorage, in County Antrim, looking east and across to the Scottish coastline and conveniently close to it, of the greatest worth in the early and successful drive to clear the Irish Sea of the U-Boats threatening the mouth of the Firth of Clyde; and Londonderry, the most northerly of the three, opening out through yet another natural anchorage, Lough Foyle, on to the Atlantic Ocean and the deciding North-west Approaches to Britain. They were, admittedly, not an all-sufficing substitute for the South Irish ports, some of which, by virtue of their being appreciably further out into the Atlantic, were better situated; but they were the only strategically placed ports available to Britain and the United States after Eire's declaration of neutrality, aside from those in distant Iceland, which would have been ineffective as main bases for the Atlantic battle. So, when the German armies had crushed and occupied Poland and during the ensuing strange lull—what came to be known at the time as 'The Phoney War'—the British Admiralty and the Ulstermen themselves began to adapt the Ulster ports and, especially, to improve and extend considerably the limited facilities of the very important harbour at Londonderry. Thanks to the lull, there were some months in which to effect what was immediately needed but the amount that required to be done was daunting. Then, with a suddenness and a daring that staggered the world, the Germans, in the most brilliantly conceived and executed military assault yet known in the history of armed conflict, seized Norway, struck at France through Holland,

[1] See *The Second World War*; also, Ulster newspapers of May 1943, when Churchill's letter to the retiring Ulster Prime Minister, J. M. Andrews, was published.

Belgium and the supposedly impassable Ardennes, rolled up and shattered the French armies by breaking through the Maginot Line, drove the British Expeditionary Force into the famous retreat to Dunkirk and threw it off the Continent. The French sued for peace and Britain found herself on her own and fighting for her very life. The Nazis were confident she would lose it. Their U-Boats, thanks to the newly-gained German possession of great stretches of European coastline, had easier, more immediate and more formidable submarine access to the Atlantic and the shipping routes the British were dependent on for their existence. The U-Boat onslaught which was to bring that race to its knees could now begin in earnest.

The author, who was then an established and exempted Civil Servant working in a London Government Department, tried to secure the essential preliminary of Treasury permission to join the British Armed Forces and do his best to fight for his country. His first six written applications, spread over a period of two years, were, with persisting disapproval and discouragement, rejected. He eventually sent in a seventh application, whereupon the irritated Treasury, waking at last to the agreeable realization that if it allowed him to go to war he might not come back, consented. He managed to persuade the Corps of Royal Marines to accept him as an elderly and slightly colour-blind volunteer and ultimately found himself in Taranto, where he was assigned to a ship's company under Combined Operations command, for what remained of the Mediterranean war, and served at sea with a not unexpected lack of distinction. However, before departing aboard a troopship for Taranto (E Deck), he was given the usual embarkation leave to see his family, entrained at Euston for Stranraer and took passage across the Irish Sea to Larne. What he saw there, as his ship was approaching the landing berth, surprised and pleased him. 'If this is the sort of thing my peculiar native Province is doing for the Allied war effort,' he murmured to himself as he stared at the swarming destroyers, corvettes, sloops, minesweepers and specially armed trawlers, 'it isn't doing too badly.' The waters of the Lough and the Harbour were crowded with small warships, some going out on U-Boat patrol, some returning, all of them quiet, grey and grim. There was a war on—and Ulster was in it.

When he arrived in Belfast and had time to look around the city of his birth, he was not so pleased. Whole areas of it had been all but obliterated by German air attack. The Luftwaffe had carried out several raids in a determined effort to knock out the big Harbour, the Harland and Wolff shipyard and the adjoining aircraft factory of Short and Harland, which was mass-producing heavy bombers and flying-boats for the Royal Air Force. In the first raids, the Luftwaffe had mistakenly dropped innumerable high explosive bombs, oil bombs and incendiaries on mainly residential districts, killing, wounding and burying the people in rubble (only Glasgow and Liverpool, of provincial cities, had a higher fatal casualty rate), shattering scores of close-packed streets, blasting the electricity power stations and plunging all into a darkness relieved only by the light of the flames and the constantly falling Luftwaffe flares, destroying the central telephone systems and the defence co-ordination dependent on them.

In the north and east of the city, the Air Wardens and the Fire Brigade were overwhelmed by the fierce and ever-spreading fires. The entire city seemed to be one mass of fire. And there were no neighbouring cities to help, as elsewhere in Britain, there was nothing outside the city boundaries but a hinterland of countryside. Belfast was on its own. Somehow, an appeal from the stricken city got through to Dublin. Could the Fire Brigade there be sent to Belfast at once? De Valera was telephoned by the Head of the Dublin Fire Service and asked if the Brigade could have permission to go to Belfast. Permission was refused. It would be a breach of neutrality, said De Valera, and replaced his night-time telephone receiver. What the Head of the Fire Service thought of the refusal has not been recorded. A few minutes later, however, his telephone rang. It was De Valera. He had changed his mind, the Brigade could answer the Belfast appeal.[1] The main Customs posts at the border between Eire and Ulster were alerted and the Dublin Fire Brigade, leaving behind it only a skeleton service in case of normal fire in Dublin itself, thundered along the darkened roads to the north, sped through the specially opened Customs posts, joined their harassed professional colleagues in Belfast and gave of their best in helping to bring the blazing city under control.

[1] See *De Valera and the March of a Nation* (Bromage), p. 278.

'After all,' said De Valera, when challenged later on his decision, 'they were our people up there.' There was an element of characteristic defensiveness in that reply. Still, he did send the Brigade. Irishmen helped Irishmen—as they should have been doing in the past and should be doing today.

If ever a city suffered wartime trouble it was Belfast. Although a small city of then about 400,000 inhabitants, the population density per square mile—particularly in the vulnerable working-class districts north and east of the dock and ship-building areas —was so intense as to make heavy casualties from air raids a certainty.[1] Some 57,000 houses all told received direct hits or were wrecked by blast, whole groups of streets disappeared from sight and almost from recollection and at least 100,000 people were made homeless—about a quarter of the entire population. Many, after the raids, managed to get shelter from relatives or friends in the countryside, many thousands 'slept rough' on the hills that looked down on the city. Something like 40,000 were accommodated in the city's Rest Centres and meals were provided in the Emergency Feeding Centres for 70,000. The Ulstermen's capital city had paid heavily for siding with the British. Not for it the neutral peace of Dublin.

But the Luftwaffe had not scored the success it so badly wanted, the one that alone could justify the risks of the long flight from its captured French airfields. It decided to make certain that it did. It came back in even greater strength and, in a few hours on a May night of perfect bombing weather, blasted the Harland and Wolff slipways and various vital construction shops so devastatingly that it seemed, when the damage was assessed next morning, that the yard would be out of production for at any rate a year. In fact, such was the determination and the round-the-clock devotion of the shipbuilding men and the other experts who set to work to repair the damage, that the yard was back in full production within six months. Those six months perforce spent mainly on repair work, though, meant a bad setback. The Harland and Wolff production had been prodigious and to have the yard at such a low production level as the air-raid devastation was being made good dangerously depleted the British Admiralty and the Royal Air Force— the Short and Harland aircraft production capacity had also been

[1] Close on 1,000 men, women and children were killed.

108

seriously reduced by the Luftwaffe raids—to the extent of many desperately needed warships, bombers and flying-boats. The Harland and Wolff yard was of the greatest importance to the British Admiralty and, if Britain's navy had not been so drastically run down since 1964 by the British Labour Government, would still be important to it. Throughout the war of 1939–45, despite the near-ruinous damage inflicted by the Luftwaffe, Harland and Wolff built ships so fast that at one stage the yard was sending corvettes down the slipways and into the water at the rate of one a week. This gave significantly relieving help to the British Admiralty. Corvettes were perhaps the most effective of all U-Boat killers because of their speed and easy manœuvrability and they were in great demand for escort convoy duty. Harland and Wolff provided the Admiralty with close on forty of them. Overall, the Belfast yard built and launched with remarkable swiftness somewhere around 150 to 200 vessels of war, from special-purpose cargo ships and big carriers of 30,000 tons to minesweepers of 1,000 tons. These were the beasts of burden of the war, unglamorous, unsung. Harland and Wolff, at Admiralty request, specialized in them but were not confined to them. They built the famous cruiser, H.M.S. *Black Prince*. The even more famous cruiser, H.M.S. *Penelope*—the much admired 'Pepper Pot', so nicknamed because it was shot full of holes in action after action—was a Harland and Wolff ship. Ulstermen may be a cross-grained, opinionated, chin-thrusting, fist-waving race, inclined to take strong dislikes and maintain them for a lifetime, but they are fine builders of ships, as the Admiralty planners in their extremity had very good reason to know. During the Nazi War, those same difficult Ulstermen provided them with ships to a total of almost 700,000 tons. In August 1945 the author returned from the Mediterranean and spent his foreign-service leave in Ulster with his family, before going back to England to await his demobilization. One evening he found himself in a typical little Belfast pub not far from the Harland and Wolff yard. There he got into conversation with a couple of shipyard men and congratulated them on the splendid job they and their workmates had done throughout the war and asked them how they had felt on V–E day. 'Bloody tired,' they said.

Of course, the English, the Welsh and the Scots worked hard, too. The whole of Britain, both native and refugee, worked hard, so why should the Ulstermen imagine they had worked so much harder than the rest? They imagine no such thing. They do ask, though, that what they did should not be stricken from the record. They want it remembered that they built up their small agricultural industry so rapidly and so well that they were able to send to those same English, Scots and Welsh in the course of the war some 2,000,000,000 eggs, many millions of gallons of milk—more than 3,000,000 gallons in one war year alone—and untold tonnages of other foodstuffs so sorely wanted by the severely rationed British. They want it remembered that a single Belfast engineering company, Mackie's, helped the British Armed Forces to the tune of 75,000,000 shot and shell, 65,000,000 general armament components, 12,000 gun barrels, 2,000,000 vital plugs for Royal Air Force bombs to drop on the enemy and an immense number of aircraft fuselages, to mention just some of the items of war manufactured by the firm and leaving unlisted the enormous quantities manufactured by other Belfast engineering concerns to swell the British armament production. They would like it remembered that the three great and famous Ulster regiments—the Royal Inniskilling Fusiliers, decimated at Waterloo and the Somme, the Royal Irish Fusiliers, and the Royal Ulster Rifles which, as the Royal Irish Rifles, had borne the worst burden of the Somme casualties—were with the British Expeditionary Force in France in 1939 and 1940, together with the 5th Inniskilling Dragoon Guards, the 3rd (Ulster) Searchlight Regiment and the 8th (Belfast) H.A.A. Regiment.

In the course of the retreat through Belgium and the harassingly invested march to Dunkirk on which the escape of the entire British Army and the safety of Britain herself depended, battalions of the Inniskillings, Irish Fusiliers and Ulster Rifles were entrusted with rearguard action after rearguard action in sacrificial efforts to cover the retirement of the main mass of the infantry. They fought with all the savagely determined Scotch–Irish doggedness so praised by General Robert E. Lee, three-quarters of a century before. They took very heavy losses in doing so. The 2nd Battalion of the Inniskillings had fought with outstanding fierceness in defence of the Ypres-Comines Canal. If the Canal position had fallen quickly, a whole British Army Corps would have been unable to withdraw to Dunkirk. It did not fall quickly, but the Inniskillings were badly mauled again and, before they were taken safely off at last from the beaches, they had been reduced from a battalion strength of around 500 or 600 men to an exhausted 150. The Inniskilling Dragoon Guards, with their tanks and armoured cars, were ordered here, there and everywhere, reinforcing wearied and thinned out regiments striving to hold the many crumbling sectors, counter-attacking when the enemy was breaking through, then steadily and stubbornly fighting their way to the waiting relief ships. They were among the last of the British troops to get away. The men of the Searchlight Regiment fought as ordinary infantry and fought well, the Heavy Anti-Aircraft Artillery Regiment used their guns ingeniously against advancing German forces and helped to defend Dunkirk itself as the dive-bombers swooped on it. Then, at long last, all but one of the patient ships had sailed for England, and a British Major-General, accom-panied by some of his staff, went walking up and down the beaches, though enemy bombs were falling all around him, searching slowly and carefully to make certain that not a man would be left behind. Satisfied that the beaches were finally clear, he embarked—the very last to quit the Dunkirk sands—and was soon walking down a gangplank in a Home Counties port, as immaculate and as unconcerned as usual. He was Harold Alexander, later Field-Marshal Earl Alexander of Tunis, born and brought up like his Ulster forebears on the family estate near the village of Caledon in County Tyrone.

Dunkirk was not the end of the war for the Ulster regiments by any means. The three infantry regiments and the Dragoon Guards, with the North Irish Horse and its light tanks, fought all through the war to its very end, through the Western Desert, Sicily, Italy, Normandy, Belgium and Germany itself. The Royal Ulster Rifles, when the Nazis finally surrendered, had advanced 700 miles since landing on the Normandy beaches. The Ulster regiments were rated as among the best fighting units in the British Army. The man who sets out to persuade Ulstermen that the Royal Inniskilling Fusiliers, the Royal Irish Fusiliers, the Royal Ulster Fusiliers, the Royal Inniskilling Dragoon Guards and the North Irish Horse have ever been anything else but *the* best regiments in the British Army is looking for trouble and will assuredly find it. Be that as it may, in the war against the Nazis they fought as Ulstermen should fight and do—obstinately in retreat, fiercely in attack. They earned their battle honours, and their campaign medals.

The Americans entered the war to the crash of bombs on their Pacific Fleet and soon were swarming into Ulster in ever-growing numbers, the advance Divisions of what was to become the biggest and most powerful army of all the combatant countries, with the exception of Soviet Russia. The white-helmeted United States Army Military Policemen—'Ike's Snowdrops'—became a familiar sight in the Ulster cities, towns and villages, but failed to relieve the anxiety many Ulster parents suddenly developed for their prettier and hitherto exemplary daughters. The Americans went at once into tough combat training, coached by an experienced British Army Division, and then thinned out as thousands of them left Ulster for the North Africa invasion, to be replaced by more and more American Divisions from every part of the United States. The programming was remarkable, one Division being 'tickled to death to have come all the way from the Middle West of America to arrive at Ballygobackwards in Ulster five minutes before schedule'. Ulster was an armed camp, clanking with heavy tanks and the innumerable other steel-clad vehicles demanded by modern war. New airfields with lengthy runways had already been made by the British; the Americans with their sophisticated construction methods and immense machines helped to make more. Lough Erne, in the beautiful westerly County of Fermanagh, was made into a flying-boat base for Royal Air Force Coastal Command and proved itself to be a damaging weapon in the intense and ever increasing fight against the U-Boats of the German Admiral Doenitz. The value of Ulster to the Allies, as the Americans now supported the British in saying, was becoming more and more decisive. General Eisenhower, when the war against Germany had ended, visited Belfast in August 1945 and, in a public speech, said this:

It was here in Northern Ireland that the American Army first began to concentrate for our share in the attack upon the citadel of Continental Europe. From here started the long hard march to Allied victory. Without Ulster I do not see how the American forces could have been concentrated to begin the invasion of Europe. If Ulster had not been a definite, co-operative part of the British Empire and had not been available for our use, I do not see how the build-up could have been carried out in England.

Let it be remembered, say the Ulstermen sadly, knowing that it is more the way of the world to forget.

The Battle of the Atlantic ebbed and flowed, as every battle usually does until one or the other side has won it. In the earlier years of the war it looked very much as if it would be Germany that would win it, for the U-Boat sinkings of Allied shipping were immense. It was then that the northerly Ulster port of Londonderry became the key to the Allied sea defence against the successful German submarines which were torpedoeing the British and American cargo ships and all-important tankers to an extent that was marked on the Admiralty graphs in hundreds of thousands of tons. By basing surface escorts on Londonderry and its natural anchorage of Lough Foyle, it was possible to increase the westward limit of convoy protection in the Atlantic by an additional hundred miles, as Captain Roskill points out in his official history of the naval side of the 1939–1945 War, *The War at Sea*. It must be said again that it could not give all the advantages that would have been given by the major Southern Irish ports, but it became the most important and effective of all the United Kingdom anti-submarine bases, with 20,000 naval and engineering support personnel, a large and comprehensive repair works installed and staffed by many of Harland and Wolff's best men to deal with wounded and weather-battered craft, 150 warships coming and going on the unceasing and wearying convoy escort duty, and a huge and complex Control and Signalling Depot. All were needed, for the Atlantic struggle was one of the grimmest and most merciless of the war.

The U-Boats, directed by their experienced and skilled commanders, would vary their tactics according to the constitution and circumstances of each convoy and the size of its escort. Usually, they would lie in wait at dusk for the nearing and darkened ships, steal up behind them, attack them with bow torpedoes, then make off at maximum knots or crash-dive as the escort protectors closed in and dropped their depth-charges. Enormous tankers would blow up in a roar of searing flame as the torpedoes smashed their hulls. Those of their crews that survived the explosions would jump into the water in a desperate hope of being picked up, only to die a terrible death in the floating and blazing oil. Convoys dared not stop to pick up the unlucky. Crowded boats from isolated, torpedoed and sinking cargo vessels would be blown to pieces by the deck guns of surfaced submarines determined to finish them off and ensure that, in accordance with the theory of total war, the number of trained and valuable Allied seamen would be reduced. The submerged German submarine crews, in their turn, their torpedoes fired, hiding silently and hopefully some fathoms down, listening to the engines of circling warships above them in the light of day, would die as horribly as the tanker men, choked by chemical fumes when the searching depth-charges found and sprang the thin-steel submarine skin, or drowned as their broken craft fell to the sea bottom and stayed there.

Everything the Ulstermen could give in this pitiless battle was given. Scores of Ulster seamen, serving in Ulster ships, died in it. Ulster is two-thirds island and her men have been taking to the sea for generations. They had served at sea in the 1914–18 War, they served at sea again in the 1939–45 War, and many of them in each of those wars did not return. Many young Ulster aircraft pilots died, too, in many an air battle in many a theatre of war. Some of them died in the Atlantic battle, flying their bombers of 502 (Ulster) Squadron of Royal Air Force Coastal Command, rarely out of the sky, relay taking over from relay, flying out into the Atlantic to furthest range, ceaselessly seeking, protecting, bombing. Lough Erne was thick with Catalina and Sunderland flying boats. The Catalinas could cover the ocean to a distance of 400 miles from shore. It was a Catalina from Lough Erne that found the German battleship *Bismarck*, when it had managed to deceive and escape from the pursuing British naval forces and was making for the safety of Brest on the German occupied French coast. The signal from the Catalina enabled the British Admiralty to plot the *Bismarck*'s position and arrange the naval concentration that resulted in her destruction.[1] The British warships that eventually killed her included H.M.S. *King George V*, captained by an Ulsterman who afterwards became an Admiral of the Royal Navy, Sir Wilfred Patterson.

As the Atlantic life-line struggle grew ever fiercer, the waters of the long broad Lough on which Belfast is situated became a key assembly and shelter point for outgoing and incoming convoys. The Luftwaffe, realizing its steadily increasing strategic importance, made several strong efforts to deny its usefulness to the British Admiralty by having the entrance to it thickly and dangerously mined. This gave the Naval Command in Ulster a lot of trouble, but the Luftwaffe did not succeed in blocking the Lough for long. The entrance was carefully swept of the many mines and constantly patrolled by sea and by air. Fighter aircraft, flying from one or other of the eighteen airfields laid down in Ulster for wartime use, saw to it that no more Luftwaffe mines came floating down by parachute. The Lough was reopened for shipping and stayed open. Ulster people living in the little towns of Bangor and Whitehead on opposite sides of the Lough would see its waters crowded in the evening with scores of deep-lying cargo ships and tankers, their escort warships taking up station and acknowledging signalled instructions from Naval Control on departure-formation and rate of knots—and wake up in the morning to find them gone and the horizon alive with still more ships, wearily and thankfully arriving. Many a master of many a ship was gladdened by the sight of Belfast Lough.

In Belfast itself—which became, among other things, the main Naval Trawler Base for the whole of the Admiralty's Western Approaches Command, with a hundred or so of the specially equipped, deadly little anti-submarine trawlers perpetually going and coming—the great harbour was packed with small and lethal vessels of war of almost every kind. A man looking down from the glowering Cave Hill that dominates the city would have felt certain he could walk across its waters by stepping from deck to deck. Destroyers, frigates, corvettes, sloops, minesweepers, patrol craft, anti-aircraft flakships, landing craft and fast commando assault craft, some of them damaged in action and under repair, most of them preparing for

[1] *Northern Ireland in the Second World War* (Blake), pp. 344–5.

renewed escort duty and whatever that duty might bring, lay side by side below and not far from the friendly arms of the enormous Harland and Wolff gantry cranes that mark the city so firmly in the mind of every Ulster man and woman, whether at home or in a foreign country. Alongside the long new berths built at speed by the Harbour Commissioners at Admiralty behest—together with nearly 200,000 square yards of additional shed storage—cargo ships of the Belfast commercial shipping lines loaded themselves with food for delivery in convoy over the Irish Sea to the Clyde, Merseyside and the Bristol Channel.

But almost everything the Port of Belfast did for the Allies throughout the war—and it did far more than has been stated here—stemmed from the Atlantic battle or was planned and controlled in such a way as to play a helpful part in it, both direct and ancillary. It was a battle that took place far out in a huge ocean, away from sight of those on land, the British people. They knew of it, of course, but did not know about it. They could not possibly take in fully its critical nature and its horror. They were aware of the Battle of Britain, fought in the very skies above their heads and capable of being watched to an extent by the assisted eye; but the Battle of the Atlantic was only really known to those whose fathers, husbands, brothers and sons were involved in it. It was a dreadful battle. Not until close on four years of hideous fighting had passed did it swing to the Allies and it was won by the gifts of Londonderry, Larne and Belfast, made gladly by those very Ulster people who are today a target for the disapproval so characteristic of the uncaring and contemptuous English. But were those ports of decisive impact or could the claim be no more than wishful-thinking, put forward by hopeful Ulster Unionists as mitigation of their guilty discrimination against the minority in their Province? The matter is beyond doubt. It is not Churchill alone who has said so. The German Admiral Doenitz, commanding all the Nazi submarine fleets, wrote his memoirs some years ago. After referring to the early sinkings his U-Boats had achieved so easily off the southerly tip of neutral Eire, he said: 'We tried to get to grips with the shipping passing to the north of Ireland, but in this we failed.' The phrasing is typical of a man more versed in the strategy and tactics of naval warfare than in the use of a pen. The final four words, however, have in them the unmistakable admission that he had been mastered and an implication of how this had happened. If there had been no special defence of 'shipping passing to the north of Ireland', if there had been no Ulster ports, no Ulster airfields, no Ulster loughs, Grand Admiral Carl Doenitz could have found himself writing very differently.

The winning of the Battle of the Atlantic made certain the winning of the war. It was an appalling struggle, though, fought to the end without a trace of the humanity that had gleamed, however momentarily, in the sea fights of the past. Because of it, a great many more dead men are lying on the Atlantic floor. A lot of them are Ulstermen. May they lie there in peace, beside the equally brave men they died with.

The Ulstermen, looking back on the war against Nazi Germany, could truly say that they had much to give and that, to the best of their resources and their ability, they gave it, despite their early inexperience in war-time organization and the most efficient use of manpower. They blundered often but learnt quickly and improved quickly, surprisingly so in view of their peace-time disinclination to accept a lesson from anyone. The women of Ulster could say that they, too, had done their best. They streamed into the linen mills and other textile mills, the shirtmaking factories, engineering works and aircraft works, the great ropeworks—one of the world's biggest—and 'wrought' hard. There is a story which perhaps only Ulster people, to whom the rasping accent and vivid language of the Belfast workers are so well and so affectionately known, would smile at. It concerns a Belfast working girl, tired out after a long day on her feet in a war-production factory, turning to a feminine colleague as they left at last for home and saying to her, 'See me? M'legs is like melodeons!' Melodeon-like or not, the legs of the Ulster women were strong enough to carry them in the making of 15,000,000 shirts and many additional millions of shirt-lengths—and to aid the men in making aircraft, trawl twine for Russia, binder twine for British agriculture, camouflage nets, cargo nets, steel boom defence nets, rocket lines, signal halyards, ropes by the mile, hand grenades, Admiralty mooring buoys, radar equipment and tank gun mountings. Some 50,000 Ulster women themselves made linen for aeroplane wing fabric, flying-suit canvas, gun-covers, nurses' uniforms, conveyor belting and other war needs. They also continued, on the encouragement of the British Government, to make luxury linen goods for the wealthy United States civilian market, thus earning for Britain many millions of the 'hard currency' dollars so urgently required to finance the British imports from America of food and weapons of war. They helped, too, in the making of the 620,000,000 yards of standard cloth produced in Ulster for use in manufacturing the utility clothing which the rationed and unfortunate British were compelled to put on their backs. And, like the Ulstermen at the benches with them, they kept their unruly Protestant tempers with the apparently innumerable Catholic men and women who flocked into the Province from Eire, where pay was poor and unemployment as depressing as a plague, to share in the higher paid jobs available in war-time Ulster.

So it went on till at last 'the rat was dead in an alley back of the Wilhelmstrasse'—and De Valera called personally at the German Legation in Dublin to express his condolences on the regretted decease of a friendly Head of State. Not even then could he see the indignity and folly of his logic. Three months after the German collapse, the Japanese Empire was beaten, too; and the Ulster people, who had given all they were able to give, were as tired as the others who had endured so much in achieving the victory.

The effort of the little Province, then, from 1939 to 1945 had not belied its claim to be loyal to Britain. And it was recognized. The English of those years, when they wanted to check the name of an Ulster town, knew where to look for it on the map. The facility did not remain with them for long, of course. Their interest in their friends is more usually displayed in time of need. But do the Ulster people overstate the case for the help they gave to Britain in the struggle with Hitler's Germany? Has it been overstated here? The author is an Ulsterman and may be prejudiced. It might be well, therefore, to learn what others had to say in the matter. First, Cyril Falls, the distinguished war historian and one-time Chichele Professor of Military History at the University of Oxford:

Had British forces not been present in Northern Ireland, I

regard it as practically certain that all Ireland would have been conquered and occupied by the Germans. In that case, the main British military effort of late 1940 and 1941 would have been diverted from North Africa to Ireland and, while this struggle was in progress, the Germans would have won immense advantages in the Battle of the Atlantic. The general effect on the war would have been incalculable.[1]

Next, General George A. Marshall, Chief of Staff of the United States Army, on the aspect of an America faced by a victorious Germany, Japan and Italy:

We were given time to gather sufficient resources to participate in the fight in a determining manner. Had Soviet Russia and the British Army been defeated early, as they well might have been if the Germans, Japanese and Italians had better co-ordinated their plans and resources and successive operations, we should have stood today in the Western Hemisphere confronted by enemies who controlled a greater part of the world. Our close approach to that terrifying situation should have a sobering influence on Americans for generations to come.[2]

General Marshall couples Russia with Britain. But where would Russia have been if Britain had fallen and been unable to help her when she herself was drawn into the war? The aid Britain gave to Russia—and Ulster work-people and Ulster sailors helped to provide it—included 5,218 tanks with the appropriate ammunition, 4,020 vehicles including lorries and ambulances, 1,721 motor-cycles, more than 7,000 weapons of various kinds, 2,560 Bren-gun carriers, 500,000,000 rounds of ammunition for small arms, a battleship, 9 destroyers, 4 submarines, 5 motor minesweepers, 9 minesweeping trawlers, 329 radar sets, 2,000 guns and enormous quantities of food and raw materials, machine tools, power plant, electrical equipment and all kinds of varied machinery and medicines.[3]

[1] Cyril Falls' *Northern Ireland as an Outpost of Defence* (H.M. Stationery Office, Belfast, and reprinted in *World Review*, London, 1951).

[2] From the Biennial Report, July 1, 1943 to June 30, 1945, to the U.S. Secretary for War.

[3] Anyone who may wish to check those figures will find them in the *Weekly Hansard*—the report of debates in the British Parliament—of April 16, 1946, No. 13, columns 2,517–2,523.

Churchill, on V–E Day, spoke exultantly to the peoples of Great Britain, the Empire and the Commonwealth. In his speech he lashed De Valera, who made public answer, saying: 'It seems strange to me that Mr. Churchill does not see that if this is accepted it would mean that Britain's necessity would become a moral code, and that when this necessity was involved other peoples' rights would not count.'[1] What rights would the victorious Germans have left to the Irish people if Britain—and Ulster—had been unable to save them from the Gestapo?

In June 1945, when the Allies had conquered Germany and the Japanese were all but finished, Churchill wrote to the Ulster Prime Minister, who was then Sir Basil Brooke, and conveyed what he thought of the Ulster men and women and the help they had given in the winning of the long and terrible war:

> We have travelled a hard and darksome road to victory in Europe and at every turn in this memorable journey the loyalty and courage of Ulster have gleamed before the eyes of men. The stand of the Government and people of Northern Ireland for the unity of the British Empire and Commonwealth and for the great cause of freedom for which we all risked our survival will never be forgotten by Great Britain.

Never be forgotten? It was forgotten the moment Japan surrendered—and it is still forgotten.

---

[1] Quoted in *Churchill and Ireland* (Bromage), p. 177.

Interlude

I. THE REAPING

IN October 1968, twenty-three years from the end of the war in which Ulster so gladly gave its help to England, the native antagonisms which had divided the Province for generations seemed to many thankful Ulster men and women to be dying away at last. Then, with a suddenness and a bitterness that dismayed the Ulster people as a whole and shocked the world, the same antagonisms, the very hatreds that so many had thought were disappearing, burst out in a volcanic violence that led to even greater violence across the Province and brought upon it a one-sided condemnation.

'They have sown the wind,' said the English disdainfully of the Ulster Unionists, 'and they are reaping the whirlwind.'

There was much of truth in this—and much of error.

The violence that erupted in 1968 established in those who watched it from the shelter of other countries a conviction that the Catholic minority in Ulster was unstained with sin, the Protestant majority exclusively culpable. The watchers took in the cleverly publicized claim that the police of the Province were in the main a recruitment of brutal men, that only the Protestant people were bigoted, that the Ulster Parliament was no more than a Protestant vested interest, the Catholics unjustifiably distrusted. They forgot the age-old saying that it always takes two to make a quarrel.

They failed to see, too, that there was a man in Ulster who remembered the ancient advice about the mote and the beam, who felt that it is not the faults of others that matter most, but the faults in oneself that must first be detected and dealt with, provided the hands that find them and spread them on the table belong to uninfluenced men. The man was Terence O'Neill, Prime Minister of Ulster, who decided in the opening months of 1969 to set up a Commission of Enquiry and accordingly submitted the necessary authorizing document to the Governor of Northern Ireland.

II. WARRANT OF APPOINTMENT
BY THE GOVERNOR OF NORTHERN IRELAND

Whereas on and since 5th October, 1968, sporadic outbreaks of violence and civil disturbances have occurred in Northern Ireland in consequence of the activities of certain bodies;

AND WHEREAS it is desired to investigate the causes and circumstances thereof:

NOW THEREFORE, I, RALPH FRANCIS ALNWICK, BARON GREY OF NAUNTON, Knight Grand Cross of the Most Distinguished Order of Saint Michael and Saint George, Knight Commander of the Royal Victorian Order, Officer of the Most Excellent Order of the British Empire, Governor of Northern Ireland, reposing great trust and confidence in your knowledge and ability hereby authorize and appoint you . . .

The Honourable Lord Cameron, D.S.C. (Chairman)
Professor Sir John Biggart, C.B.E.
James Joseph Campbell, M.A.

Commissioners to hold an enquiry into and to report upon the course of events leading to, and the immediate causes and nature of the violence and civil disturbance in Northern Ireland on and since 5th October, 1968; and to assess the composition, conduct and aims of those bodies involved in the current agitation and in any incidents arising out of it...
....
....

Given at Government House, Hillsborough,
this 3rd day of March 1969,
By His Excellency's Command

PART TWO

E*

Chapter Seven

ON October 5, 1968, in the ugly and unlikeable City of Londonderry, so famous in the political history of Britain, the anger of the misused local Catholic population exploded in the face of the Ulster Unionist Party and made the first of many breaches in the hitherto impregnable fortifications it had built over a period of almost half a century to keep at a distance all who would threaten its Protestant domination of the cherished city and the Province. Thousands of men and women of the Ulster Catholic minority, marching in protest procession under the sponsorship and banners of the Civil Rights Association, were confronted by detachments of the Royal Ulster Constabulary assigned to stop them from entering certain zones of the city in defiance of a prohibiting Order made by the Ulster Government. Banner poles were thrown at the policemen's eyes, placards at their legs, stones were flung at them in greater and greater number, striking and injuring many constables, there was a raging and shouting uproar, a surging forward and a thrusting back, a batoning of heads and shoulders, a violence that appalled the Ulster people when they saw it on their television screens and read the accounts of it in their newspapers.

The 5th of October did not see the end of it. All that night and next day there was even worse violence, beginning when the police forcibly removed a provocative banner from Civil Rights protesters who were approaching the War Memorial. There was a vicious clash, swiftly joined in by innumerable hooligans spoiling for trouble. The hooligans were from the Bogside district of the city, the Catholic area made famous by the dramatic activities of Bernadette Devlin, and the police, using batons and water-cannons, managed to contain them and eventually drive them back to where they had come from. There was trouble, too, from an increasing mob of Protestant hooligans—all the Christian Churches in Ireland are strongly supported by followings of faithful guttersnipes—and the fighting throughout the city continued for a stretch of thirty hours, exhausting the forces of the outnumbered police. Catholics stoned Protestants, the Protestants stoned the Catholics, both Catholics and Protestants stoned the police, who charged and batoned them both impartially. Television cameramen were endangered, reporters mobbed and knocked to the ground. Altogether eighteen policemen, some of them badly injured, were treated in hospital casualty departments. No fewer than seventy-seven civilians were hurt. The Casualty doctors were kept busy, stitching up lacerated craniums, legs and arms and saving the damaged eyes of young policemen. Ulster hung its head in shame.

Terence O'Neill, elected Prime Minister in 1963, saw his chance to introduce the reforms he had set his heart on. He would have introduced them earlier—almost as soon as he had taken office, in fact—if he had not been frustrated by die-hard Unionist elements in his Cabinet. Now, however, he was reinforced by the very violence he had foreseen and wished to avoid. He announced a series of five important reforms, designed to assuage the Catholic minority by meeting their just demands. The reforms covered the appointment of an Ombudsman to investigate grievances; the organization of housing allocation on a points system; the appointment of a Development Commission to replace the Londonderry Corporation (ruled by a Unionist junta in its own questionable interests and in the even more questionable interests of its equally blind supporters); abolition of the hated pluralistic and selective voting right in local government elections, and an eventual withdrawal of certain sections of the even more fiercely hated Special Powers Act under which suspects could be arrested and imprisoned without charge and trial. This was as far as he dared go at the time—politically, he had to walk carefully, in view of the reactionary thinking of the Unionists in the constituency associations, the watchful grass-roots prowlers—but he was known to be a man of liberal mind, integrity and warmth of heart, determined to bring in further reforms as quickly as he found it practicable to do so. He had first to educate his ossified Party in Parliament, the cities and the countryside, no easy and swift task. The moderate leaders of the Civil Rights movement knew this. Not all the leaders were moderate men, of course, but those who were responsible and gifted with judgment were well aware that O'Neill was to be trusted. The Opposition Members in the Ulster Parliament knew it, too, but showed themselves shallow in their thinking and mistaken in their tactics. Although they were aware that O'Neill was their best hope in the matter of continuing and enlarging reform, they preferred to stoop to Party manœuvring rather than buttress him by urging restraint on the part of the Catholic minority. They suffered later— stupidity has a habit of bringing retribution—when O'Neill was ejected from office by the jackals of his own Parliamentary Party, and the spreading violence in Ulster reacted heavily and tragically against the Catholics in Belfast. The Catholic Nationalist and Republican mentality, however, has always been one of the weightiest crosses the Ulster people have had to carry.

O'Neill was deeply convinced that only through treating the Ulster Catholics with justice and unvarying fairness could they be turned from enmity to friendship, from an attitude of angry and suspicious non-co-operation to a willingness to join with the Protestants in building a better and happier country. It is possible that he was not entirely right in this, as the minority in Ulster was generally and emotionally in favour of an all-Ireland Republic, but, whatever the overall political preference of the minority might have been then, he was clearly provident in his undoubted desire to make the effort to win them over to a constructive sharing in the shaping and life of the Province. There is always wisdom in behaving honourably. O'Neill, beyond question, was an honourable man, ultimately beaten by the folly of his Party. He went down fighting, though, and before resigning from office did much to set the feet of the Ulster people on the path they should properly follow.

This cannot be said of the Catholic minority, which caught the scent of blood, changed its objectives and embarked on a campaign to destroy the Ulster State. The Civil Rights movement was infiltrated by extremists whose passion for civil justice was subordinate to their determination to wreck the structure in entirety. Opposition Members of Parliament who were on its committees and who directed its course saw the chance of smashing the Unionist Party and decided to take it. Ulster, as violence broke out all over the Province, went from bad to worse. Militant students of Queen's University of Belfast formed a movement called People's Democracy (the stone-breaking Bernadette Devlin was a founder member of it[1]) which carried out a riot-causing march to Londonderry in January 1969, led by Young Socialist Alliance members, Revolutionary Socialists, members of illegal Irish Republican Clubs, other Irish Republican sympathizers, Irish Republican Army men keeping well in the background, together with a number of Anarchists—as repellent a gathering of inadequately informed, immature and self-satisfied troublemakers as one could find in Britain, the kind that raise the roof for Tariq Ali and believe him to be the Prophet of Prophets.

On their protest march to Londonderry, they were ambushed and stoned brutally by extreme Protestant guttersnipes of almost insane fundamentalist Biblical conviction—one of the most disgraceful episodes in the recent story of Ulster[2]—and many of them were seriously hurt. It must be remembered, however, that the march was provocative. On their way through a little country town called Toomebridge, a Republican flag was unfurled and flaunted. This angered the Protestant Unionist majority in the neighbourhood and the escorting police had difficulty in saving the marchers from attack. The object of the march, the students claimed, was to protest peacefully against the Unionist neglect of Londonderry,[3] where unemployment was demoralizing thousands of the people and mostly Catholic people. There was truth in the accusation about unemployment —in Londonderry it was shocking and the demoralization of the unemployed men there was unquestionable—but the real object of the march was to strike a blow at the Unionist Party and advance the cause of an all-Ireland Workers' Republic. Any idea that the marchers consisted entirely of starry-eyed student idealists may be discarded. There were no stars in the eyes of the marching Revolutionary Socialists, Anarchists, Young

[1] See the picture of her, reproduced in world newspapers, breaking up stones for throwing at the police.

[2] The ambush took place at the now notorious Burntollet Bridge.

[3] The allegation of Governmental neglect of Londonderry was spurious. The Ulster Government, in a period of roughly four years prior to October 1968, had spent £15,000,000 on industrial development and housing in the city and immediately outside it. Londonderry, because of its geographical situation, presents difficult problems in the securing of employment.

Socialist Alliance members and Irish Republican Army men. The arrival of the marchers in Londonderry stirred up intense violence and the police were again in action, struggling to contain and disperse the Protestant and Catholic mobs of hooligans inflamed by the march and by political and religious antagonisms into further stone throwing, smashing of shop windows, burning and looting. Again the Ulster people hung their heads in shame. The top correspondents of the world's newspapers were giving the story of Ulster's disgrace to thousands upon thousands of readers in country after country, the cameramen were filming the dreadful scenes for showing on network after network. Millions of men and women were horrified by the barbarism and assumed it to be characteristic of the Province.

And still the violence spread. Ulster was aflame with it. A branch of People's Democracy in the small country town of Newry in County Down—it had a Catholic majority and its Urban District Council showed as much bias in its handling of civic affairs as any similarly bigoted council with a Unionist majority—decided to stage a protest march. Its objective was to draw attention to the denial of civil rights to the Catholic minority in Ulster, although O'Neill had already made it plain that the rights were being granted and more concessions were on the way. The People's Democracy branch in Newry, however, cared nothing for O'Neill, had little regard for civil rights, cared more—and a great deal more—for its chance of damaging Ulster. The Ulster Government gave permission for the march to take place but insisted by a prohibiting Order that a certain route was to be avoided by the marchers. It was a route through a quarter almost entirely inhabited by Protestants, who probably would not have opposed the march. The Government feared, though, that Protestants might come into the town from outside and attack the marchers. It persisted in its ban.

The author of this book went specially to Newry on the day of the march to see for himself. He arrived in the town an hour before the march was due to start, walked around the significant parts of it, eyed the crush barriers, the detachments of police in strategic positions, felt the acute tension in the air and made his way to the main barricade set up to bar the marchers from entering the disputed area. This barricade consisted of small crush-barriers as the first line of defence. A few yards back from it were placed five police tenders stretched nose to tail in a line across the road, a solid block of them, impossible to pass through. The only way to get past and into the road was by climbing over them or by knocking them down. Behind the tenders stood a double row of quiet and expectant policemen and behind them, equally expectant, a water-jet wagon. Alongside the water-cannon stood a special tender containing reinforced helmets for the police to put on if stones were thrown at them. The author was allowed by the police to station himself immediately behind the crush-barrier until the marchers arrived, after which he was to stand behind the tenders.

As the time drew near for the marchers to reach the barricade, the tension became more and more palpable, the waiting and watching crowds—hitherto unexpectedly and strangely silent—began to murmur and everyone wondered if the marchers would accept the prohibiting Order or attempt to smash through the barricade and the lines of police and march in triumphant procession along the banned route. Suddenly, word was given that the marchers had set out from their assembly point—there were about 3,000 of them—and that the head of the column would soon be in sight. A monotonous chanting roar was heard in the distance—'One man one Vote—One man one Vote!', the principal slogan of the People's Democracy and Civil Rights marchers of the time, aimed at the plurality voting in local government elections—growing louder. It was the first occasion on which the author had heard the voice of a mob and it made him remember, with a shudder, the words of W. B. Yeats, 'And what rough beast, its hour come round at last, slouches towards Bethlehem to be born?'

The head of the column, preceded by stewards wearing arm-bands, came nearer and nearer until at last, with a sort of convulsive and menacing movement, it halted within a few yards of the barricade. An immaculately uniformed District Inspector of the Royal Ulster Constabulary stepped forward and politely read out the warning that defiance of the Government's Order prohibiting the marchers from the specified route would be an offence. There was an equally polite refusal to accept the necessity of the Order by the Chief Steward, who then turned to the marchers, explained what had happened and appealed to them to accept the ban and disperse. Many of them did. But the revolutionary element among the marchers had no intention of dispersing. The Young Socialist Alliance members, Revolutionary Socialists, Anarchists and assorted Republicans, their faces inflamed with anger, surged towards the barricade, seized the crush-barriers, threw them aside and hurled themselves on the tenders. The author, in obedience to a firm request from the police, had now taken up his station behind the tenders, about ten yards from them and in front of the first shock-line of policemen. 'In the name of God,' an American television cameraman said to him, 'what is the matter with your country?' The tenders were rocking as infuriated marchers struggled to overturn them, beating with their hands, thrashing with sticks, kicking, cursing and almost screaming with rage as they swayed them and swayed them until at last the tenders fell over on their sides and lay on the road like wounded heavy beasts, as the democrats swarmed round them and cursed them again and started to smash them before setting them on fire later in the day. The police, who had put on their reinforced helmets, stood quietly and expressionlessly in their ranks and made no move to save the tenders. Obviously, it had been decided officially that the tenders were expendable. Obviously, too, it had been decided by the Government that the effectively publicized claim of the People's Democracy and the Civil Rights movement to be non-violent should be exposed as a lie. And a lie it certainly was, as those who watched the television screens that evening—the attack on the barricade was filmed—could see. The marchers, however, prudently stayed back from the police.

As night fell, Newry went mad. Mobs of hooligans ran amok, police made repeated baton charges, the air was thick with jagged stones and venomously dangerous missiles of every kind, injured policemen fell to the ground and were hurried to hospital by ambulance, shop windows were smashed, attempts were made to set buildings and houses on fire, police tenders went up in flames that lighted much of the whole vicious and damnable scene—while spokesmen for People's Democracy and the Civil Rights Association tried to convince newsmen that the fault lay exclusively with the Government for issuing its prohibiting Order and with the police for their 'brutality'.

Increasingly the people of Ulster were made to feel ashamed, as more violence and more horrible scenes occurred all over the Province. There was a disgraceful confrontation between Civil Rights marchers and extreme Protestants in the charming old City of Armagh, ecclesiastical capital of Ireland since the time of Saint Patrick. Wherever the decent men and women of Ulster turned their eyes there were confrontations and stonings and outbursts of the hatred that so many had hoped was gone for ever. Ulster was sinking lower and lower. In Londonderry the Catholics barricaded themselves into the Bogside district and fought a full-scale battle with the Royal Ulster Constabulary, battering them with stones and worse than stones, hurling petrol bombs at them, setting many of them on fire, inflicting severe burns on them. The police, faced with about 2,000 or 3,000 Bogsiders, were hopelessly outnumbered, strained to breaking point.[1] The Army had to be called in. Inevitably, as Ulster Protestants saw the Bogside struggle on their television screens and read of it in their morning newspapers, there came a backlash. Appalling rioting broke out in Belfast, many Catholic houses in the quarter known as 'The Falls' were petrol-bombed and burnt to the ground, whole streets were gutted, people were shot dead as bullets from illegally-held weapons swept into blocks of flats. The hard-line Protestant Unionists in the Ulster Parliament had earlier intrigued against Terence O'Neill and removed him from office. He was succeeded by Major James Chichester-Clark. The situation became out of control, many more Army troops were called in, the Westminster Parliament intervened. It almost seemed as if the terrible times of the early 1920s had returned to plague the people and debase the Province. Men wondered if Ulster could recover, if the Province would be taken over and governed by Westminster. They wondered if they would be thrust against their will into an all-Ireland Republic. There was a smuggling in of guns along the sea-coasts by extreme organizations of opposing persuasions, preparing for a last-ditch struggle in the name of legitimate defence. Protestant ultra-extremists slipped into the Irish Republic and blew up the headstone on the grave at Bodenstown in which the eighteenth-century Irish rebel, Wolfe Tone, was buried. This was the first occasion, in more than a hundred

[1] The Royal Ulster Constabulary was so stretched that it could manage to assign only a few hundred policemen to contain the Bogsiders.

years, on which Ulstermen had committed such a folly. An attempt was made by the same ultra-extreme organization to blow up the great power installation near Ballyshannon in County Donegal, also in the Irish Republic. Ulster was heading, through the stupidity of its mindless extremists, for a madness that could destroy it. The Unionist chickens were coming home to roost.

Terence O'Neill, before being forced to resign the Premiership at the end of April 1969, when the diehard Unionists of his Parliamentary Party succeeded in whittling away his support, had given much of his thought to the paramount need of the Ulster people to see themselves as others saw them. In his opinion, the Province could not hope to regain its health until the Protestant majority were made drastically and dramatically aware of their shortcomings, of the faults they had committed in the oppression of the Catholic minority, of their supine toleration of wrongs against a third of their fellow-citizens. The Protestant Unionists must take stock of themselves, however shocked they might be by a public revelation of their all but unbelievable lack of vision and intelligence. There must be an assessment, too, of the forces ranged against the majority, such forces as People's Democracy and the Civil Rights movement. How genuine were they? What were they and who were they? What were their real objectives? There must be an awakening. Let there be fresh air in the Province, clean air. Let there be a properly constituted impartial enquiry into the causes of the violence and civil disturbance in Ulster, which could bring a cleansing and a hope. Let there be truth, a new start, a new direction.

So, on March 3, 1969, there was set up, on O'Neill's instigation, the body that became known in Ulster as the Cameron Commission. It was set up by Warrant of the Governor of Northern Ireland. Its Chairman, Lord Cameron, was a Scottish High Court Judge with long experience in the Courts of Justice and other households of the law, a practised legal referee of accepted ability and disinterestedness, held in considerable respect throughout Scotland and by the British Government at Westminster. No one could accuse him of prejudice. His fellow Commissioners were Professor Sir John Biggart, a Protestant

Ulsterman, then Dean of the Faculty of Medicine at the Queen's University of Belfast, and James Joseph Campbell, a Roman Catholic Ulsterman and a leading Belfast educationalist. Both he and Biggart had deserved reputations as men of trained and impartial mind in their professions and in spheres outside them. The Commission sat for many hard-worked hours each day and heard evidence submitted by numerous bodies, associations and groups involved, as well as by individual men and women, of every shade of political and religious opinion in Ulster. Its report, when published in August 1969, staggered and shamed the better men and women of the Province and roused the reactionary Unionists to intense anger. It confirmed the existence of serious discrimination by the Protestant Unionist majority against the Catholic minority and, in Paragraph 229, summarized the discrimination in language so clear that no one could misread or ignore the message:

(1) A rising sense of continuing injustice and grievance among large sections of the Catholic population in Northern Ireland, in particular in Londonderry and Dungannon, in respect of (*a*) inadequacy of housing provision by certain local authorities, (*b*) unfair methods of allocation of houses built and let by such authorities, refusals and omissions to adopt a points system in determining priorities and making allocations, (*c*) misuse in certain cases of discretionary powers of allocations of houses in order to perpetuate Unionist control of the local authority;

(2) Complaints, now well documented in fact, of discrimination in the making of local government appointments, at all levels but especially in senior posts, to the prejudice of non-Unionists and especially Catholic members of the community, in some Unionist controlled authorities;

(3) Complaints, again well documented, in some cases of deliberate manipulation of local government electoral boundaries and, in others, a refusal to apply for their necessary extension, in order to achieve and maintain Unionist control of local authorities and so to deny to Catholics an influence in local government proportionate to their numbers;

(4) A growing and powerful sense of resentment and frustration among the Catholic population at failure to achieve either acceptance on the part of the Government of any need to investigate these complaints or to provide and enforce a remedy for them;

(5) Resentment, particularly among Catholics, as to the existence of the Ulster Special Constabulary [the 'B' Specials] as a partisan and para-military force recruited exclusively from Protestants;

(6) Widespread resentment among Catholics in particular at the continuing in force of regulations made under the Special Powers Act and of the continued presence in the statute book of the Act itself.

Six damning sub-paragraphs, each of them unarguably true and telling, each of them confirming the Catholic case against the Protestant Unionist majority. None of them, however, conveys the basic reason for the Protestant majority's reaction to the Catholic minority over the years since the Ulster State had come into being in 1921. The omission was partly made good, however, in the final sub-paragraph of the section:

(7) Fears and apprehensions among Protestants of a threat to Unionist domination and of *control of Government by increase of Catholic population and powers* . . .

The missing words will be added and considered later in Chapter Nine.

The Commission's report ends with these significant full paragraphs:

235. There have been and are at work within Northern Ireland persons whose immediate and deliberate intention is to prepare, plan and provoke violence, reckless of the consequences to human-beings or property. Their purpose is not to secure peace by way of reform and within the structure of the State. At the same time, there are others who by their appeal to sectarian prejudice and bigotry have assisted in inflaming passions and keeping alive ancient hatreds that have readily led to the unleashing of lawless and uncontrolled violence.

From the aimless and vicious hooligans of the streets
and alleys to the extremists of right or left, of whatever
creed, Catholic or Protestant, all would appear to bear
a share of the blame for the tragic events which have
occurred and in which the vast majority of the population of Northern Ireland have neither hand nor concern
and which we have no doubt they most deeply deplore;
236. In a situation which contains so many grave possibilities
we would draw particular attention to the complexity of
the causes of those disorders which we were called on to
investigate and to the dangers which over-emphasis or
over-simplification in Press or other report or comment
on particular facets of these causes could so readily
produce. These unhappy events have already received
very wide Press and television coverage which, as we
have observed, sometimes high-lighted intentionally or
by chance incidents the reporting of which may well
have distorted or tended to distort the accuracy of the
picture as a whole.

'Extremists of right or left, of whatever creed, Catholic or
Protestant, all would appear to bear a share of the blame,' says
Cameron. But the People's Democracy and the Civil Rights
Association have taken very great care to avoid saying it. In
their view, trumpeted everywhere, only the Unionists were to
blame. The view has been repeated over and over again until,
like Goebbels' lie, it has come to be accepted. The fact is that
both People's Democracy and the Civil Rights Association are
deeply suspect. The People's Democracy was and remains a
collection of unpleasant and unscrupulous exploiters, fishers in
troubled waters, unversed juveniles in relation to the practi-
calities of the world and the ways of humankind, unknowingly
fascist in their thinking and their policies, strongly opposed to free
speech as understood in any true democracy, jesuitically in favour
of mob violence. The Cameron Commission report exposes the
double-think of People's Democracy in the matter of violence:

Although the Civil Rights Association is especially dedicated
to non-violence, the phrase is given a particular and limited
meaning among some at least of its supporters and the same

136

limited interpretation is adopted by certain of the leaders of the People's Democracy. In their vocabulary it is not violence to link arms and by sheer weight and pressure of numbers and bodies to press through and break an opposing cordon of police. If the police resist such pressure, then it is the police who are guilty of violence—and if such 'violence' is offered by the police, then a defensive violent reaction is permissible. This doctrine was presented to us by several witnesses. With all respect to those who hold and express these views, we cannot consider them other than metaphysical nonsense and divorced from the world of reality. They may provide a salve to tender consciences, but are, we suspect, an argumentative justification for bringing about what those who hold them desire—publicity from violent confrontation with the police and the stirring up of passions and hostilities within the community. The battering ram pressure of a crowd with linked arms to breach a physical barrier in the shape of a cordon of police is in its way just as much the use of force to achieve an object as the use of batons by police to achieve the dispersal of a hostile and recalcitrant crowd.[1]

That reads uncommonly like sense. It is not accepted by People's Democracy, however, which knows very well that its methods when confronting the police are not in accord with the 'metaphysical nonsense' it submitted to the Commission. Many have watched the People's Democracy men when they were confronted by a police cordon. There was no linking of arms, no steady and noble pressing forward in the name of noble ideals. There was a brutal showering of the police with every flingable missile the People's Democracy men could lay their hands on. They included sharpened pennies for slashing open the policemen's faces, paper bags of pepper to blind them with, keen-pointed banner poles. The men of People's Democracy are by no means nice in their methods and if some of them had their heads rapped by a baton they got no more than they deserved.

They show, too, the naïvety of the Leftist youth of today. In a political manifesto put out by People's Democracy in the 1969 Ulster election, demands were made for—'an emergency programme of direct state investment in industry to provide

[1] Cameron Commission report, paragraph 204.

137

permanent full employment and to halt emigration, a massive injection of capital by the Government to set up industries under workers' control in those state-owned factories vacated by short-term private industrialists, the extension of workers' control to all branches of industry'. That is the sort of stuff one expects from a school debating society, not from grown and responsible men setting themselves forward as candidates in a Parliamentary election; yet the People's Democracy, through deliberately fomented violence and skilful handling of gullible newspaper correspondents and television men, has done untold harm to Ulster. As Cameron says, 'there is evidence of close association between prominent personalities in the People's Democracy movement and members of the Revolutionary Socialist Students Federation from England—these have aims which go far beyond reform and involve the total destruction of the current constitutional structure of the State in favour of what is called a Workers Socialist Republic'.[1] The leaders of the People's Democracy movement—and it might be as well to name them—have been Michael Farrell, Cyril Toman, Eamonn McCann and Bernadette Devlin. They subscribed to the terms of the People's Democracy election manifesto.

The Cameron Commission took a gentler view of the Civil Rights Association. It had some grounds for doing so, as in the main the aims and methods of the Association have been legitimate. In one aspect, however, the Commission was surprisingly and perhaps naïvely gentle. This concerns the Irish Republican Army. The Commission says: 'There is no doubt that the Irish Republican Army has taken a close interest in the Civil Rights Association from its inception.'[2] Why? Why should the Army have interested itself in the Association, if it had nothing to gain? Had it no more than an altruistic interest in the securing of civil rights for the Catholic minority in Ulster? That seems unlikely, in the light of the Army's history. Cameron goes on to say in the same paragraph: 'Among the stewards at Civil Rights Association demonstrations there have been known members of the Irish Republican Army. They have been efficient stewards, maintaining discipline and checking any disposition to disorder.' This really is naïve. How did it happen that the Cameron Com-

[1] Paragraph 197.
[2] Paragraph 212.

mission failed to realize the significance of the fact that the Association had been infiltrated and was being actively served by men of an organization known to be subversive, a body *proscribed by the governments of both Ulster and the Irish Republic*? If the sole intention of the Association were to secure civil rights for Ulster Catholics while accepting and loyally supporting the lawful constitution of the Ulster State—the Association's leaders, some of whom are known to be in close and constant touch with the Irish Republican Army, have been carefully non-committal in this matter of acceptance—why has it admitted to its counsels and membership, as it unqestionably has, a number of men from an organization pledged to the destruction of that State? This, to phrase it very mildly indeed, is suspicious. As Cameron says: 'Here is an Association which could without any excessive difficulty be successfully infiltrated by those whose intentions are far other than peaceful and constitutional. We have already commented on the presence of Irish Republican Army sympathizers and members within the Association . . . at the same time there is little doubt that left-wing extremists of the type already closely associated with the control of People's Democracy would be ready to take over, if they could, the real direction of the Civil Rights Association and divert its activities from a reformist policy to a much more radical course which would not exclude the deliberate use of force and the provocation of disorder as an instrument of policy.'[1]

Cameron's language is characteristic of the cautious lawyer. The Bogside Catholic district of Londonderry had been made into a barricaded enclave by its residents on the grounds that they had to defend themselves from being battered into the ground by the Royal Ulster Constabulary. Neither the Constabulary nor the troops of the British Army were permitted to enter, and the national flag of the Irish Republic—the tricolour, which is banned by the Ulster Government—was proudly and publicly flown to show the district's political adherence, with the knowledge and full approval of the Civil Rights Association. There is nothing surprising in this. The membership of the Civil Rights Association is almost entirely Catholic—understandably so, in view of the fact that the Association's objective is to have the Catholic disabilities lifted—and the great majority

[1] Paragraph 193.

of Catholics in Ulster are emotionally attached to the idea of an all-Ireland Republic. That has already been said here. It can bear repeating, for the emotional nationalism of the Ulster Catholics could be a deciding factor in the choice of political direction the Irish, north and south, are bound to take in the not too distant future. There is much in the material sense to induce Catholics to prefer to remain in an Ulster connected with prosperous Britain—the higher social benefits are only one of the inducements—but no wise Irishman would care to forecast the result if the Ulster Catholics had an opportunity of voting in a referendum on whether they wished to stay in an Ulster State or would prefer a merging of Ulster in an all-Ireland Republic.[1] And it is a fact beyond argument that a lot of Catholics in Ulster have a romantic sympathy for the men of the Irish Republican Army. Their fathers sheltered and hid those men in the early years of the 1920s when the Army was attacking Ulster, a large number of them fought side by side with the attackers and many of the aims of the Army are persistingly dear to the Catholic Irish heart. The indoctrinated political faiths of the Irish, be those faiths Republican or Unionist, rarely diminish. There is substance, therefore, in the belief of many Protestant Ulstermen that the Civil Rights Association, while probably initially intent on securing concessions to the Ulster Catholic population, was simultaneously determined to bring down the Ulster State and that, having gained its first end, it is now working to achieve the goal of a unified Ireland independent of Britain.

The Association, said Cameron, 'could without excessive difficulty be successfully infiltrated by those whose intentions are far other than peaceful and constitutional'. This implied that the Association had not yet been seriously infiltrated, which is contrary to the known facts. The infiltration, indeed, has been admitted in other sections of the Cameron Commission report. Its nature and its danger do not seem to have been fully grasped by the Commission, however. Michael Farrell, whose intentions are most certainly not peaceful and constitutional and who has been connected with much of the recent trouble in Ulster, was a

[1] In about fifteen years' time, the Ulster Catholic middle class, which has a higher birth rate than the Catholic lower classes, will be the decisive factor in any such referendum.

member of the controlling body of the Civil Rights movement. He advocates outright revolution in Ireland.[1] With Cyril Toman, another People's Democracy revolutionary, he frankly informed the Cameron Commission that he meant to use the Civil Rights movement for his own purposes and to further his political objectives.[2] Anyone who wishes to understand what subversives like Farrell, Toman and Bernadette Devlin are really seeking should obtain a copy of the *New Left Review*, No. 55, from 7 Carlisle Street, London, W.1, and read in it the verbatim report of a discussion—it took place in April 1969, while the Cameron Commission was sitting and hearing evidence—between Farrell, Toman, Bernadette Devlin and two other equally mischievous Leftists. It is a pompous, humourless and depressing farrago of Marxism, Maoism, Trotskyism, Castroism and additional mixed-up 'isms' of the fashionably Left-wing and jargon-ridden visionaries of today, unrelieved anywhere by knowledge or intelligence. Bernadette Devlin leans towards Castroism. She stated at the Overseas Press Club in London in May 1969 that the kind of Ireland she would like to see is a Socialist republic on Cuban lines. It is unlikely that she admitted this to the susceptible Irish–Americans who gave money to her 'cause' when she stumped the United States in 1969.

The Cameron Commission suggests that the People's Democracy is declining in appeal and in numbers. This may well be but the fact is not significant. Farrell, Toman, Bernadette Devlin and a fellow agitator called Eamonn McCann,[3] a Londonderry labourer of very dubious political connections, are active and first-class speakers with a cleverly calculated approach to the ignorant. They have done much damage and could do more. They are unscrupulous, like all revolutionaries, and they are expert in the employment of 'the big lie'. The Cameron Commission inclined towards playing them down. This was a mistake. It was also a mistake for the Commission to play down the impact of the Irish Republican Army on the Civil Rights

---

[1] 'We don't want reform of Northern Ireland, we want a revolution in Ireland.' (See *New Left Review*.)

[2] Cameron Commission report, paragraph 200.

[3] McCann has been associated with the Irish Workers' Group in London, and the Irish Workers' League in Dublin—see Cameron Commission report, paragraph 201.

movement. Many Catholics in Ulster argue that the Irish Republican Army is no longer an effective force, that stories of its activities in Ulster today are more mythological than factual, that its recruitment is insignificant, its capacity for harm even more insignificant. This is wishful-thinking or, perhaps, something else. There are probably about 1,000 men in the Irish Republican Army now. If there were only 500, it could still be dangerous. 500 well-armed men in a small community can blow up a lot of key installations and inflame a lot of people. But does it have a real influence within the Civil Rights movement? It most certainly has. In February 1969, a man called Frank Gogarty was elected Chairman of the Civil Rights Association. Mr. Gogarty is a very interesting man. When violent rioting broke out in Belfast in 1969—the Protestant backlash to the Catholic provocation in Londonderry's Bogside—Gogarty admitted to a British national newspaper[1] that he had been in 'regular touch' with the Irish Republican Army. He added, referring to the Belfast rioting: 'Everything exploded so suddenly that the Irish Republican Army were at first only able to muster six revolvers. They managed to find one machine gun but were unable to reach their stocks, hidden on the outskirts of the city.' No one familiar with Ulster would doubt that the Irish Republican Army has taken good care since then to make good the omission. This statement by Gogarty disproves the assertions of Ulster Catholics that the inhabitants of the areas attacked by Belfast Protestants in that dreadful August were totally unarmed and consequently defenceless. Why was the Chairman of the non-violent and constitutional Civil Rights Association in 'regular touch' with gunmen hostile to the Ulster State? Why was Dominic Behan recently in the United States to buy guns if they were wanted for no more than ornamental purposes?[2] Dominic Behan is a brother of the late Brendan Behan, the Irish playwright. Brendan Behan was an active member of the Irish Republic Army. Is Dominic Behan a member of it? If not, for whom are the guns he wants to buy intended? Assuredly, it was an error on the part of the Cameron

[1] *Daily Mail*, London, August 19, 1969.

[2] *Sunday Express*, London, October 26, 1969, Philadelphia dateline: 'Dominic Behan told students here he was in America to buy guns for an illegal organization. He said 300 armed men of the organization threw petrol bombs in Ulster during recent riots to defend people.'

Commission to play down the Irish Republican Army and it was also an error to decry or belittle the influence of the Army on the Civil Rights Association.

But there was a need for the Association, as only the most reactionary and bigoted Ulster Protestants—and there are far too many such Protestants in the Province—will refuse to allow. Something had to be done to attract influential attention to the discrimination practised against the Catholics. The Civil Rights Association was formed to attract that attention in the first case, whatever else it may have had in mind, and the Protestant Ulstermen have only themselves to blame for the fact that the Association had to come into existence at all. The Association's original protest demonstration was directed at discrimination in the little town of Dungannon in County Tyrone, but the bias there was nothing compared with the ruthlessly engineered Unionist discrimination in Londonderry. This was a scandal and conscientious men and women of the Ulster majority had tolerated it for much too long. Londonderry has a big Catholic preponderance in the city's population, yet the local government ward boundaries were so manipulated by the powerful Unionists as to give them control of the Londonderry Corporation. This enabled them to corner the patronage market, particularly in the matter of housing allocation, for their own benefit and for that of their similarly blind and stupid followers. Some 15,000 Catholic voters were deliberately so placed that they could not possibly win more than eight Council seats against the twelve seats unvaryingly won by some 9,000 Unionist voters.[1] Whatever excuses may be made by protagonists of the Unionist Party, this was gerrymandering at its worst. Londonderry, of course, has an appeal of high emotional intensity to thousands of Protestant Ulstermen, especially those who are members of the Orange Order. It is the historic walled city which Protestant Irish adherents of William of Orange held so heroically against the besieging troops of the Catholic King James II of England—thus helping to establish the Protestant Succession for the English. The siege was a long and desperate one and the defenders came close to total starvation before the city was at last relieved and the besiegers forced to withdraw in defeat.

[1] For the story of local government manipulation in Londonderry, see *Orange and Green, A Quaker Study of Community Relations in Northern Ireland.*

Ever since then, Londonderry has been near sacred to Protestant Ulstermen, who are much more sentimental than their manner reveals. They always remember with pride the famous episode when the courageous Londonderry apprentice boys of the time slammed the great gate in the faces of the emissaries who were trying to persuade the pliable City Governor, 'Traitor Lundy', to surrender the city to King James and save it from the hardships of a siege. The idea of allowing Catholics to take over the governance of Londonderry appears to die-hard Protestant Ulstermen today as a form of blasphemy. Hence the manipulation of the wards. The 'fall' of Londonderry is imminent, though. It will soon be under the local government of Catholics. The reforming Development Commission, set up by Terence O'Neill, will see to it, with the aid of an impartial Boundaries Commission to ensure fair representation.

Whatever arguments there may be on the original intentions of the Civil Rights Association, there can be little if any doubt— the author has none—that it decided some time in 1969 to tighten the screw still further in the hope that the Ulster State, already badly weakened by the street rioting, might collapse. The Association's leaders, far from co-operating with the Government by helping to stabilize the situation after the reforms were granted, suddenly raised the stakes. It submitted more and more demands, all of them unreasonable, all of them pointed like a pistol at the Government's head. The Opposition members of the Ulster House of Commons, who had worked closely with the Civil Rights movement since its beginning, became obstructive with similar suddenness. In June 1969, the Government had laid before them its reform programme in full —a generous programme—and invited them to approve it, together with the time schedule for its legislative implementation. The Opposition members officially, appreciatively and publicly declared their approval of both. Then, without warning, they withdrew their approval and joined with the Civil Rights leaders in the game of submitting further demands. This was sharp practice, politics at its dirtiest. The Opposition members of the Ulster Parliament, of course, lack the ballast of clear sight and clear thinking. They cannot be regarded as responsible. They are led by such men as Gerard Fitt and Austin Currie. Fitt, who belongs to what he calls the Republican

Labour Party, was described in the Cameron Commission report as 'seeking publicity for himself and his political views . . . guilty of reckless and wholly irresponsible conduct'[1] during the October 5 Civil Rights march in Londonderry. In the United States, during 1969, he stated publicly that Catholics in Ulster were treated worse than negroes in America.[2] This was a monstrous lie and he later tried unavailingly to deny that he had made the statement. Currie, a young and untravelled Irish Nationalist whose knowledge of Irish history is nothing if not superficial, was also referred to in the Cameron Commission's report. In its analysis of the October march, it remarks that Currie 'gave what could be interpreted as more or less guarded encouragement to the use of violence to break the police barrier'. Usually, such strictures would bring a man face to face with himself, compel him to look inside himself and think. There was no sign, however, on the part of Fitt and Currie that Cameron had in any way abashed them. They pursued their path with seeming disregard of all save their political objectives.

The vast majority of the Ulster people, said Cameron, have neither hand nor concern in the ugliness inflicted recently on their Province. He might have added that the Ulster people have had much to put up with from the Civil Rights Association and the members of Her Majesty's Opposition in the Ulster House of Commons.

[1] Paragraph 46.
[2] Reported in the *Belfast Telegraph* and other Belfast newspapers during 1969.

Chapter Eight

We still get a lot of support from Catholic
capitalists and bigots. Although I personally
believe there is very little Christianity in
Ireland, there is a lot of religion and the one
way to unite Protestants and Catholics is by
trying to get rid of both churches at once.
                                    Bernadette Devlin
                                    New Left Review,
                                    No. 55

DIVORCE is forbidden by law in the Irish Republic. The use
of the oral contraceptive pill is forbidden there, the sale of
contraceptives generally is forbidden. The books you may or
may not read are decided by a Censorship Board, the films you
may see in the cinemas are subjected to official censorship, the
plays you may see in the theatres are subject to an unofficial
censorship, as Sean O'Casey and other equally shamefully
treated Irish dramatists discovered to their cost. In the capital
city of Dublin and in every corner of the Republic there is a
disapproving puritanism not unlike the repressive puritanism
that pervades the public and private life of men and women in
Spain. This puritanism and State dictatorialism in the Irish
Republic stem from its written Constitution, mostly drawn up
by De Valera, which came into effect in December 1937 and
was largely framed in accordance with the wishes of the most
dominating and powerful force in the Republic—the Roman
Catholic Church. The Church had no difficulty in gaining
observance of its wishes, as 95 per cent of the people of the
Republic are respectful Roman Catholics. It even had its status
explicitly laid down in the Constitution. Article 44 acknowledges
that:

The State recognizes the special position of the Holy Catholic
Apostolic and Roman Church as the guardian of the Faith
as professed by the great majority of its citizens.

The Article goes on to say:

The State also recognizes the Church of Ireland, the Presbyterian Church in Ireland, the Methodist Church in Ireland, the Religious Society of Friends in Ireland, as well as the Jewish Congregations and the other religious denominations existing in Ireland at the date of the coming into operation of this Constitution.

Having made this concession to the lesser faiths, the Constitution then states in the clearest language that:

Freedom of conscience and the free profession and practice of religion are, subject to public order and morality, guaranteed to every citizen.

It is admirable to find in the written Constitution that every citizen is guaranteed the free profession and practice of his religion. Most civilized nations do not consider it necessary to give such a guarantee in writing. They allow the freedom as a matter of course. Not the Irish Republic, however. There the guarantee must be categorically stated. There is one important objection to this specific assurance, though. It is not honoured. The profession and practice of religion in the Republic of Ireland are by no means fully free, far less free than in 'bigoted' Ulster, as members of that strange but harmless little sect known as Jehovah's Witnesses will tell you, if you choose to ask them. You might seek out two of them, if they are still alive—Stephen Miller and Henry Bond—who were attacked and beaten by the villagers of Clonlara in County Clare and had a number of their books and pamphlets publicly burned in the village square on the instigation of the local parish priest, the Reverend Patrick Ryan. The priest and nine of the villagers were sued by Miller and Bond and the case was heard on July 27, 1956, at the Limerick City Court. A Catholic Bishop and several Catholic clergy were interested spectators. The District Justice who heard the case found it proved but applied to the charges against Father Ryan and the nine villagers the Probation of Offenders Act. He then bound over the two Jehovah's Witnesses to keep the peace and required each of them to find security of £200 for their good behaviour. Religious tolerance, it was said, did not extend to acceptance in an Irish village of the gospels being disseminated by the Witnesses. The Irish Catholic faith, it was pointed out, was something that had been tempered in the fires of persecution and was not only a religion but a tradition, a legend and a way of life. Its roots were in the lonely vigils kept by Irishmen on the run, in prisons and death cells and on the scaffold. That was the faith which Miller and Bond sought to attack, challenge and destroy. In the Catholic understanding, they preached blasphemy. Were the people of the village of Clonlara to lie down before it? Certainly not. The appellants were lucky to escape as lightly as they had for the assault that had been made against them by Father Ryan and the villagers. Let this be a lesson to them.

The *Irish Times*, commenting on the case, said: 'Mr. Miller and Mr. Bond had the same right as any other religious sect, whether Christian, Jewish, Mohammedan, Taoist or Hindu, to propagate their faith by peaceful means and any denial of that right is a reflection on the state of freedom in this country.'[1] The *Irish Times* is a Dublin newspaper. However, the case had at least the beneficial effect of alerting Jehovah's Witnesses to the nature of the freedom they would have, to profess and practice their religion in the Republic of Ireland. Many Mormons have found themselves in considerable unpleasantness, too, in their missionary efforts throughout the Republic. Their elders have discovered that it is oddly difficult for them to purchase land on which to build churches, and there are no Mormon churches in the Irish Republic.[2] The fact is that the faith of the Jehovah's Witnesses and the Mormons runs counter to Roman Catholicism and will not be tolerated. Also, when the Constitution came into operation, these faiths did not officially exist. The Constitution very carefully defined such faiths, churches and congregations as would be granted State toleration. The faiths held by Jehovah's Witnesses and the Mormons were not among them. Then there is the additional constitutional safeguard that freedom of conscience and the free practice of religion shall be subject to public order and morality. What was meant

[1] July 28, 1956.
[2] The fact that Mormons find it strangely difficult to buy land-sites for their churches in the Irish Republic was confirmed to the author in November 1969 by a member of the Mormon Mission in Ulster.

by 'morality' and who is to define it as occasion arises? Obviously, only the State of the Irish Republic could define it and that State is influenced by the Roman Catholic Church, which regards all other churches as mistaken. The State is still influenced by it—and in the opinion of the Ulstermen, who have no objection to Jehovah's Witnesses and who have allowed the building of Mormon Churches in Ulster, it will remain so.

Divorce is permitted in Britain. Ulster is a part of Britain, so divorce is permitted in Ulster. Not in the Irish Republic, however. The Roman Catholic Church does not approve of divorce and does not allow it. This being the case, Article 41 of the Constitution of the Republic of Ireland lays it down that:

No law shall be enacted providing for the grant of a dissolution of marriage.

The same Article continues with these words, which constitute a severe sentence, perhaps covering many years:

No person whose marriage has been dissolved under the civil law of any other State but is a subsisting valid marriage under the law for the time being in force within the jurisdiction of the Government and Parliament established by this Constitution shall be capable of contracting a valid marriage within that jurisdiction during the lifetime of the other party to the marriage so dissolved.

The Constitution is pierced through and through with the arrogance and obscurantism of the Roman Catholic Church, which, in Ireland, is persistently reactionary. That same Article 41 has much to say about the importance of the family and it is not hard to see whence the Constitution makers received their prompting:

The State recognizes the Family as the natural primary and fundamental unit group of Society and as a moral institution possessing inalienable and imprescriptible rights, antecedent and superior to all positive law.

Very nice, too, say the Ulstermen—but what is meant by 'antecedent and superior to all positive law'? What sort of law is it that consents to be subordinate to family rights? The pragmatic Ulstermen are further puzzled—and amused—by the Constitutional undertaking that:

> The State recognizes that, by her life within the home, woman gives to the State a support without which the common good cannot be achieved. The State shall, therefore, endeavour to ensure that mothers shall not be obliged by economic necessity to engage in labour.

What do the many young mothers of the Irish Republic who have to go out to work to earn enough money to make certain that the marriage home and the children are maintained in security and dignity think of that particular clause in their Constitution? The State seems to have fallen down a trifle on its undertaking. To the Ulstermen, this is medieval Roman Catholicism at its most absurd. What is wrong, they ask, with the idea of a young, healthy, intelligent mother helping her husband by taking a job, provided proper arrangements are made for the children to be looked after when she is working? The marriage could be better and happier and the children unharmed if she accepts a well-paid job and takes some of the burden from her husband's shoulders.

There is much, too, in the Constitution that concerns itself with the language. The Government of the Irish Republic has long been anxious to revive the use of the Gaelic tongue, which was the language generally used in Ireland centuries ago and which is still used in certain remote areas of the countryside. So Article 8 declares that:

> The Irish language, as the national language, is the first official language. The English language is recognized as a second official language. Provision may, however, be made by law for the exclusive use of either of the said languages for any one or more official purposes, either throughout the State or in any part thereof.

The Irish language is the national language? When one visits Ireland does one hear the people everywhere speaking Gaelic? Of course not. They speak English. This stuff about the national language is wishful-thinking at its silliest. The Gaelic tongue is dead. The number of men and women in the Irish Republic who can speak and write it is small and growing smaller every year. The Government's obsession[1] with it has led to insistence that candidates for posts in the Civil Service of the Republic must be able to speak and write in Gaelic, although the successful applicants immediately drop the language the moment they enter the Service. Then there is the condition that every actor and actress who wishes to become a member of the Abbey Theatre Company must also be fluent in Gaelic. The Government is again in a strong position to be insistent, as it has given a financial subsidy to the Abbey Theatre for some years now. The Abbey Theatre Company was once one of the finest ensembles in Europe, despite the inability of most of its players to speak without an Irish brogue, and many experienced and perceptive Irish people have noticed that the unhappy decline in the quality and reputation of the Company—which today is unimaginative and routine, trading on the renown of the past—coincided with the arrival of the subsidy and the over-riding condition in regard to familiarity with Gaelic. The Government's meddling cold hand has laid a chill on the theatre.

It has laid a chill, too, on the Press, Radio and Television in the Republic. Its ability to do so is born of Article 40 of the Constitution:

> The State guarantees liberty to the right of the citizens to express freely their convictions and opinions. The education of public opinion being, however, a matter of such grave import to the common good, the State shall endeavour to ensure that organs of public opinion, such as the radio, the Press, the cinema, while preserving their rightful liberty of expression, including criticism of Government policy, shall not be used to undermine public order or morality or the authority of the State.

This is in accord with the age-old conviction of the Catholic Church that, as Tertullian, one of the Fathers of the Church, said in the second century, thought is evil. Independence of mind is unwelcome to the Catholic Church in Ireland, criticism even more so, whatever its apologists may say as they point to

[1] Not only the Government is obsessed; if any member of the Gaelic Athletic Association of Ireland is caught playing in or even watching a game of rugby football, soccer or cricket, he is instantly expelled from the Association for taking an interest in English games.

the subjects of discussion at the recent Vatican Councils. The room for critical manœuvre in the Catholic Church is limited and will stay that way. The Government Ministers of the Irish Republic, obedient sons of Mother Church and very astute politicians, possessed of the political animal's normal yearning for continuance in office, share the Church's view on the need to protect public opinion from the vulgarity of error. They have firm views, too, usually conveyed with considerable undercover skill, on the matter of open criticism of Government policies. In 1969, however, their finesse seems to have deserted them, or they were out of luck. Several senior executives of the News and Current Affairs Division of the Republic's television service— Telefis Eireann, substantially subsidized from Government funds—resigned from their well-paid posts on the grounds that there was increasing and intolerable behind-the-scenes Government pressure on the Division to amend its critical attitude towards the policies of the Government on some aspects of considerable public concern. There was a flaming row and the Division has since been noticeably more circumspect. Thought is evil.

Opinion is free in Ulster. This was not always the case, of course. Over many years, honest public criticism of the Unionist Government or the Unionist Party or both could bring sudden and mysteriously originated ill-luck to a man in his business or professional career and in his social life. Today, though, the atmosphere is healthy. Both the Government and the Party have been fired on from many directions. They have learnt to stand up openly and face the fire, whether it comes from the Westminster Government, from their own Unionist right-wing die-hards determined on obstructionism or from the moderates determined to press through more and more moderate policies. The criticism heard in public in Ulster now is astonishing to anyone who has known the Province for the past forty odd years. In this respect, Ulster has gone ahead of the Irish Republic. And there is no official censorship there to declare what books the Ulstermen may not read, what films they may not see. Some interfering puritans and unpleasant busybodies have tried at local government level to impose a film censorship, but by and large they have failed. There is no Church-inspired censorship to force an impresario to withhold a play from public performance.

This happened in Dublin not long ago. The Roman Catholic Archbishop of Dublin compelled the withdrawal of two plays from the Dublin Theatre Festival. One was a play by the great Irish dramatist, Sean O'Casey, which contained some gentle strictures on the Catholic Church in Ireland. The other was an adaptation for the stage of James Joyce's *Ulysses*. The plain fact is that the Irish Republic is a highly intolerant country. To all who know it, its claim to be clear of discrimination is nothing short of blazing hypocrisy. One of the Republic's best writers, Sean O'Faolain, who fought in the Irish Republican Army against the British and has no love for Ulster, has written this:

> Whatever pious aspirations or resolutions may be found in the Constitution of Ireland about religious tolerance, it is a matter of common knowledge to those who care to enquire or even observe that the Protestant in the south has as little chance of getting his fair share of public appointments as the Catholic in the north. Neither north nor south need pretend that the other is alone in penalization on account of religion and private opinion. Religion in the south is just as solidly organized as in the north and is no less narrow-minded.[1]

Sean O'Faolain is a Roman Catholic.

On September 15, 1958, an interesting case came before the Killaloe District Court in the Irish Republic. Three men— Michael Boland, John McKenna and Patrick Daly—were charged with assaulting Robert Lindsay, Samuel Lindsay and Christopher Rowe, thereby causing them actual bodily harm. It was stated by the police that the Lindsays and Rowe, Protestant evangelists, had gone to Killaloe to hold a religious meeting. Rowe was holding a Bible in his hand. It was snatched from him by Boland and kicked along the street. The three evangelists were then attacked with sticks and fists. One of the Lindsays was knocked to the ground unconscious, lost two teeth and suffered concussion. Boland, McKenna and Daly pleaded guilty to the assault, but their solicitor submitted that they had been under 'great provocation'. They had been confronted by men 'vending Christianity and it was fantastic that

[1] To be found in O'Faolain's biography of De Valera, published as a Penguin Special, p. 155, written more than three years ago. He now feels that the Irish Republic 'has moved on, whereas Ulster has not'.

these men should vend Christianity to a people steeped in it'. The District Justice applied the Probation Act to the benefit of the accused and said: 'When men come into an Irish village and provoke the people by foisting religious views on them, they are abusing whatever rights they have under the Constitution, which guarantees freedom of religious worship.' No admonishment was issued by the Roman Catholic hierarchy or clergy. The Minister for Justice in the Government of the Republic remained silent. The Protestant Bishop of Limerick referred to the case and said:

It is not the wisdom or the consideration of the would-be preachers that matters, it is not the vigour or brutality of the attackers—it is the pronouncement of the District Justice appointed by the Government . . . speaking in his official capacity, ignoring the injuries of citizens and defining the rights of freedom and protection belonging to those who profess a minority religion in the Republic. The question at issue is the right of the citizen to the protection of the law. The words spoken by the three evangelists were not seditious or treasonable. The main question is—can the citizen depend upon the protection of the law to preserve him from bodily harm if he expresses views thought unacceptable to the religious loyalties of persons who happen to be present in the public street when the words are used? Apparently not. He can be mobbed and battered with impunity by anyone who is provoked by the words used.[1]

But that case occurred a long time ago, say the Catholics of the Irish Republic, and Sean O'Faolain's words were written in 1939. Things are different now. Catholicism in the Irish Republic is tolerant today and the Protestants of Ulster need have no fear of discrimination against them if they agree to an all-Ireland Republic. The Ulstermen do not believe this. The Catholic Church in an all-Ireland Republic, they say, would have to be even more discriminatory and repressive to maintain its position in the face of an influx of a million extra Protestants, independent in their thinking, energetic, refusing to accept the

[1] September 29, 1958, in an address to the Church of Ireland clergy of the combined sees—the United Dioceses.

ban on divorce, the ban on contraceptives, the censorship. Would the Catholic Church in Ireland agree to shift its position on such matters? The Ulstermen are convinced that it would not. It might budge an inch or two in regard to censorship but not on such aspects as divorce and the public sale of contraceptives. These are central to Catholic doctrine. Then there is the Ne Temere decree of the Catholic Church, which might be still more doggedly adhered to in the event of an all-Ireland Republic. This was the decree, regarded by Ulster Protestants and indeed by Protestants everywhere as infamous, under which the Catholic Church declared that any marriage between a Roman Catholic and a Protestant if celebrated otherwise than according to the rites of the Roman Catholic Church was invalid.[1] Although legally binding, it was not considered by the Roman Church to be a marriage at all and the man and woman who lived together after such a marriage were said by the Church to be living in sin. Is it conceivable that the Catholic Church in Ireland will diminish this decree if the Ulster Protestants agree to an all-Ireland Republic? This, too, is important to Catholic belief and the Ulstermen will never accept it. It angers them. They are angered, also, by the Catholic insistence that the children of a marriage between a Protestant and a Catholic should be brought up in the religion of the Roman Church. The Ulstermen, through their unusually close experience of the Roman Church, believe that it will not give an inch of ground in any matter of doctrinal importance to it—especially in Ireland; that it unalteringly considers itself to be the only legitimate heir and guardian of the one true faith; that its conviction that outside it there can be no salvation has not changed and will never change, however discreetly reticent its clergy may be on the point; that its interpretation of the unity of Christendom implies no more than the return of the straying Protestant Churches to Rome and their total subservience to it. In Ireland, the hierarchy and clergy of the Roman Church are generally less subtle than in other countries, less diplomatic, due to their inferior schooling and consequent lower standard of education. That is a statement of fact, unfortunately for Ireland, not an indication of prejudice

[1] The Archbishop of Canterbury spoke strongly against the decree, at the Assembly of The World Council of Churches, Uppsala, July 1968; see newspaper reports in Britain.

and a wish to be offensive. The notorious Fethard affair in Ireland supports the statement.

The village of Fethard is in the Irish Republic. In 1957, Mrs. Sheila Cloney,[1] whose husband was a Roman Catholic, had a dispute with her husband over the schooling of the elder of their two children. Taking the children with her, she left home and was thought to have gone to Ulster. The husband took a habeas corpus action in the Ulster Courts but it had to be disallowed as he was unable to trace and inform the Court of the whereabouts of his wife and children. From this family disagreement there arose a campaign of victimization that was to last for many months. It took the form of a boycott by Fethard Roman Catholics of the few Protestant shops in that village on the grounds that there had been Protestant connivance in the disappearance of Mrs. Cloney and her children. In a village so small, the effect on the livelihood of the Protestant shopkeepers was serious but appeals by the local Protestant clergy and public demands from all over Ulster and the Irish Republic that the Roman Catholic clergy should intervene fell on deaf ears. Eventually, however, a representative of the Catholic hierarchy did speak on the boycott. Dr. Browne, Roman Catholic Bishop of Galway, publicly declared that there seemed to be a concerted campaign to entice or kidnap Roman Catholic children and deprive them of their faith. He made this declaration—which was reported throughout the United Kingdom—to a congregation which included the then Roman Catholic Primate of All Ireland, Cardinal D'Alton, and other members of the Irish Catholic Hierarchy, and went on to say:

Non-Catholics, with one or two honourable exceptions, do not protest against the crime of conspiring to steal the children of a Catholic father, but they try to make political capital when a Catholic people make a peaceful and moderate protest. Those who see the mote in their neighbours' eyes but not the beam in their own are hypocrites and Pharisees. At the present time, Catholics need knowledge, loyalty and courage. They need confidence in their own Catholic people, clergy and bishops. They need courage to stand up for their faith.[2]

[1] Mrs. Cloney was a Protestant.
[2] June 30, 1957, in Wexford, at a special service.

Before the Catholic Bishop of Galway had delivered this questionable statement to his approving congregation, the *Irish Times* of Dublin said, in a bluntly worded leading article:

The indiscriminate apportionment of suffering is contrary to the equity of civilized states. It is just as certainly opposed to the lofty teaching of the Roman Catholic Church and we must confess to some surprise that the clerical authorities of Fethard have not yet succeeded in persuading their flock of the great injustice it is committing. To penalize a whole group of people for the sake of one of its members is unjust and un-Christian. It is the sort of conduct which, while official practice in nations under the Communist yoke, has no place in a 20th-century democracy. That fact would be reason enough in itself for condemning the whole deplorable business. Added to it, unhappily, is the suspicion which it is bound to engender—that the vaunted religious tolerance of the Irish Republic is little more than skin deep.[1]

De Valera, as Head of the Government, was appealed to in the Parliament of the Irish Republic. His Parliamentary Secretary replied for him:

I have made no public statement because I have clung to the hope that good sense and decent neighbourly feeling would, of themselves, bring this business to an end. I regard this boycott as ill-conceived, ill-considered and futile for the achievement of the purpose for which it seems to have been intended. I regard it as unjust and cruel to confound the innocent with the guilty. I repudiate any suggestion that the boycott is typical of the attitude or conduct of our people. I am convinced that ninety per cent of them look on the matter as I do and I beg all who have regard for the fair name, good repute and well being of our nation to use their influence to bring this deplorable affair to a speedy end.[2]

The Roman Catholic hierarchy paid not the least attention to the Head of State. The boycott of the Protestant shopkeepers of Fethard, who were brought to ruin in some cases, continued. The same attitude of tacit approval was maintained by the

[1] June 11, 1957.
[2] July 4, 1957, in Dail Eireann.

hierarchy until Mrs. Cloney was driven into returning to Fethard with her children a year later. And all this happened while the Irish Republican Army was engaged in attacking Ulster, murdering policemen and civilians and blowing up houses. The attacks were condemned by the Catholic hierarchy but it seemed to the Ulster people, who suffered cruelly from them, that the condemnation could and should have been made sooner and much more firmly.

Let it be repeated here that the author, as he made clear in the Foreword to this book, is not himself a member of any Christian Church and is not attempting, from an aspect of bias, to denigrate the Catholic Church. He is an Irishman who believes that the Christian Churches in Ireland have been rather more interested in political and theological quarrelling than in spreading the all-loving goodness of God. Protestant Churches in Ulster have shown a similarly unyielding attitude in many matters and their un-Christian intolerance will be dealt with in the next chapter. But, where the Catholic Church in Ireland is concerned, it is time and more than time for some very plain speaking, for all the fact that criticism of that Church infuriates its Irish followers, who are convinced that it nestles in the exclusive confidence and authority of the Almighty. If the Irish people are to solve the exceptionally difficult problems of their country, there must first be an honest stock-taking, with nothing left lying on the shelves. The fruit of the spirit, says St. Paul, is in righteousness and truth. The truth in Ireland is that as regards religious discrimination there is a case of six of one and half a dozen of the other.[1] Yet the Catholic Church in Ireland and the Catholic people of Ireland persist in placing the blame for religious discrimination entirely on the shoulders of the Protestant Ulster people. This is not all. There is a very large number of Irish Catholic priests stationed throughout the world. They have almost all of them been indoctrinated in youth with Irish Republican predilections and anti-Ulster prejudices. They supplement the anti-Ulster propaganda of their Catholic colleagues at home in Ireland by striving to turn world

[1] The (Protestant) Church of Ireland Gazette of October 30, 1969, says: 'Any grievances are not concerned exclusively with the minority Protestants in the Irish Republic. They concern those areas of law and administration where it may be said that the State is more concerned to uphold Roman Catholic teaching than the interests and welfare of all the citizens.'

opinion against Ulster through unceasing iteration of the claim that in the Irish Republic there is no discrimination of any kind against Protestants, whereas the Catholics in Ulster have been forced into the position of second-class citizens and are kept in that position by the weight of unjust laws. This is a lie as monstrous and offensive as Gerard Fitt's assertion that Catholics in Ulster are treated worse than negroes in America, but it is disseminated so cleverly, convincingly and unwearyingly that it is believed by an increasing body of men and women in an increasing range of countries.

Since the Ulster Government introduced its reform programme in 1969, there has been much talk by leading Irish Republic politicians and by leading Irish Catholic churchmen to the effect that the path could be smoothed for the Ulstermen to join in an all-Ireland Republic. A Commission has already been set up in Dublin to examine the 1937 Constitution of the Irish Republic and amend it where necessary, especially in the light of Articles in it which are objected to by the Ulstermen. Indeed, following upon the introduction of the reforms in Ulster, there has been specific mention of the possibility of removal of the clause in Article 44 allotting to the Catholic Church its special position in the Republic. Cardinal Conway, today's Roman Catholic Primate of All Ireland, has said that the removal of the clause would not cost him a pang. He has also said that, if the removal of it would help to reassure the Ulster people, he would be glad of its disappearance. This makes the Ulster people smile. They know where Cardinal Conway's political sympathies incline, and they are not so gullible as to believe for a moment that the disappearance of the clause would make the slightest difference. Changing the goods in the shop window does not automatically alter the nature of the business carried on in the store and the influence, power and determination of the Catholic Church in Ireland would not be abated an iota if the Constitution of the Irish Republic were rewritten from beginning to end. It stands in need of rewriting, of course, in the interests of the people of the Irish Republic. That does not concern the Ulstermen, however. They are engaged in remedying the faults of their own small State and ask only that they be left in peace while they are doing so. They suggest that the English should take the trouble to read their Act of Settlement of 1701, by

159

which they precluded in perpetuity all Catholic claimants to the English Crown and established the Protestant Succession. They remind the English that Prince Charles, as heir to the English throne, would not be allowed to marry a Roman Catholic. They then suggest that the English should take the additional trouble to read the Irish Republic's Constitution, study its dangerous Articles and indicate whether they themselves would consent to live beneath the shadow of such a document. The Ulstermen know very well what the English reply would be. All right, then, say the Ulstermen—please understand why we grind our teeth as we listen to Labour Party Members of your Westminster Parliament prating about the sins of Ulster and urging the desirability of Irish unification. Can it be purely coincidental, ask the Ulstermen, that those of your Labour Party Members who are most vociferous on the Irish question are those who have a significantly large Irish Catholic vote in their Parliamentary constituencies?

It was Coventry Patmore, the English poet, who wrote these words:

Some who do not consider that Christianity has proved a failure, do, nevertheless, hold that it is open to question whether the race, as a race, has been much affected by it, and whether the external and visible evil and good which have come of it do not pretty nearly balance each other.

The Christian Churches in Ireland, with their long record of arrogance and bad behaviour, could profitably consider those words of Patmore's. They could also profitably remind themselves that such questions as the existence of God, the nature of God if he does exist, the intentions of God, have baffled the finest minds the human race has yet managed to produce, that men have only inhabited the planet called Earth for less than a second in evolutionary time, that the divinity of Jesus of Nazareth is open to honest doubt by honest men. Additionally, they could remind themselves that their Christian religion is in a minority, that a great many more millions of equally sincere and searching human beings adhere to the other world religions than adhere to Christianity, that religion of every kind is a matter of faith and not of the certitude displayed by Catholic and

Protestant clergy in all places and particularly in the minute and unsophisticated parishes of Ireland. They might ponder the worth of humility. They might ponder, too, the instruction that they should render unto Caesar the things that are Caesar's and render unto God the things that are God's. In other words, they should concentrate on Christian leadership and put their political prejudices behind them. Unfortunately, they have not done this in the past in Ireland or of late. During the Belfast religious fighting in August 1969 between the Catholic district known as 'The Falls' and the Protestant district of 'The Shankill'—two working-class areas notorious in the story of the unhappy city— men and women suffered terribly. There was killing, wounding, blinding, a burning of houses, a driving of people from homes they had lived in and loved for a lifetime, a ruining of what was left of the lives of many of the elderly and the old. It was appalling. What did the church leaders do to bring the people to their senses and the tragedy to an end? Did they join together, go to the scene of the fighting, place themselves between the warring sides and call to them, 'If you must take lives, take ours'? The people, enraged though they were, would not have killed them, but the leaders stayed away. Did they join together in an urgent television appeal to the people in the name of God to stop attacking one another? They did not.

Splendid individual Catholic parish priests and Protestant parsons did what they could to reason with the people, but in the churches' leaders the vision and humanity of old Pope John were lacking. If he had been alive and could have gone to Belfast during the rioting, he would have wanted to walk through the hate-filled districts with his arms outspread to embrace both Catholics and Protestants as being all of them the children of God. He would have shown the wisdom, the simple loving goodness and intellectual courage he showed to all he met in the course of his kindly life, he would somehow have got through to the hearts of the people, he would have tried with all his moral strength to lead them from their brutality to better things. Could he have had an effect on people wild with rage? He could. In Londonderry at a time of bad fighting there, earlier in the year, the local Catholic and Church of Ireland bishops, with the heads of the Presbyterian and Methodist Churches in the city, walked among the angry people in an attempt to calm them.

The attempt succeeded. The people crowded round the church-men and were thankful for their presence. This could have been done in Belfast. It was not done. The church leaders there were not men of intellectual courage.

Did William, Cardinal Conway, himself born of a poor family in the Catholic district of the Falls and risen to be Roman Catholic Primate of All Ireland and a Prince of the Church, try with all his moral strength and intellectual courage to bring home to the uneducated and enraged people that, regardless of creed, they were children of the same God and that hate is perhaps the worst of all the mortal sins? Did he walk among his people in the Falls before or after the fighting? Did he call on all leading churchmen in Ulster to come together in the name of their Christian God, forget their past quarrels and join in an effort to create a lasting peace in the Province? He did not. Has he done so since? He has not. Has he ascribed the blame for the Belfast rioting fairly? Many will deny it. He put his name to a public statement which attributed the blame in entirety to the Protestants, although the onus of responsibility for the rioting had not yet been investigated by the Tribunal appointed by the Ulster Government to go into it and report on it truthfully and fearlessly. Why did he put his name to such a statement? Let the question be left, let all the questions be left, to the conscience of the Cardinal himself. If he decides to examine his conscience, he will assuredly bear in mind as he does so the advice of Marcus Aurelius that a man should not look to see what his neighbour says or thinks but only at what he does himself, to make it just and holy.

It was the same Marcus Aurelius who said that if any man could convince him that he did not think or act aright he would gladly change, for he was searching after truth, by which no man was ever harmed. It was Tertullian, the second-century Father of the Church, who said, 'See how these Christians love one another.' Had he lived in Ireland, he might have said it with his tongue in his cheek. Maybe he did say it with his tongue in his cheek, maybe the Christians of his day were very like the Christians in Ireland now. Probably not, though. The Christians in Ireland do not love one another and their churches stand greatly in need of change. Will those churches change and, as Aurelius would have done, change gladly? It is possible perhaps that the religious rioting in Ulster has come home to them as evidence of their failure, that it has startled them into something in the nature of self-examination and that from this probing may come an improvement. Possible but unlikely. Not long after the worst of the Belfast rioting in August 1969, three Irish church leaders shared a television programme. They were Cardinal Conway, Archbishop Simms of the Church of Ireland and the Reverend John Carson, head of the Presbyterian Church in Ireland at the time. There was one aspect on which they were agreed—that the savage fighting throughout the Province stemmed from a political quarrel and not from a religious one. It was hardly to be expected that three prominent churchmen would admit that the fighting was born of a religious quarrel. That would have been a public admission that their churches were scandalously divided and that they had failed to persuade the people to live in accordance with the standards laid down by Jesus of Nazareth. The discussion between the three clerics was civil, cautious and evasive. There was an interesting moment when the Reverend John Carson hinted gently that the Catholic Church in Ulster might begin to show the official courtesies customarily given to the State. The Cardinal looked embarrassed and made no comment. He must have known the scorn and rudeness habitually directed at the Ulster State by his church and his Catholic flock in the Province. He must have known, too, that it compares ill with the good manners shown by Ulster people and Ulster church representatives of the Protestant faith when they visit and have dealings in the Irish Republic. Politically, however, it could have been dangerous for him to admit before the television cameras the justice of the considerately hinted reproof. An Irish Cardinal must ever be mindful of Irish political considerations.

Those who know Ireland will appreciate the Cardinal's difficulty. It is twofold. First, it is always hard, perhaps impossible, to emancipate ourselves intellectually from the indoctrination imposed on us in boyhood. Children born in the poor Catholic district of the Falls and the equally poor district of the Shankill are exposed to opposing political indoctrination of an extreme and persisting kind. Second, it is expected of an Irish Cardinal and Primate of All Ireland that he should be an adamant champion of the Republican cause in Ulster. The

Republican politicians in Dublin keep a steady eye on him and he must be perpetually peering nervously over his shoulder in their direction. But the world looks for rather more in all the Princes of the Church than attention to the politics of petty men. The British Home Secretary, James Callaghan, who visited Ulster twice in 1969 to help the Ulster Government in the initiation of reforms, saw this clearly and called for a gesture from the Ulster Catholics. You have been given your reforms, he said to them, now show yourselves possessed of vision and generosity, let us have a worthwhile response from you. He was disappointed. There was no response. The Ulster Catholics, ruled by their intractable Republicanism, have so far shown themselves incapable of the wider outlook, of forgetting their inherited political ambitions. It was here again that Cardinal Conway might have given the leadership which the Ulster people, both Protestant and Catholic, had a right to expect of him. He has not yet given it. If many Ulster people consequently and sadly believe him to be more of a political priest than a Christian leader of men, can he blame them?

Some will insist that it is unreasonable to say that the Christian Churches in Ireland have been more ineffective than in other countries. Humankind, they will maintain, has proved throughout 2,000 years to be generally unreceptive to the teachings of Jesus of Nazareth. But the history of Ireland shows unarguably that the churches there have failed disastrously. They have been inward-looking, implacable, they have helped to perpetuate highly un-Christian quarrels among their people by the affixing of differing national flags above their doorways, they have wrongly informed the young through false tuition in their schools,[1] they have forgotten, if they ever grasped it, the

[1] On August 12, 1969, the author wrote to the Department of Education of the Irish Republic, in Dublin, and asked it to tell him what Irish history is taught in Catholic schools throughout Ireland; the Department has not answered. The fact is that Irish history is scarcely taught at all in Irish schools, whatever the denomination. Some effort is made to teach it in Ulster Protestant schools, but the overall situation is seriously unsatisfactory. In Irish Catholic schools the subject is left mainly in the hands of teachers who have little if any knowledge of the history of their country and who give their pupils a slanted and untruthful version, especially of the 'English brutality' in Ireland; nothing is taught them of the Irish Civil War and the atrocities committed by the Irish Republican Army. This is particularly and unhappily true of the schools run by the Irish Christian Brothers—a Roman Catholic Order.

essence of Christ's message—'By this shall it be known ye are My disciples, that ye love your fellow men.'

Many Irish men and women who care for their country, who know its story and are not deceived, will agree that if the Christian Churches of all denominations could be removed from it until such time as they have truly learnt to identify the path that Jesus of Nazareth referred to, Ireland would be the better for their absence.

Chapter Nine

> The glorious, pious and immortal memory of the great and good King William, who saved us from popery, slavery, knavery, brass money and wooden shoes.
>
> *Famous Orange Toast*[1]

THE Orange Order, formed in Ulster in 1795 for the defence of the Protestant religion, is said to have a membership of around 100,000 in the Province alone, although it is believed that the real figure is well below that total. Its constituent unit is the Lodge, like the lodges of Freemasonry, and there are many lodges in the Province, in Scotland and in countries overseas. On July 12 each year there are massive public processional marches by the Lodges to celebrate the victory in 1690 of the army of Protestant William of Orange over the army of the Catholic King James II of England in a battle fought at the Boyne River near Drogheda in what is now the Irish Republic. It was a decisive battle, which confirmed William on the English throne from which he had expelled King James, and it changed the course of European history. In Belfast, the annual procession is made up of many Lodges, headed by bands of every kind and carrying their great painted Lodge banners, marching through the crowded streets to what is known by all self-respecting and God-fearing Protestant Ulster people as The Field. Speeches, usually predictable, are delivered there to the assembled brethren by political and other leaders, telegrams of loyalty are despatched to the British Royal Family, sandwiches are eaten, bottles of beer and stout are emptied, and the Lodges march back through the still-crowded streets to the dispersal point. It is the most colourful event of the year in Ulster, traditionally part of the Ulster way of life, even recog-

[1] The 'brass money' refers to King James's coinage and 'wooden shoes' to his French allies.

nized as such by the tight-lipped Ulster Catholics, who have an equivalent association known as The Ancient Order of Hibernians, which stages a similar procession every August. It is said—and it may well be true, for anything is possible in Ireland—that the rival lodges have been known to borrow one another's drums.

What exactly is the Orange Order? According to its Constitution, Laws and Ordinances:

> The Institution is composed of Protestants, united and resolved to the utmost of their power to support and defend the rightful Sovereign, the Protestant Religion, the Laws of the Realm, and the Succession to the Throne in the House of Windsor, BEING PROTESTANT, and united further for the defence of their own Persons and Properties, and the maintenance of the Public Peace. It is exclusively an Association of those who are attached to the religion of the Reformation, and will not admit into its brotherhood persons whom an intolerant spirit leads to persecute, injure, or upbraid any man on account of his religious opinions. They associate also in honour of KING WILLIAM THE THIRD, Prince of Orange, whose name they bear, as supporters of his glorious memory.

A man seeking admission to the Order must first satisfy the Master and Members of the Lodge to which he wishes to be admitted that he fulfils the following qualifications:

> A sincere love and veneration for his Heavenly Father; an humble and steadfast faith in Jesus Christ, the Saviour of Mankind, believing in Him as the only Mediator between God and man. He should cultivate truth and justice, brotherly kindness and charity, devotion and piety, concord and unity, and obedience to the laws; his deportment should be gentle and compassionate, kind and courteous; he should seek the society of the virtuous, and avoid that of the evil; he should honour and diligently study the Holy Scriptures, and make them the rule of his faith and practice; he should love, uphold and defend the Protestant religion, and sincerely desire and endeavour to propagate its doctrines and precepts; he should strenuously oppose the fatal errors and doctrines of the Church of Rome, and scrupulously avoid countenancing

167

(by his presence or otherwise) any act or ceremony of Popish Worship; he should, by all lawful means, resist the ascendancy of that Church, its encroachments, and the extension of its power, ever abstaining from all uncharitable words, actions or sentiments towards his Roman Catholic brethren; he should remember to keep holy the Sabbath day, and attend the public worship of God, and diligently train up his offspring, and all under his control, in the fear of God, and in the Protestant faith; he should never take the name of God in vain, but abstain from all cursing and profane language, and use every opportunity of discouraging those, and all other sinful practices, in others; his conduct should be guided by wisdom and prudence, and marked by honesty, temperance, and sobriety; the glory of God and the welfare of man, the honour of his Sovereign, and the good of his country, should be the motives of his actions.

That is not all. It is firmly laid down that:

No person who at any time has been a Roman Catholic or married to one, shall be admitted into the Institution, except after permission given by a vote of seventy-five per cent of the members present at a meeting of the Grand Orange Lodge of Ireland and of the District and County Grand Lodges respectively, founded on testimonials of good character and a Certificate of his having been duly elected in the Lodge in which he is proposed.

Two things follow from these ordinances. First, a man should not attempt to join the Orange Order unless he is a saint or possessed of the capacity to become a saint. This is absurd. Second, should a member of the Order so much as attend a ceremony in a Roman Catholic Church, he is liable to expulsion. This is tyrannical. It is also counter to the ordinance that an Orangeman should ever cultivate charity. Yet men have been expelled from the Order for the offence of setting foot within a Roman Catholic Church. In 1967, a senior Unionist Member of Parliament in the Ulster House of Commons was put out of the Order. A Community Week had been organized in a small country town within his Parliamentary constituency, one of those get-togethers which country folk throughout the United

168

Kingdom are for ever arranging, with such features as flower shows, vegetable marrow competitions, sports meetings and other un-sinister events. Special services were arranged to mark the occasion and were given by the local Church of Ireland, Presbyterian Church and Roman Catholic Church. The Member of Parliament, as was his duty, attended all three services. A few weeks later, when the Grand Orange Lodge had met to consider the matter, he was expelled from the Order. There have been other expulsions for similarly trifling and uncharitable reasons. The leaders of the Order argue in justification that all Orders expect their rules to be obeyed and that if a man does not feel that he can observe the rules of the Orange Order he should not apply for membership. They also argue that men who live in democratic countries have the democratic right to form any law-abiding association they may choose to form. Both arguments would be unobjectionable if the Orange Order in Ulster did not seek to interefere with the democratic rights of such of its fellow citizens as are not members of it. But it does interfere. Its influence intrudes into almost every aspect of life in the Province.

This is especially true of the Province's political life. The Order has a grip on the Unionist Party that is coming near to a stranglehold through an ever-increasing infiltration of the Unionist Constituency Associations. Any man who wishes to take up a political career in Ulster is pretty well under compulsion to join the Orange Order if he is to have any hope of winning a constituency nomination. It is even more necessary to be a member of the Order if he is aiming at Cabinet rank. Admittedly, this is beginning to change. Since the Parliamentary election of February, 1969, called by Terence O'Neill in an effort to gain support for his programme of legislative reform, there have been some Unionist members of the Ulster House of Commons who are not Orangemen and who have no intention of joining the Order. The fact that at least one of them is an officially adopted Unionist who secured the nomination of his Unionist Constituency Association despite his known refusal to join the Order is a straw in the wind. It is no more than a straw, however. These 'unauthorized' Unionist members will have difficulty in retaining the nomination at the next election. There is still a long long way to go before the fingers are prised loose.

The Ulster Catholics attack the Orange Order on the grounds that it has a seriously prejudicial effect not only in Ulster but in London as well. One of the twelve Members of Parliament Ulster is entitled to send to Westminster holds a very high position in the Order and his colleagues are almost all of them Orangemen. The Catholics accuse the Order of a bigoted determination, consistently maintained, to limit Catholic representation in Ulster at every level, to compel them to accept inferior citizenship, to deny them the higher and more responsible posts in the public services and in the judiciary.[1] They assert that the Order is run by ignorant and bitter Protestants from the less educated classes, who do not fulfil and have no ambition to fulfil the high-sounding qualifications for membership, whose principal objective is not merely to defend the Protestant faith but to assail and diminish those of the Catholic faith. They say that the Order has a disproportionate influence, through automatic right of delegation, on the Unionist Council, which is the 800-strong governing body of the Unionist Party in matters of policy. It has powerful influence, too, they say, in the Standing and Executive Committees of the Council. Above all, they argue, its influence is strongest and most prejudicially effective in a great many of the Unionist Constituency Associations which select in the rural areas the more illiberal Unionist candidates for the Ulster House of Commons. It is so deeply entrenched in those areas, the Catholics say, that it will not be dislodged for many years to come. They insist that every Unionist should resign from the Order on election to the Ulster House of Commons and particularly when appointed to Cabinet rank. Indeed, they argue that the Order is an anachronism and that it stands in the way of a rapprochement between the Catholic and Protestant sections of the community. In short, they detest the Orange Order.

Can the Order refute these charges? They are exaggerated, but there is truth in many of them and the Order does not help its argument or its cause by playing straight into its opponents' hands. The annual July 12 procession, whatever the Order may

[1] High Court Judges in Ulster are selected and appointed by the British Government at Westminster. The appointment rests with the Lord Chancellor of England and the Ulster Government has no decisive voice in the matter; indeed it is questionable if it has any influence at all.

say about its non-violent and law-observing nature, is provocative. Why should the Order insist on an annual public celebration of a battle which took place more than two and a half centuries ago? Why should it insist on exultantly reviving the memory of a bitter and unhappy phase of Irish history? Many brave Irishmen fought at the Boyne on the side of James II. They had a right to do so and their views on the shape and allegiance of their country were as legitimate as those of the equally brave Irishmen who fought for William of Orange. Why should they be ridiculed? The bands that lead the Lodges of the Orange Order to The Field in July of every year play songs with words that are bound to be insulting to a lot of Catholics. Why should the Order offend its fellow citizens in Ulster by insisting on the playing of such provocative party tunes? And the swaggering braggadocio of many of the drum-majors during the march has to be seen to be believed. How does the Order reconcile all this with the ordinance that the deportment of an Orangeman shall be gentle, compassionate, kind and courteous, that his conduct shall be guided by wisdom and prudence? Or reconcile it with the declaration that it will not admit into its brotherhood such persons as an intolerant spirit may lead to persecute, injure or upbraid a man on account of his religious opinions? The annual July procession of the Orange Order reeks of triumphal intolerance. It is as if the British Army insisted on marching through Paris every June 18 in celebration of its victory over the French at Waterloo, its bands playing songs that insult the memory of Napoleon and denigrate the courage of the French soldiers who fought so gallantly for him. The Orangemen cannot justify their procession by arguing that the Catholics in their annual August march of the Ancient Order of Hibernians are just as provocative. It is questionable whether they are. But, however provocative and childish the Hibernians may be—and they are both—two follies have never yet made sense. The Orange Order has lost the respect of many thoughtful, moderate and kindly-minded Ulster men and women of varying religious and political outlooks. They know that the Order contains numerous fine and honourable men in its higher, middle and lower ranks. They also know that it contains far too many men who bring shame to the Order and to the good name of Ulster, that however necessary its

171

existence may have been in the past its excessively anti-Catholic rules and its processional posturing are now a nembarrassment and a possible danger to the continuance of the Ulster State. Its intolerance forges a weapon for the enemies of that State, who seize on it for the purposes of their propaganda and broadcast it to the world.

The leaders of the Order—let this be repeated, for it is important—argue that men who live in democratic countries have the democratic right to form any law-abiding association they may choose to form. Well and good. The argument is sound. But is the Order law-abiding in the democratic meaning? Is it even democratic? There are many in Ulster who believe that its leaders should give careful thought to its present structure and future activities, who believe that it will not fully recover respect or truly serve the State until it cancels provocative public marches, purges itself of the many members who discredit it, amends its rules to exclude such un-Christian rigidity as the refusal to allow a member to step inside a Roman Catholic Church and agrees to slacken its grip on the political structure of the Province.

It is possible, of course, that the July 12 processional march of the Orange Order does not give so much offence to Ulster Catholics as a section of the Ulster people are convinced it does. The procession is a long-established feature in Ulster life and certainly there are Catholics who have an affection for it, who would regret its passing. But the march tunes should be changed. For them there is no excuse. There is never an excuse for the wilful playing of aggressive party songs in a place so politically and religiously sensitive as Ulster. This applies with especial truth since the rioting and fighting of 1968 and 1969. The worst of the fighting began on August 12, 1969, when an organization known as The Apprentice Boys of Derry staged its traditional march in celebration of the relief of besieged Londonderry in 1688–89. The Apprentice Boys association is not connected in any way with the Orange Order but its marchers are preceded by bands playing the very same party tunes as are played by the bands that precede the Orange Lodges and they are unquestionably provocative. In view of the serious tension in Londonderry on August 12, 1969, the organizers of the march should have known that the strident playing of the Protestant party songs would inevitably lead to trouble. It did lead to trouble, very serious trouble indeed. The Catholics of the Bogside district of Londonderry suddenly flamed into anger and began to stone the marchers, the police and the bystanders. That night, next day and for many days and nights, all hell broke loose in Londonderry. The national newspapers and the national and international television services gave the fighting immense coverage—and Ulster suffered untold damage to its reputation. Was it really worth it to play those songs? Should the march have taken place at all? How did the Apprentice Boys advance the cause of the Protestant religion, or defend it, by their march? The rioting that resulted from the march diminished the name of Protestantism in Ulster. But the Apprentice Boys could not see this, still cannot see it.

The more thoughtful Ulster people, just as patriotic as the Apprentice Boys—more so, perhaps, because their vision is keener and they are more aware of dangers—feel that such associations as the Apprentice Boys and the Orange Order should take a long and thorough look at themselves and consider whether they stand in need of alteration. They feel particularly that the Orange Order should free itself from the justified accusation that it is behaving undemocratically by flooding and controlling so many Unionist Party Constituency Associations, by influencing the Province's political life in favour of reactionary Unionist candidates for election to the Ulster Parliament. The Order need not deny that this is happening. It knows very well that it is happening. It should put a stop to it, before it changes the political direction of the Province so much for the worse that the end-product could be disaster. It has served Ulster well in the past.[1] Let it serve it better— now and in the future.

Ulster has been much exposed, unfortunately, to zealots. One of the most prominent of these religious and political zealots is a man called Paisley. He is a most interesting product of the seventeenth-century religious fervour that obtains in Ulster, anti-Roman Catholic almost to the point of frenzy, with a mind that is closed tight shut against all that differs from a literal interpretation of the Protestant Bible. An enormous man

[1] The 36th (Ulster) Division which fought so superbly at the Somme in 1916 consisted very largely of Orangemen.

physically, with a voice like a trumpeting elephant, he stumps the Province calling on the faithful—and there are many of them—to aid him in resisting the devilish encroachments of the Scarlet Woman of Rome, abhorred of all true followers of the Lord Jesus. In May 1969, the annual General Assembly of the Church of Scotland—Protestant, of course—took place in Edinburgh and was attended in person by Her Majesty, Queen Elizabeth II of England. It was also attended, on the invitation of the Assembly, by a Roman Catholic priest, Father John Dalrymple, as an observer. This desecration of a Protestant Assembly angered Paisley. Together with the Reverend Jack Glass, Chairman of the Twentieth Century Reformation Movement in Scotland, he decided to lodge an objection by way of petition to the Queen at Holyrood Palace, the historic residence of former Scottish monarchs. The petition reads:[1]

Your Gracious Majesty,
On behalf of many thousands of your most loyal subjects, we address this petition to you.

These subjects have requested us to assure you that they pray continually to Almighty God that you may be given grace and wisdom to govern all your subjects in the way that shall bring both upon you and them the benediction and blessing of Heaven.

Your visit to this particular General Assembly, when a representative of the Church of Rome is for the first time being received, gravely alarms those for whom we have the honour and authority to speak. We would respectfully remind Your Majesty that the last occasion on which you visited the Assembly was to commemorate the glorious Reformation of the 16th century. We submit that all that glorious event accomplished for the Scottish Kirk is now jeopardized by this intention to make you a party to the welcoming of a representative of that Church from whose fetters John Knox was raised up by God to deliver us. We condemn the action of the Assembly's hierarchy in using Your Gracious Person and Royal Authority to accomplish their false ecumenical ends. These actions we most solemnly protest. They are neither

---

[1] See the *Protestant Telegraph*, Belfast (Paisley's journal) of May 31, 1969, obtainable from Puritan Printing Co., Ltd., 67 Ravenhill Road, Belfast 6.

in keeping with Bible Christianity nor with the laws of your realm. Further, they ignore the whole basis and spirit of the Coronation ceremony and the safeguards of the Bill of Rights.

We humbly request that Your Majesty will make it abundantly clear that you will not consent to any deviation from or violation of your Coronation oath, but will ever maintain the Protestant Religion.

John Knox said that he feared one Mass in Scotland more than a regiment of the enemy. Your subjects fear the result of the proposed welcome to this idolatrous Mass-mongering representative of the Papal Antichrist and look to you to fulfil for them the words of the prophecy of Isaiah concerning the Church in Chapter 49, Verse 23—'And kings shall be thy nursing fathers, and their queens thy nursing mothers.'

The General Assembly made a moderately phrased reply[1] to Paisley, acknowledging the right of anyone to disagree with its decisions but pointing out that 'controversy, however, must be conducted in a spirit of mutual respect, for where bitterness and violence are allowed to take the place of tolerance and freedom only damage can be done to the cause of truth itself. Moreover, a Christian is under an obligation not only to search for truth, but to proclaim and practise love. The Church of Scotland believes that it must . . . re-examine the teaching of other Communions . . . this can be achieved through dialogue, so that a clearer understanding of the other's standpoint may lead to closer contacts and, wherever possible, to co-operation in charitable and other works for the welfare of the community. It was within such a context that the invitation to the Roman Catholic Church to send an official visitor was extended.' Paisley's answer to this was given in his Belfast journal, the *Protestant Telegraph*:[2] 'The Church of Scotland has failed completely to answer the petition. Instead it declares that it is on a quest for truth which is leading it to re-examine its own basis of teaching and to enter into dialogue with Rome. Having abandoned the sheet anchor of God's word, it is falling an easy prey to the Roman conspiracy. Alas, alas, for the church of John Knox'.

Who is this Ian R. K. Paisley, who protests in Edinburgh

[1] *Protestant Telegraph* of June 28, 1969.
[2] The same issue of the *Protestant Telegraph*.

and who protests against the visit in June 1969 of Pope Paul to Geneva? He is a man of commanding presence and personality, approaching his middle forties, and he is an Ulsterman—which is not surprising, as Ulster is the Bible Belt of Britain—the son of an Ulster minister of the Baptist Church. He holds an honorary doctorate from the Bob Jones University of South Carolina in the United States of America,[1] where he studied for a while before returning to Ulster and eventually setting up what he calls The Free Presbyterian Church. There are now several churches of this peculiar denomination in Ulster and Paisley describes himself as Moderator. He was ordained by his father, his religious beliefs are obviously unsubtle and his qualifications are regarded by the official Presbyterian Church in Ireland as falling short of the minimum requirements for ordination. He has a large and growing simple-minded Ulster following—the Paisleyites—and is consequently, thanks to the existence of the ballot box, a significant political influence in Ulster. There are Ulstermen who near despairingly consider him to be the greatest danger to it. He does not agree.

He conducted a bitter campaign against the reformist Prime Minister of Ulster, Captain Terence O'Neill, accused him of truckling to Rome, accused him of yielding to the Irish Republican Army, the Civil Rights Association and other subversive elements intent on destroying Ulster—all of which was untrue—and publicly gave thanks to God when he was at last and shamefully hounded from office. No one strove harder to bring about O'Neill's downfall. By doing so, he did the Province a serious disservice. Again, he does not agree. He cannot agree, either, for all his Biblical literalism, that in his Father's house there are many mansions. In his opinion, always forthrightly expressed, the other mansions are jerrybuilt—unsubstantial and of inferior material. Only the Free Presbyterian Church of Ulster is meet for Divine approval. He has a most astute legal adviser and he is a born publicist and organizer. When he calls a meeting of his supporters in an Ulster countryside town, a large cavalcade of his Belfast faithful are there too, which gives

[1] See *Belfast Newsletter* of October 7, 1969, when Dr. Bob Jones II was in Belfast for the opening of Paisley's new £175,000 church; Dr. Jones said: 'We gave him an honorary degree. It was as simple as that. He never studied with us and we don't have a correspondence school.' This contradicts other statements that Paisley did study there.

the impression that his local following is larger than it really is. Just how many supporters he has in Ulster is difficult to estimate, but they form a substantial pressure group, recruited mostly from the narrowest and most unpleasant section of the community. Many of them—too many—are members of the Orange Order and, following the example of hard-line Orangemen, they are flooding the Constituency Associations of moderate Unionist Members of the Ulster Parliament in order to deny them the nomination for the next election and replace them with candidates who share their limited thinking on the direction the Province should take. This could result in what Bismarck called 'government of a household by its nursery'. It could also result in the ruin of the Province and may very well do so.

Paisley's right-hand man in Ulster was Major Ronald Bunting. Between them they formed The Ulster Constitution Defence Committee and an organization known as The Ulster Protestant Volunteers. Each organization is closely connected with the other. The Chairman of the first is Ian Paisley and the Commandant of the Volunteers was Major Bunting, who arranged them in what he called Divisions—taking their names from the Parliamentary Divisions in which they are situated. Both men were present in various Ulster towns when rioting and general disorder took place. The Cameron Commission report[1] has this to say:

> In face of the mass of evidence from both police and civilian sources as to the extent to which the supporters of Dr. Paisley and Major Bunting were armed at Armagh and on the occasion of the People's Democracy march to Londonderry, it is idle to pretend that these were peacefully directed protest meetings. On neither occasion were the Civil Rights or People's Democracy marchers armed. On neither occasion had they offered violence towards others, on neither occasion was the march or demonstration routed through streets or areas traditionally Protestant or 'loyalist'.

> We are left in no doubt that the interventions of Dr. Paisley and Major Bunting in Londonderry and Armagh and the threatened marches of Major Bunting elsewhere were not designed merely to register a peaceful protest against those

[1] See paragraph 216 et seq.

engaged in Civil Rights or People's Democracy activities, however much they profess the contrary. It is our considered opinion that these counter-demonstrations were organized under the auspices of the Ulster Constitution Defence Committee and the Ulster Protestant Volunteers and that their true purpose was either to cause a legal prohibition of the proposed Civil Rights or People's Democracy demonstrations by the threat of a counter-demonstration, or, if this move failed, to harass, hinder and, if possible, break up the demonstration. It must have been quite apparent to Dr. Paisley at least that, in the existing state of the law and having regard to the available strength of the police and to political realities in Ulster, it would not be practicable to prevent congregation or concentration of 'loyalists' or to disperse them once gathered together on the route or in the vicinity of a proposed Civil Rights demonstration, meeting or march.

That the use of force was contemplated or expected and prepared for both in Armagh on 30th November, 1968 and in Londonderry on 4th January, 1969 is amply proved by evidence of the weapons and missiles seen by the police and others to be carried and used by those concerned in the counter-demonstration in Armagh and at Burntollet Bridge. In addition, having regard to circumstances which must have been known to them, we can only condemn as an act of the greatest irresponsibility the decision to hold a meeting of the nature of that conducted by Dr. Paisley and Major Bunting in Londonderry on the 3rd January, 1969. Both these men and the organizations with which they are so closely and authoritatively concerned must, in our opinion, bear a heavy share of direct responsibility for the disorders in Armagh and at Burntollet Bridge and also for inflaming passions and engineering opposition to lawful and what would in all probability otherwise have been peaceful demonstrations or at least have attracted only modified and easily controlled opposition.

What were the weapons with which the Paisleyite counter-demonstrators were armed in the city of Armagh? Cudgels of all kinds, some of which were studded with nails.[1] A television

[1] See paragraphs 72 to 88, inclusive, of the Cameron Commission report.

cameraman was clubbed with a home-made baton which had been lead-filled and taped. The Paisleyites had many other ugly weapons which the Cameron Commission does not specify. It has this to say in the matter of Paisley's organizational gifts:

That the organization was widespread and effective is shown by the conveyance to Armagh through the night and in the early hours of the morning of people from widely separated areas of the Province.

It then says this:

The fact remains that the police could not guarantee the physical safety of the Civil Rights marchers against the obvious menace of unlawful violence. For this, the actions of Dr. Paisley, Major Bunting and their associates and supporters bear direct responsibility.

Such was the work of the men of God, ever in the service of their Lord and Saviour. A few aspects need to be clarified. Burntollet Bridge is on the route taken by the People's Democracy marchers on their way to Londonderry on January 4, 1969. It was a provocative march, as explained in Chapter 7, but the stoning of it at Burntollet Bridge by Protestant guttersnipes and hooligans was a shame that Ulster will not recover from for a long time. According to Cameron, Major Bunting himself was seen to take part in the activities at the bridge.[1] The meeting in the Londonderry Guildhall on January 3, 1969, led to scenes of shocking anger and violence, for which Paisley and Bunting had direct responsibility. Bunting, it should be remarked, was a fervent convert to Free Presbyterianism and one of Paisley's most convinced disciples. One other point must now be cleared. In Chapter Seven some words were omitted from sub-paragraph seven of the Cameron Commission's listed causes of the disorders in Ulster. Let the sub-paragraph now be given in full:

Fears and apprehensions among Protestants of a threat to Unionist domination and control of Government by increase of Catholic population and powers, inflamed in particular by the activities of the Ulster Constitutional Defence Committee

[1] See paragraph 222.

and the Ulster Protestant Volunteers, provoked strong hostile reaction to Civil Rights claims as asserted by the Civil Rights Association and later by the People's Democracy which was readily translated into physical violence against Civil Rights demonstrators.

Ulster, of course, is not the only part of Britain afflicted by those who regard themselves as The Chosen of the Lord. But the Chosen in England, Wales and Scotland are no more than harmless cranks. In Ulster they have a viciousness that has already led to the deaths of innocent people, including a child of nine and a policeman of twenty-nine, killed by bullets during the 1969 rioting in Belfast. They have the mentality of the seventeenth-century Puritans in England who looted and smashed 'idolatrous' churches, executed Anglicans on false charges, shouted Biblical texts as they massacred garrisons. They will tolerate no liberalism of thought in Ulster. It was men of their mentality who forced the resignation from Parliament of Richard Ferguson, Unionist Member for South Antrim, because he had withdrawn from the Orange Order. Ferguson, representative of the best and most liberally minded of the younger entrants to the Ulster House of Commons following the O'Neill election in February 1969, is an able barrister in his early thirties. He felt that his membership of Parliament was incompatible with that of the sectarian Orange Order and publicly announced his retirement from it, a most courageous act. This outraged the Chosen who lived in or around his constituency. They demanded a meeting of the local Constituency Association, packed it and succeeded in passing a vote of No Confidence in him, thus compelling him to resign his seat. Before this, they subjected him and his wife and children to despicable anonymous and criminal abuse and even threatened his life, just as they have threatened the life of the author of this book for different reasons. Will the Orange Order in Ulster assert that members of the Order had nothing to do with the manœuvre that packed the Constituency Association meeting with opponents of Ferguson's liberal ideas? Will Paisley assert that his followers had nothing to do with it? Ferguson's health broke down under the strain and for a time he was unable to practise his profession. What have The Chosen of the Lord to say to that, as they sink to their knees in their churches and give thanks to God that they are not as others are?

There are dispassionate observers who will point out that the Ulster men and women of moderate views, who wish to see the Province at peace and all of its citizens living in harmony with one another, have in their hands the power to defeat these Protestant extremists. Nothing could be more true. But the moderate Ulster people are like the moderate people of other countries—indifferent to their long-term interests, unnoticing of what is happening around them, stupid and apathetic. They will not look closely, they will not rise from their comfortable evening chairs, attend their Constituency Associations and repel the bigots determined to capture and control the electoral machinery. They are doing nothing, while the extremists are sweeping like an incoming tide across the sands. The moderates will continue to do nothing, until at last they wake to discover that Ulster has been taken over by the extremists and has become something unpleasantly like a Fascist State.[1] This could be a too pessimistic forecast, of course, but the signs are unmistakably in sight. More and more moderate Unionist Party members are being thrust out of their Constituency Associations on pretext after pretext. The Prime Minister himself, Major Chichester-Clark, has been removed from office in his own Association because of the reforming measures introduced by his Government. Everywhere the extremists are gaining ground. They will be putting up candidates at the next election, which will be the most crucial ever fought in Ulster.

What do these extremists object to? What do they want? They object to the reforms brought in by the Ulster Government since October 1968. They say they make too many concessions to the Catholic minority and they want them rescinded. The reforms cover allocation of houses on an equitable points system to make certain that Catholics are not precluded and 'ghettoed'; redrawing of gerrymandered ward boundaries in the field of local government; abolition of the pluralistic vote

[1] In the late autumn of 1969, after this chapter was written, the Ulster Unionist Party woke up to the danger; it tried to persuade the Constituency Associations to reframe their membership rules so as to admit only those with a genuine stake in the constituency and to abolish plural membership of Association Branches.

in local government which Catholics say discriminate unfairly against them although the system operates against Protestants to a similar degree and is still used in some British Commonwealth countries; appointment of an Ombudsman to investigate complaints at Government Department level and ensure that injustices are detected and remedied; establishment of machinery for examination of grievances against public bodies and authorities; appointment of an uncommitted Development Commission to replace the Londonderry Corporation; reshaping of the Royal Ulster Constabulary into an unarmed civil police force no longer made responsible for security duties; supersession of the Ulster Special Constabulary by an Ulster Defence Regiment under the control of the General Officer Commanding British Army troops in Ulster; the setting up of a Ministry of Community Relations—the Minister, Dr. Robert Simpson, resigned his membership of the Orange Order when appointed and will most certainly run into trouble in his Parliamentary constituency for doing so; and a promise by the liberal-minded Minister of Home Affairs, Mr. Robert Porter, Q.C., that the Government will consider amending aspects of the Special Act when conditions in Ulster have returned to normal sufficiently to allow this to be done without danger.

That is a generous programme and a wise one. It strikes the swords from the hands of Ulster's enemies and strengthens the State in the eyes of honest men, despite the cavilling of the Opposition members in the Ulster House of Commons, who sullenly and pettily strive to have it augmented to an unreasonable extent. They are unworthy and they decry the programme unworthily. But they are as nothing compared with the unteachable hard-line Unionists and Paisleyites who would abrogate it altogether. Let this chapter end with the words of Paisley's petition[1] of May 1969 to the Moderator of the Church of Scotland in General Assembly:

In the Name of Jesus Christ, the Great King and only Head of the Church, on our behalf and on behalf of many thousands of Protestants, we solemnly protest against the representative of the Pope (whom your own Confession identifies as the man of sin and son of perdition) being welcomed into this

[1] See *Protestant Telegraph* of May 31, 1969.

Assembly. This act of yours is a grave betrayal of the Gospel; an insult to the prerogatives of Jesus Christ, the only Redeemer of God's elect; a slur on the work and ministry of John Knox, the great reformer and founder minister of your Church; and a tragic capitulation of Presbyterianism to prelacy and Popery . . .

The Bible and its testimony, the spirit of John Knox, the blood of the martyrs, and the Spirit of the Lord within our hearts unitedly cry out against this courtship with the Mother of Harlots and the Abomination of the Earth. Any further betrayal by you will lead to the most serious consequences in our nation. No peace with Rome till Rome makes peace with God!

If the Ulster people do not wake to a realization of what Paisleyism stands for and will bring to their country, they will pay a bitter price.

Chapter Ten

Their purpose is not to secure peace by way of
reform and within the bounds of the constitution,
but to subvert and destroy the constitutional
structure of the State.

Cameron Commission

THE Irish Republic is a small and backward country, totally
dependent on England for its existence. If England were overwhelmed tomorrow, the Irish Republicans, who perpetually
revile her, could not survive. This is something they refuse to
face and it is time the ignorance and mythological rubbish that
befog their minds were dispersed.

The currency of the Irish Republic is inextricably interwoven
with the currency of England, its banking system is similarly
interwoven with the English banking system and is lubricated
by it.[1] The vital currency reserves of the Irish Republic are
held in English Government securities. Interest rates in the two
countries are inter-connected, the capital markets of the two
countries are almost identical. The banks of the Irish Republic
must hold substantial investments in English currency in order
to ensure that they can meet either balance of payments deficits
or public withdrawal of deposits. The dependence of the
Republican currency and banking system on England is mani-
fest in the inescapable fact that the Republic had no alternative
but to devalue its currency at the same moment and by the same
amount as England in November 1967, so as to maintain the
essential parity with sterling. English insurance companies
dominate the insurance market in the Republic. Between 70 per
cent and 75 per cent of the Republic's trade is with the United
Kingdom. Without the United Kingdom market for its exports,

[1] Readers who wish to verify this and subsequent statements made above will
have to study various statistical reports issued by the Government of the Irish
Republic, the British Government, and other bodies. They should also study the
admirably researched Outline Policy of the Irish Labour Party.

the economy of the Irish Republic would collapse. Without the generous admission to England of many thousands of emigrant Republican Irishmen who are allowed to engage in well-paid work there, the unemployment figure in the Irish Republic would be disastrously worse than it is already—which is the highest percentage unemployment rate in Western Europe. Despite the emigration of more than a million since the Republic —then known as the Irish Free State—came into being in 1922, it is the only Western country to register a persistent fall in the work-force. Its annual growth rate in Gross National Product over the long term is the lowest in Europe. Its income per head is the fourth lowest in Europe. Its house building rate is the lowest in Europe. The national housing stock contains a high percentage of houses over a hundred years old and of houses without running water and internal sanitation. Only half the estimated housing requirements are being met annually.

It is mainly an agricultural country, yet, while its agriculture has shown improvement over the past ten years, it is still far behind Ulster, where the agricultural industry is uniformly much more prosperous and is one of the most forward-looking and highly mechanized in Europe. The Ulstermen are the best livestock farmers in the United Kingdom and among the very best in the Western world. If the United Kingdom enters the European Common Market, the Ulster farmers will be better able to survive the competition than the farmers of the Irish Republic, which must enter the Common Market simultaneously with the United Kingdom or fall into economic ruin. Already, it is suffering from severe currency inflation. And its social welfare benefits are necessarily lower than those in Ulster, which are the same as those payable in the United Kingdom. Ulster, being a part of the United Kingdom, keeps parity with it in all such matters. Here are some random examples of variations in welfare benefits.[1] In the Irish Republic an adult single man draws £3 5s 0d per week in unemployment benefit, against £4 10s 0d in Ulster, while an unemployed man with two children draws £9 4s 0d per week in Ulster against £7 8s 6d in the Republic. A widow's weekly pension in the Republic is £3 5s 0d compared with £4 10s 0d per week in Ulster, where a widow with two children receives £8 3s 0d per

[1] The *Financial Times*, London, August 29, 1969.

week against only £4 18s 6d in the Republic. The maternity grant in the Republic is a mere £4, in Ulster it is £22. The maternity allowance in the Republic is £3 7s 6d per week for twelve weeks, in Ulster it is £4 10s 0d per week for eighteen weeks. Children's allowances also show a considerable difference. In the Republic they are 2s 6d per week for the first child, 7s 6d for the second and 10s 0d for the third. In Ulster, as in the United Kingdom, there is no allowance for the first child, but the allowance per week for the second child is 18s 0d, with £1 per week for the third child and each subsequent child.

The *Financial Times* recently had some hard-hitting things to say about the failure of Irish Republicans to confront the financial and economic difficulties in the way of an all-Ireland Republic:

Political and religious considerations apart, there is no logical reason why most people in Ulster should throw in their lot with the Republic if they were to be losers by the process. This they certainly would be in terms of social welfare benefit. A completely reliable comparison between the benefits payable in the two parts of the country is not possible in many sectors because of discrepancies in contribution levels and in the qualifications for benefits, though children's allowances and maternity grants are two areas where it clearly is possible, but the cash difference in Ulster's favour is obviously sizeable. If health and education are also taken into consideration, it is a reasonable estimate that Dublin's spending in these three areas alone would need to rise to at least £350,000,000 per annum, or more than double present expenditure, in order to maintain services broadly similar to those now available in Ulster. The differences do not end there. Personal income per head in Ulster is still one-third higher than in the Republic. For every £1 spent by the Republic on its universities, Ulster spends £2 10s 0d. The number of pupils in post-primary schools in Ulster and the Republic is roughly the same, but the Republic has double the population. Agriculture, the largest single industry on both sides of the border, employs one in ten in Ulster against one in three in the Republic. Farming is heavily subsidized in both areas, but the £81,000,000 earmarked in the Republic's

1969–70 budget for agriculture would need to be at least doubled to provide farmers in the Republic with the kind of benefits Ulster's farmers get under the British farm support system. It is next to impossible to put a figure on all this to measure accurately what it would cost the Dublin Government in additional expenditure to bring subsidies and support costs in general up to the levels in Ulster. A figure in the £300,000,000–£400,000,000 range cannot be very far off the mark. Finding this additional revenue would require draconian fiscal measures.

Draconian fiscal measures would indeed be required. But would Southern Irish politicians impose such an additional taxation burden on their countrymen as an inducement to Ulster to join in an all-Ireland Republic? It is arguable. It is more than arguable, it is unlikely. The author of this book recently mentioned the matter of the extra three or four hundred millions to an Irish Republican and asked him how the money would be raised. The Republican, of course, had given no thought to the problem. On being pressed for an answer, he revealed the dream world in which he and his kind prefer to live. 'We wouldn't have to raise it,' he said, 'we'd get it from the English.' In return for another declaration of neutrality, no doubt.

The word 'neutrality' again brings up the question of Irish national defence. This is another facet of life in which Irish Republicans refuse to look facts in the face. They just will not allow themselves to confront the unpalatable truth that they are incapable of defending their country, that they are in a position where their defence lies completely in the hands of England. Their navy is non-existent, their air force consists of a handful of obsolete machines. Their national army could not possibly stand up to modern troops, combat-experienced and possessed of devastating modern firepower. However bravely its men might fight—and Irishmen always fight bravely—it would be wiped out in a week, if not sooner. When, oh when, the Ulstermen wonder, will the Irish Republicans grow out of their childhood and begin to look at this difficult and dangerous world through adult eyes? And when will they realize the folly of their Catholic Republican policy in Ulster? When will they learn that constant lying about Ulster is hardly the way to win over the Ulstermen, who are not afraid to look facts in the face? The lies are many and are easily exposed. Let us take a look at the major untruths.

Has there been discrimination by the Protestant majority against the Catholics in Ulster? There certainly has, but not to the extent the Catholics claim. And they themselves have been to blame for most of it, have brought it on themselves. Does the Cameron Commission report support the Catholic claims in full? It would seem so. But the Commission was so restricted by its warrant that it could not compel witnesses to attend, could not compel them to give evidence on oath. Its constitution was not that of a British Court of Justice. It had to invite evidence, through advertisements in the local newspapers and through public announcements on other media. The Catholic side seized its opportunity and crowded every session the Commission held. The Unionist Ulstermen, as usual, failed to put their case as thoroughly. The Commission's report refers to discrimination at local government level and found that it existed 'in some Unionist-controlled authorities'. This was unquestionably true and it is a reproach to the good Ulster name. But how many is 'some'? While the Commission was hearing evidence, there were sixty-eight local councils in Ulster. Did the Commission hear evidence in regard to all of those councils? It would not seem so. And what about the Catholic controlled councils, where there is serious discrimination against Protestants? The Commission give them only a half-hearted mention. Did the Commission go into the basic reason for Protestant discrimination, fully and authoritatively? It did not. Nowhere in its report will there be found an analysis of the grounds for anger on the part of Protestant Ulstermen—the deadly Irish Republican Army attacks on Ulster in the past, the assistance given to that Army by Ulster Catholics, the unceasing attempts by Catholic Nationalists to bring down the State, the refusal of the Catholics to play a full and friendly part in the life of the State. Nowhere does it extensively examine and report on the untenable claim of the Catholics that the Protestant Ulstermen forced them into the role of second-class citizens and bullyingly kept them there. In short, the Commission did not investigate the Ulster question in depth.

Take, for example, the Catholic claim about second-class citizenship. The truth is that the official Catholic policy, inspired

188

from Dublin, was to opt out of the Ulster State from its inception. The Catholic Nationalists led the Catholic population generally in refusing to recognize the State, refusing to attend State functions, avoiding the necessity of standing for the playing of the British National Anthem by staying away from all occasions when it would be played or walking out of a hall when its opening notes were sounded. This compares very badly indeed with the behaviour of Ulster people who visit the Irish Republic. They always show respect to the State by rising to their feet for its national anthem—'The Soldier's Song'—and would not dream of omitting to do so. In 1969, the General Assembly of the Presbyterian Church in Ireland was held in Dublin. The Assembly invited De Valera, as President and Head of State, to attend. He accepted the invitation and the Assembly arranged for the Republic's national anthem to be played when he arrived. Every Ulsterman in the gathering stood up and showed respect. In Ulster, a Catholic gathering would never behave with similar consideration and good-breeding. The Catholic Nationalists, and their political bosses in Dublin, refer to the Ulster State, with characteristic churlishness and stupidity, as 'the British-occupied Six Counties'. The Irish Nationalist Party in the Ulster House of Commons for many years declined to accept the status of Official Opposition, although it was the largest party on the anti-Government benches, because acceptance might imply some distant recognition of the British Monarchy. The Roman Catholic Hierarchy in Ulster has refused from the very beginning to appoint a Roman Catholic chaplain to the Ulster House of Commons although repeatedly invited to do so. The Hierarchy and its Catholic flock in Ulster has consistently refused to recognize the Ulster Constitution, hoping—with typical foolishness—that their refusal would somehow result in its disappearance or hasten it. What has William, Cardinal Conway, to say on the matter of recognizing the Ulster Constitution? In March 1969, he was interviewed by the late John E. Sayers, Editor in Chief of the *Belfast Telegraph*,[1] who put many considerately phrased questions to him. Sayers put this question to the Cardinal:

It is sometimes said that the Roman Catholic Bishops have

[1] Issues of March 27 and 28.

189

never recognized the Constitution of Northern Ireland. Have you any reservations about it?

The Cardinal's answer was a masterpiece of evasion, the sort of thing that makes intelligent Protestant Ulstermen despair. Here it is, quoted in full:

A Protestant layman put this matter about the Constitution to me the other day and I asked him—'When did you recognize the Constitution?' and he scratched his head and said—'That's a good question'. I think there is a touch of Gilbert and Sullivan about this whole thing. There is almost the implication that there is some kind of printed form recognizing the Government, which everyone is expected to sign when he reaches the age of twenty-one and that the Catholic bishops have refused to sign it. The normal way to recognize an authority is to respect its lawful directives and, if the occasion arises, negotiate with it as an authority. The problem in the Middle East, for example, is that the Arab States will not negotiate with the Jews because they do not recognize the State of Israel. The Catholic bishops have done both these things. They could not have demonstrated this more clearly than when they condemned the armed [Irish Republican Army] campaign of the 1950s. Moreover, they have negotiated with the Government as such—most recently on the Education Act—and in all correspondence the Governor, the Prime Minister and members of the Government are given their proper titles. It is difficult to see why all this is not regarded as sufficient. I cannot help feeling that what many people want is a political declaration from the bishops— or something that could be construed in a political sense— like telling their people that they should give up all hope of a united Ireland. That, of course, would be quite improper for the bishops to do, just as it would be wrong for the Scottish bishops to condemn Scottish Nationalism as a political standpoint.

With the highest respect to the Cardinal's rank, that answer —as all informed Ulstermen are well aware—was jesuitical and downright dishonest, in the sense of intellectual dishonesty. Cardinal Conway is a publicly admitted and unalterably convinced believer in the desirability of an all-Ireland Republic. His bishops in Ulster share his political ambitions to a man and there is not a single experienced Protestant Ulsterman who will trust them. John E. Sayers followed up his question about recognition of the Ulster Constitution by putting this further question:

Captain O'Neill [then Ulster Prime Minister] said on January 29, 1969, to the leaders of the Roman Catholic community—'Has not the time come for you to render unto Caesar the things that are Caesar's, to observe the normal courtesies towards the authorities of this State?'

Is it true that the leaders of the Roman Catholic community do not observe the normal courtesies towards the authorities of the State?

Here is the Cardinal's reply, again given in full:

Frankly, I do not think we have been lacking in courtesy in our dealings with the State, as I have just tried to indicate. What many people think of in this context is that we do not attend certain social functions like receptions or garden parties. I can state quite categorically that there is no political significance whatever in this and—equally categorically—that there would be no political significance if we were to change our practice and start to attend some of them. Some years ago, one of the bishops paid a special visit to the Governor to make this crystal clear. He spelled out quite explicitly that the practice of not attending these functions was meant to be a silent protest at the way Catholics were treated in Ulster and had no political significance whatever.

No political significance whatever? Shades of Cardinal Mac-Rory and his hatred of England! Cardinal Conway must indeed believe that the majority in Ulster are ingenuous if he thinks they will swallow that. In the course of the interview he referred to the refusal to appoint a Roman Catholic chaplain to the Ulster House of Commons and said: 'There is no difficulty in principle about this and it may well come in due course when certain practical difficulties have been resolved.' Practical difficulties? What *practical difficulties* could possibly stand in the way of appointing a Roman Catholic chaplain to the Ulster Parliament?

All the Hierarchy has to do is name one and send him there.'[1]

The responsible Protestant Ulster people have been pressing increasingly of late for the de-segregation of the Ulster schools. In their opinion, the barriers between Protestants and Catholics are built at a very early age and the best way to ensure that there will be no barriers at all is by educating all children together from the age of five upwards. Let the children, Protestant and Catholic, get to know one another and become friendly with one another at the outset. This will lead to understanding and the establishment of relationships free of religious prejudice. There would be obstacles in the way, of course. The schools administration system would have to be changed, school buildings adapted and re-sited. But the problems are no more than administrative and could be solved. The benefit to the Ulster people as a whole would be immense. Cardinal Conway, however, will have none of it. When Sayers placed the matter before him, he said:

> You know as well as I do that all this talk about separate education being the major cause of division in the community is largely a political gimmick, an attempt to put the boot on the other foot.
>
> They gerrymander the local government constituencies, rigidly segregate Catholics into so-called Nationalist wards, keep Catholics down to a fraction on their committees, practically exclude them from decent local authority jobs, put people out of the Orange Order for even attending a Catholic ceremony—and then blame the whole thing on Catholic schools.

That answer was shocking. Blame the whole thing on Catholic schools? Educated and responsible Protestant Ulster people, in their tolerant and decent wish to bring an end to religious bigotry through co-education of Protestant and Catholic children, regard that answer as nothing short of insolence. It was more than insolent, it was insulting and deeply stupid. Catholic schools in Ulster are given very generous financial grants, as generous as any in the United Kingdom and in many instances even more generous. Where the handing out of money to

---

[1] If a Catholic chaplain has been appointed before this book is published, as perhaps may happen, it will be—the Ulstermen think—almost half a century overdue.

Catholic Ulster schools is concerned, there is no prejudiced reluctance on the part of the Ulster Ministry of Education and Ministry of Finance. For Cardinal Conway to accuse Protestant Ulster people of trying to maintain that segregated education is 'the major cause of division in the community' was irrelevant and inaccurate. The Ulster people have made no such statement. The fact is that the Roman Catholic Hierarchy in Ulster refuse to agree to co-education of Catholic and Protestant children in any circumstances, from a mixture of arrogance and fear. Arrogance, because they believe that the Roman Catholic religion is the only true faith. Fear, because they are afraid that if their Catholic children are associated in school with Protestant children they may lose their faith.[1] They never allow themselves to forget the saying attributed to the Jesuits—'Give us a child until it is seven . . .'—and they have no intention of permitting their children to be exposed to the danger of heresy. Cardinal Conway should make himself aware of the fact that a great number of good and very sincere Ulster Roman Catholics are saddened by his intransigence. They are anxious to have their children educated side by side with Protestant children, but the Cardinal will not allow it. He has spoken.

Next? What next in the catalogue of Catholic Nationalist misrepresentation, in the Catholic claim that all the wrong-doing in Ulster is perpetrated by the bigoted Protestants? Let us deal with the Catholic Nationalist blackening of the Royal Ulster Constabulary and the Ulster Special Constabulary, one of the nastiest lies of the many that have contributed to the diminishment of the Ulster name since October 1968. To damage the confidence in which the police force of a State is held is a well-known tactic on the part of men who wish to injure the State. As James Callaghan, British Home Secretary, said during the summer of 1969 on one of his visits to Belfast: 'The police force of a State is its cement. Weaken the cement and you may cause the State to fall.' Have the Catholic Nationalists succeeded in weakening the cement? Did they set out to do so? They did set

[1] 'The Roman Catholic school system is necessary for the growth and survival of the Catholic faith and the only possible system in practice in Ulster conditions as they are' (The Rev. T. P. Donelly, headmaster of St. Patrick's High School, Maghera, Co. Londonderry—a Catholic school; speech on prizegiving day; see *Belfast Telegraph* of November 29, 1969). Cardinal Conway did not publicly refute Fr. Donelly.

out to do so and they have very definitely gained their objective. They have persuaded the rest of the United Kingdom and the peoples of many countries of the Western world that both forces have been guilty of serious and indefensible brutality, while saying nothing at all, of course, concerning their own vicious and dangerous attacks on them.

The Royal Ulster Constabulary replaced the old Royal Irish Constabulary in 1922 and its strength has circled around the 3,000 mark ever since. Many of them were shot dead or badly wounded in the fighting with the Irish Republican Army, as stated in an earlier chapter. They constituted Ulster's main security force in the protection of the State and, until 1969, they were armed with heavy service revolvers worn on their belts. Their uniform was a dark green. The Ulster Special Constabulary, which also came into existence in the dark days of the Irish Republican Army attack, was an organization of patriotically inclined volunteers who could be called out as emergencies arose, to guard the border between Ulster and the Irish Republic and keep armed watch on key installations. Many of them, too, lost their lives in repelling the Irish Republican Army. They served long and dangerous hours for nominal pay, they were armed with rifles, revolvers and with a few machine-guns and they were allowed to keep their weapons in their homes to ensure that there would be no delay in their arriving, fully prepared, at the place or places where they were urgently needed. There were many occasions on which they were urgently needed and they never failed to get there in time. They numbered about 30,000 and they were vital in helping the regular police and the Army troops in the defence of the Province. Be it ever remembered that there would have been no need to call them into existence at all had it not been for the Republican attacks and the hostility of so many of the Ulster Catholic Nationalists. For some years now, the strength of the Special Constabulary has been around 8,000. They have been so successful in the protection of the State that they have become an obvious target for the smear tactics of the Ulster Republicans, who have long been highly anxious—for reasons easily apparent —to get rid of them. Since October 1968, therefore, the Republicans have been engaged in an exceptionally malicious campaign to brand them publicly as entirely consisting of dangerous bullies, continually batoning, stoning and otherwise maltreating innocent Catholics. The same damnable smear has been fastened on the Royal Ulster Constabulary. These Nationalist accusations made against the main police force since 1968 have been exhaustively investigated by County Inspector Harold Baillie, an officer of proven and known integrity. His report has not been published and this has led to further Nationalist smears, of course. But the English, Welsh and Scottish police forces, which have had to bring a great many disciplinary charges against their men[1]—far more, proportionately, than could have been brought against the men of the Royal Ulster Constabulary—hold steadily to the practice of non-publication of similar investigations. The Ulster people are aware, however, that the Baillie Report recommended disciplinary action against some sixteen constables for misbehaviour.[2] This, taking the overall strength of the force as 3,000, represents 0·5 per cent. If fifty constables had misbehaved, the figure would be 1·6 per cent. How many police forces throughout the Western world would be thankful if they could claim that such an infinitesimal number of their men had been guilty of behaving badly? Can the New York, Chicago, Paris, Madrid, Berlin, London and Glasgow police forces truthfully claim so few? And were their men so outnumbered and so attacked that more than a third of their total forces were injured?

Let there be no misunderstanding. The author, like every other informed and experienced Ulsterman, is not oblivious of the fact that members of the Royal Ulster Constabulary and the Special Constabulary lost their heads and shamed their uniform during some of the rioting in Ulster since 1968. There is a relevant passage in the Cameron Commission's report:

> While we fully realize that the police had been working without adequate relief or rest for long hours and were under great stress, we are afraid that not only do we find that allegations of misconduct are substantiated but that for such conduct among members of a disciplined and well-led force

[1] There have been many charges of planting false evidence on criminals, of bribery and corruption, etc.; in December 1969, four London police officers were suspended for investigation of charges of corruption.

[2] The charges have since been dropped, as they could not be substantiated by the complainants.

there can be no acceptable justification or excuse. We have also considered the full and careful report of County Inspector Baillie, which has been made available to us (and whose evidence we have heard) and we note, with some satisfaction, though with regret, that his independent investigation has led him to reach the same conclusions as to the gravity and nature of the misconduct as those at which we have arrived in our consideration of the evidence before us. Although this unfortunate and temporary breakdown of discipline was limited in extent, its effect in rousing passions and inspiring hostility towards the police was regrettably great and obscures the restraint, under conditions of severe strain, displayed by the large majority of the police concerned. It has always to be kept in view, when considering the police action and reaction in the situations which arose, that the number of police at any given time and place was limited and not always adequate for the difficult task they had to perform. The extent to which the available police forces were stretched may be gauged from an example drawn from the period of the People's Democracy Belfast-Londonderry march. One police platoon was continuously on duty from 9 a.m. on the Friday until 3 a.m. on Sunday without rest or relief.

Or, it should be added, without proper food. Would English policemen tolerate such a spell of continuous duty without complaint? Would the English people allow it to happen without protest at such treatment of their police?

The Cameron Commission, in noting the police misbehaviour, fell below its generally maintained standard of clarity and fairness. It could have stated that the overall number of policemen guilty of misbehaviour was so small as to be insignificant. The Baillie report was in the Commission's possession, it knew the facts. Why did it not give the facts in greater detail, why did it not give a percentage? Men of the Royal Ulster Constabulary trying to contain mobs of Catholics from invading Protestant districts—which was attempted again and again, whatever the Catholics may say in an effort to prove the contrary—were outnumbered by forty and fifty to one and had to stay at their posts until many of them were almost dropping from exhaustion. In the confusion and shifting circumstances, it was impossible to feed them adequately and ensure that they got hot drinks. They were under intolerable pressure and attack. The weapons and missiles[1] the Catholics used against them included stones, jagged bricks, portions of concrete flagstones, marbles shot at them from catapults—a direct hit with a catapulted marble can fracture a man's skull—knife-edged pennies, ball bearings, pointed iron bars, pieces of wood used as spears, empty milk bottles, broken bottles, lemonade bottles made heavier by being filled with water, fire bombs containing sugar and syrup to make them burn more adheringly, cudgels with nails sticking out of them, heavy spanners and even hammers. Petrol bombs were flung at the police in hundreds, many of whom were set on fire and very badly burned.[2] One policeman was struck on the head with a hurley stick—hurley is a sort of Gaelic hockey, played by Catholic men in Ireland—and knocked unconscious. As he lay on the ground he was savagely kicked. Another policeman was struck in the mouth by a stone which forced his teeth through his left cheek. Scores of policemen were taken to hospital. Their injuries would have shocked the English people. Would they have allowed their police forces to have been so battered day after day, week after week? They certainly would not. They would have raised a very angry uproar if they had seen their policemen so appallingly attacked and wounded and, if only 0·5 per cent or 1·6 per cent of their police had been provoked into temporary indiscipline, they would not have thrown up their hands in horror. Yet those same English threw up their hands in horror when they were assured by Ulster Catholic Nationalists that all the constables in Ulster are violent blackguards. The fact that only about 200 civilians have been injured in the rioting compared with rather more than 800 police hardly brands the Royal Ulster Constabulary as the aggressors. Nothing justifies a loss of discipline and restraint by a constabulary. But how would the English police have reacted to such savagery? Since 1945, there have been many complaints of brutality against civilians by the English police, although they

[1] The author has personally inspected many of these weapons, retained in the Royal Ulster Constabulary 'museum'.

[2] On August 12, 1969, in Londonderry, Sergeant Duncan of the Royal Ulster Constabulary was turned into a human torch when a petrol bomb was flung at him by a Catholic rioter; his trunk and head were ablaze and he was only just saved from death by incineration.

were not under such provocation. Can the English be certain their policemen would not, in a few instances, have fallen from their customary high standard of control?

In Ulster, there are only 3,000 Royal Ulster Constabulary men to cover a population of 1,500,000. This obviously places a heavy burden on the force. Things are much less difficult for the police in England. A few years ago, a huge Left Wing anti-American mob attempted to storm the United States Embassy in Grosvenor Square, London. The Embassy was saved by the London Metropolitan Police Force, which succeeded in keeping the mob back from it. It managed this by simply filling the square and its immediate surroundings with more policemen than are to be found in the entire strength of the Royal Ulster Constabulary. The London police chiefs were able to flood the vicinity with about 5,000 policemen. It was easy for them. The suppression of riots is never easy for the Ulster police. They are armed with pistols—which they may not use except in certain desperate situations—batons, riot shields and protective visors which are not very effective. On some occasions during the rioting, when they were being heavily stoned by Catholic mobs, they flung the stones back at their attackers. This was deplorable, as everyone who saw it on the television screens will agree. But what else could the policemen do? They had to contain the mobs somehow, had to stop them from breaking through the police cordons, so they threw the stones back until at last they were given gas canisters to use. They hated throwing the stones back, but they had no option for a long time. They were impossibly outnumbered and would have been overwhelmed. If they had been, the consequences would have been dreadful.

Those who have met and talked with Royal Ulster Constabulary men—as the author has done over many years—know them to be as disciplined a force as you could find. They are now to be transformed into a purely civil police force. No longer are they to carry their service revolvers on daily duty. Are they sorry? On the contrary, they are delighted. They wanted to shed their guns a long time ago but the Ulster Government feared that such disarmament would invite a renewal of trouble from the Irish Republican Army and other elements. That was possibly a mistake. It might not have been, however. Who is to say with certainty? The Ulster Special Constabulary is to disappear in its present form and will contribute a nucleus for the Ulster Defence Regiment. The Catholic Nationalists are making a loud noise about this, although it is the hope of the Ulster Government and the military command in Ulster that many Catholics will join the Regiment. Truly, both forces have been defamed—and are still being defamed—to an insufferable extent.

How many of the people of the United Kingdom know that the Royal Ulster Constabulary has an outstanding crime detection record, probably by far the highest in the whole of the United Kingdom and certainly much higher than that of the English and Welsh police, for instance. Over the years 1964 to 1968, the Royal Ulster Constabulary detection rate percentages were: 1964, 59·7 per cent; 1965, 61·2 per cent; 1966, 52·7 per cent; 1967, 54·2 per cent; 1968, 58·3 per cent. The corresponding figures for England and Wales were: 39·6 per cent, 39·2 per cent, 40·2 per cent, 41·2 per cent and 41·9 per cent. The differences, whatever the English and Welsh police may say, are telling.

Yet this is the force which has been so successfully blackened by Ulster Catholics that the English have gulped down every calculated lie about it. In 1969, in the course of its British-designed reorganization, its Inspector General—the Head of the Force, an Ulsterman—was arbitrarily replaced by an Englishman from the City of London Police. The Englishman is a most experienced and efficient police officer, but the replacement was unnecessary. What does an Englishman, moreover, know of Ulster? Shortly after the replacement came into effect, an attempt was made to put the Royal Ulster Constabulary into London Metropolitan police uniforms, with a view to pleasing the complaining Catholic sections in the Province. Batches of these London police uniforms were sent to Belfast and found to be ill-fitting. The Royal Ulster Constabulary, which had worn its distinctive dark green uniform honourably for almost half a century, was to be compelled by outsiders to wear the clothing of some other police force. The Royal Ulster Constabulary protested. Its men felt themselves insulted. They were angered. All Ulstermen who knew the true quality of the force were equally angered. The English should have shown more understanding, more common sense, more awareness of the attachment men feel to their own traditional uniform. If they had looked into the facts, they would have come to realize that the Royal Ulster Constabulary had had to endure such slanders as no other British police force has had to endure, without being allowed to enter an open defence of its name and record. That name and record are now under close examination by a body set up by the Ulster Government in 1969. This is the Scarman Tribunal, presided over by Lord Justice Scarman, an English judge, a much more judicially and properly constituted body than the Cameron Commission. The Tribunal's report will not be available until after this book has been completed and sent to the printers, so the author cannot now say what degree of Royal Ulster Constabulary culpability will be established in the way of ill behaviour during the rioting of 1968 and 1969. He believes, however, that it will not be much greater than he has suggested. Time will tell. In the meanwhile, the English might accept the fact—and it is a fact—that the Royal Ulster Constabulary, despite being let down momentarily by a minute handful of hotheads who reacted wrongly and discreditably in near intolerable conditions and under great provocation, has long been one of the best police forces in Britain and still is.

The twentieth century is now old and cynical. It was to have been the first truly liberal century, the era of understanding, when man would free himself from the curse of war and the whole of humankind would advance together in peace, confidence and mutually beneficial achievement. Yet, before it had attained its majority, it had rushed insanely into the 1914–18 War and, in middle-age, brought on itself the even more terrible war with Hitler and the Nazis. In these and other wars of the time there died at least a hundred million men, women and children. Man was still stupid, still blind, still made mistakes.

Very well, say the Protestant Ulstermen—as all men make mistakes why should we be expected to be infallible? We have certainly made mistakes, but so has every other race. The Ulsterman taps the Englishman on the chest and says to him, with typical Ulster directness: 'We are tired of being condemned by those who know nothing of the situation we are in, especially by you English who look down on all other peoples as inferior and so speedily forget the peoples who helped you. We Ulstermen have been guilty of discrimination, you say? You are right and we admit it. But all other races have been guilty of discrimination against those within the State who strove to wreck it. The history of your own country shows that you, too, have again and again been guilty of discrimination for religious and political reasons. And not only on those grounds. You have been so discriminatory against coloured immigrants into your country that you have had to pass an Act of Parliament to stop you from treating them badly. What would be your reaction towards a 33⅓ per cent minority who refused to co-operate and tried for fifty years to do away with your Parliament and drive you under the governance of the Welsh? Would you welcome them into your highest counsels? You would not and you know it. We Ulstermen are accused of bias against every Catholic in every field of work. That is untrue. The Catholics are free to join our Civil Service, which asks no questions regarding the religion of any applicant. Hundreds of Catholics join it and are free to rise in it—many of them do—if they have the ability, personality and presence. A lot of them lack all three and blame their promotion failure on discrimination. They should blame it on their inadequate education and limited outlook. Protestants who are similarly lacking are not promoted, either. The modern Civil Service is demanding and severely competitive. Cameron speaks of discrimination at local government level. He is right but in an appreciable number of our local councils there is little if any discrimination. The Catholics complain of discrimination against them in the matter of appointments to the medical staffs of our hospitals. This has been denied by our consultants and medical superintendents, all of them men of the highest reputation and integrity in their profession. The appointments, they say, are given to the best qualified. Religion does not enter into it. Why should it be automatically believed that they are lying, merely because disappointed applicants of lesser qualification and experience assert that they are? We suggest that the Catholics should look to their schools in the first instance and ask themselves honestly if they are of such all-round excellence as the Protestant schools. The blunt answer is that they are not.[1]

[1] See the article in the *Daily Telegraph*, London, of May 7, 1969, by Stephen Preston.

The Catholics complain of our Special Powers Act, which gives drastic rights of arrest and detention. The Act was passed to defend the State against the dangerous men who worked to destroy it and still work to destroy it. Why do you never hear any serious complaint from our Catholics against the special powers legislation in the Irish Republic? You English should take a look at the Irish Republic's Offences Against the State Act of 1939 and its Criminal Justice Act, introduced as a Bill in 1967. If you do, you will find that the Republic is not a whit behind Ulster in determination to protect itself, that its powers of arrest and internment are also drastic. The Irish Republic takes very good care to keep these powers on its statute book. It takes equally good care to keep quiet about them. Let us have a little less reproving talk about the Ulster special powers until the Republic has amended and lessened its own powers, as we have promised to do with ours. You say we should have reduced our discrimination by introducing our general reforms a number of years ago? You are right. We should have introduced them shortly after the Hitler War. But we are human. Our ruling Unionist Party, our governing Party, has always been unassailable. There has never been any possibility of its being defeated at the polls since the State came into existence in 1921, democratically ousted from office. So it inevitably became complacent, arrogant, diminished in purpose and directive. Is there a political party in the Western world that would not have become arrogant and complacent after half a century of continuous office and persistingly ineffective opposition? Please to remember that spontaneous generosity is rare and that—as we have pointed out again and again—we have always had very good reason to distrust the people you say we should not have discriminated against. Those people should have said to themselves in 1921: 'The Ulster State is in being. Let us make the best of it, let us give all we can to help build its prosperity, let us live in peace and increasing trust with the Protestants and let us leave the unification of Ireland until such time as the Protestant Ulstermen have been given unarguable proof that we are their friends and may be relied on.' Did they say this? They did not. They snarled and fought and then stayed back. They should have entered the industrial world of Ulster, they should have built factories, capitalized them, given employment to both Catholics and Protestants as we did and are still doing. We would not have stopped them. On the contrary, we would have been more than pleased.

Coming back again to the matter of discrimination, there is no prejudice, no discrimination, among the educated middle-class Ulster people on either side, Protestant and Catholic. There is none against Catholics in our universities. Some Catholic boys and girls attend our Protestant Ulster schools and no one bothers about their religion. And the Catholics should have peacefully and pleasantly insisted on securing more appointments in the higher official reaches of the life of the community. This could have been done if the approach had been right. It would not have taken the Catholic minority long to establish their intent as dependable. But the Catholics refused to make the right approach. Among other mistakes, they persisted in painting a ludicrous picture of the benefits to be gained from an all-Ireland Republic. What benefits? Industrial and trade benefits? In the year 1924, the total value of the external trade of the *twenty-six counties* of what was then the Irish Free State and is now the Irish Republic was £120,000,000 against our Ulster *six-county* total of £131,000,000. For the year 1968, our total of external trade was £1,250,000,000 against the mere £822,000,000 of the Irish Republic. Ulster is the world's major centre for man-made fibres and probably the world's centre for the modern textile industry generally. The giants in the manufacture of synthetics have large factories in Ulster. Imperial Chemical Industries, Courtaulds, Du Pont, Monsanto, British Enkalon and the great German firm of Hoechst are with us, employing thousands of our workpeople. The world's biggest single shipbuilding yard is in Ulster and it has installed what will be for some time to come the world's biggest graving dock. Industrially, Ulster is important to Britain and the Western world and is growing ever more so. Why, then, should it allow itself to sink from sight in an all-Ireland Republic? Do you English want to lose *all* the Irish ports when the next world war breaks out? It will not necessarily be a nuclear war, all over in a moment. It is more likely, because of the mutual destructiveness of nuclear armaments, to be a conventional war, with enemy forces dominating Europe. The Atlantic routes will be as vital as before, especially as Russia, for instance, has an enormous submarine fleet, three or four times larger than the German U-Boat fleet that so nearly beat us in 1939–45. What would you English do then, if our Ulster ports were buried in an all-Ireland Republic? Trust to the Republican Irish to see more clearly? Don't be so damned naïve! We know the Republican Irish mind a great deal better than you have ever known it and we tell you it will be generations before it rids itself of its stupidity and hostility. You should remember that. You should remember, too, that we Ulstermen are good fighters, a useful lot to have at your side when the going gets rough. We've proved that many times already and we're prepared to prove it again. We'll stand by you. Whatever pressure is brought to bear on us, we will *not* go into an all-Ireland Republic. Why should we? To learn Gaelic?'

But prosperity, say the Catholic Ulstermen, would soon attend the formation of an all-Ireland Republic. Would it? The Ulstermen doubt it. They say that they know the Southern Irish nature, temperament, lack of time-sense and application. The Province of Ulster, the Ulstermen say, has done well and means to do better. But the Province of Ulster, say the Republicans, would not be prosperous if it were not sustained by 'massive financial subventions' from Britain. This, the Ulstermen reply, is nonsense. These 'massive subventions' are not massive at all. Ulster, as a United Kingdom area with development difficulties, certainly gets financial help from the British Government, but no more and perhaps less than is given to such other development areas as Scotland and Tyneside. And the Ulstermen carry the same heavy burden of income tax as the British, much heavier than the income tax burden of the Irish Republic. Besides, what right have the Irish Republicans to be scornful about such financial aid as Ulster may obtain from the English? Ulster could ultimately work herself into a position where she could do without it, whereas the Irish Republic would be shipwrecked if it were not for the favoured treatment it receives from England despite the fact that the Republic deliberately and unpleasantly took itself out of the British Commonwealth of Nations and thus forfeited its claim to special treatment. As this final chapter is being revised—December 1969—a trade delegation from the Government of the Irish Republic is in London, shamelessly begging for even greater concessions from the English. The Irish Republic's industrial and commercial condition, say the Ulstermen, is very shaky indeed. If England ceased to exist or if she stopped showing the Southern Irish such exceptional and undeserved generosity, the Republicans would not know which way to turn.

So why, the Ulstermen ask again, should they join an all-Ireland Republic?

The Ulstermen are struggling to put their house in order. They own their mistakes, their obduracy, their guilt. They plead extenuating circumstances and who will truthfully argue that the extenuation did not exist? They remind those that would condemn them that it has always taken two to make a quarrel and always will. They are struggling to cleanse their stable, to rid their ruling Unionist Party of its hard-line members, its extremists. It will be a long struggle but the moderates will eventually win. They look to the Catholic minority in Ulster to show wisdom and fairness, to respond, to help. Will the Catholics do so? Again, only time will tell. Many Ulstermen, if they read this book, with its candid description of the faults on the Protestant Unionist side, will dislike it. The Irish Republicans, the Southern Irish generally, if they read the book in their turn, will dislike it even more. They will be very angry. The Southern Irish mind does not take kindly to criticism. As Heywood Broun says, the Southern Irish are the cry-babies of the Western world, even the mildest quip will set them off into resolutions and protests. They have a liking for savage denigration of others, but rage when someone exposes their faults and refutes the propaganda with which they blacken those they disagree with. Whether they will clean out their stable, as the Ulstermen are trying to do, whether they will rid themselves of their rancorous politicians and church-men, is questionable, this side of many years. They are still the prisoners of their self-created political myths. They will learn, of course—most peoples acquire common sense eventually, or something approximating to it, as younger and more unprejudiced minds take over—and the day may come when the Southern Irish will respond to the plea of King George V of England as he addressed the elected Members of the newly-formed Ulster Government almost half a century ago:

I appeal to all Irishmen to pause, to stretch out the hand of forbearance and conciliation, to forgive and forget, and to join in making for the land which they love a new era of peace, contentment and goodwill.

Wise words, already quoted in this book. Let them serve as its curtain-fall. Better still—let all Irishmen who care for their country, north and south, think of them as the cue for curtain-rise.

Bibliography

Beaslai, Piaras: *Michael Collins and the Making of a New Ireland,*
   1926

Beckett, J. C.: *The Making of Modern Ireland, 1966*

Blake, John W.: *Northern Ireland in the Second World War, 1956*

Bolton, G. C.: *The Passing of the Irish Act of Union, 1966*

Bromage, Mary C.: *De Valera and the March of a Nation, 1956*

Bromage, Mary C.: *Churchill and Ireland, 1964*

Bryant, Sir Arthur: *Turn of the Tide, 1957*

Calvert, Harry: *Constitutional Law in Northern Ireland, 1968*

Carty, James: *Ireland (1783–1850), 1949*

Churchill, Winston: *The Second World War, 1951*

Edwards-Rees, Desiree: *Ireland's Story, 1967*

Ervine, St. John: *Craigavon, 1949*

Falls, Cyril: *History of the 36th (Ulster) Division, 1922*

Falls, Cyril: *Northern Ireland as an Outpost of Defence, 1965*

Feiling, Keith: *Life of Neville Chamberlain, 1947*

Gwynn, Denis: *Life of John Redmond, 1932*

Hastings, Sir Patrick: *Autobiography, 1948*

Holt, Edgar: *Protest in Arms, 1960*

Hyde, H. Montgomery: *Carson, 1953*

Leybourn, James G.: *The Scotch–Irish—A Social History, 1962*

Macardle, Dorothy: *Tragedies of Kerry, 1924*

Marjoribanks and Colvin: *Life of Lord Carson, 1932*

Marshall, W. F.: *Ulster Sails West, 1943*

Moles, T. H.: *Lord Carson of Duncairn, 1925*

Montgomery, Eric: *The Scotch–Irish and Ulster, 1965*

Morley, John: *Life of Gladstone, 1903*

McGrath, Fergal: *Newman in Dublin, 1969*

McNeill, Ronald: *Ulster's Stand for Union, 1922*

Neeson, Eoin: *The Civil War in Ireland, 1966*

O'Brien, William: *The Irish Revolution, 1923*

O'Casey, Sean: *Blasts and Benedictions, 1967*

O'Hegarty, P. S.: *Victory of Sinn Fein, 1924*

Robb, Nesca A.: *William of Orange, 1962*
Roskill, S. W.: *The War at Sea 1939–1945,* H.M. Stationery Office, *1959*
Samuels, A. P. I.: *With the Ulster Division in France* (privately printed)
Stephan, Enno: *Spies in Ireland, 1963*
Stewart, A. T. Q.: *Craig and the Ulster Volunteer Force, 1967*
Stewart, A. T. Q.: *The Ulster Crisis, 1967*
Taylor, Rex: *Michael Collins, 1968*

Commentary by the Government of Northern Ireland to Accompany The Cameron Report, 1969
Constitution of Ireland, 1937
Constitution, Laws and Ordinances of the Loyal Orange Institution of Ireland, *1967*
Disturbances in Northern Ireland: Report of the Cameron Commission, 1969
Labour Party Outline Policy (Irish Republic), 1969
Memoirs of Cordell Hull, 1948
New Left Review No. 55, 1969
Orange and Green, A Quaker Study of Community Relations in Ulster, 1969
Report of the Advisory Committee on Police in Northern Ireland, The Hunt Report, 1969

Parliamentary Debates of the Ulster House of Commons and the *Oireachtas* of the Irish Republic
Various Belfast and Dublin newspapers
The *Protestant Telegraph* of Belfast
The *New York Times*